SCHOOLING SEXUALITIES

Debbie Epstein
and
Richard Johnson

Open University Press
Buckingham · Philadelphia

Open University Press
Celtic Court
22 Ballmoor
Buckingham
MK18 1XW

and

1900 Frost Road, Suite 101
Bristol, PA 19007, USA

First Published 1998

A catalogue record of this book is available from the British Library

ISBN   0 335 195369 (pb)   0 335 19537 7 (hb)

Library of Congress Cataloging-in-Publication Data
Epstein, Debbie, 1945–
      Schooling sexualities/by Debbie Epstein and Richard Johnson.
          p.   cm.
      Includes bibliographical references (p.) and index.
      ISBN 0-335-19537-7 (hardcover) — ISBN 0-335-19536-9 (pbk.)
      1. Gender Identity—Great Britain.   2. Educational sociology—
Great Britain.   3. Sex instruction—Great Britain.   4. Sex differences
in education—Great Britain.   5. Feminism and education—Great Britain.
6. Homosexuality and education—Great Britain.
I. Johnson, Richard, 1939–   .   II. Title.
LC192.2.E67   1997
306.43'2—dc21

                                                                                    97–23198
                                                                                         CIP

Typeset by Type Study, Scarborough
Printed in Great Britain by Biddles Ltd, Guildford and King's Lynn

Contents

This book is dedicated, with love, respect, and memories of their schooling, to our respective children:
Judith Green and Diana Paton;
Becky Johnson and Paul Johnson

Acknowledgements

Books are never written alone (or even by just two people). We owe debts of gratitude to a number of people, but especially:

- all the members of the Politics of Sexuality Group from the Department of Cultural Studies, Birmingham University, particularly Mary Kehily, Peter Redman and Deborah Steinberg, with whom we have been in constant discussion and who have read and commented on our work on sexuality, including chapters of this book, over a number of years;
- Judith Green, Frances Maher, Diana Paton for reading earlier drafts of various chapters;
- Shona Mullen, Pat Lee and Anita West at Open University Press, for their extended patience while waiting for the book to appear and continued belief that it would be worth it in the end;
- East Birmingham Health Authority, the University of Birmingham and the University of Central England for providing us with the money for help with interviewing, observation and transcription in the early stages of the research;
- the Institute of Education for funding the employment of a researcher to help with the search for newspaper cuttings;
- Alistair Chisholm, Louise Curry, Mary Kehily, Gurjit Minhas, Anoop Nayak and Shruti Tanna for their contributions to interviewing and observation and Judith Green for doing the press research.

Debbie would also like to thank:

- members of and visiting fellows to the Centre for Research and Education on Gender who have provided intellectual stimulation and personal friendship since she jointed the staff at the Institute of Education;

- Gunther Kress for making it possible for her to spend significant amounts of the Spring Term 1997 working on the book;
- students taking the MA in Women's Studies and Education during 1996/7, on whom she tried out many of our ideas during the final phase of writing.

Richard would also like to thank:

- Mariette Clare, Bob Bennett and Iris Johnson for discussions, support and putting up with 'deadline-itis';
- members of the Thesis Writers Group and the Research Practice course, Faculty of Humanities, Nottingham Trent University for discussion of examples from the book, including 'interviewing powerful people';
- Nottingham Trent University and Roger Bromley for a job where he can write.

CHAPTER I

Introduction: schooling sexualities/sexuality and schooling

Schooling and sexuality

Putting the terms 'schooling' and 'sexuality' together is the stuff of which scandal can be, and often is, made. After all, as the popular press would have us believe (see, for example, *Daily Mail*, 2 March 1996), sexuality is not a proper part of schooling, neither are schoolchildren ready to learn about sexuality. But almost every reader of this book will undoubtedly have memories of sexuality playing a big part in their experiences of schooling from the earliest days at school. These memories may take many forms: the (in)famous game of 'doctors and nurses' played by young children; those chasing games in which gender is emphasized, like kiss-chase played in most infant playgrounds; skipping and clapping rhymes like the well-known 'When Suzie was a . . .';[1] the agonies and ecstasies of dating, first boyfriends/girlfriends; the gossip, jokes and innuendo; the sexualized teasing and bullying that takes place in classrooms and playgrounds; crushes on teachers and harassment by teachers. All these and more contribute, in different ways, to experiences of schooling.

Given the ubiquity of such memories of schooling, it may seem surprising that talking about sexuality and schooling in the same breath can seem so disturbing (particularly to journalists and politicians). This may be partly because schooling stands rather on the 'public' side of public/private divisions, while sexuality is definitely on the private side. But schools are not only public or state institutions; they are also closely associated with childhood and with child–adult relations. They are therefore associated with all the discourses of childhood, which construct the child as pre- or asexual, as 'innocent', at least as an ideal. One of the key arguments of this book is that the idea of childhood sexual innocence inhibits attempts to alter, in more hopeful and progressive ways, the terrible and oppressive tangles which form part of child–adult relations in our culture.[2]

Actually schooling is associated with sexuality in particularly rich and complicated ways. These connections work at two levels, themselves inter-connected. The first level corresponds to the school itself. As places of every-day-life activity as well as public or state institutions, schools are sites where sexual and other identities are developed, practised and actively produced. Pupils, but also teachers and to a lesser extent other participants (parents, usually mothers, and other carers for example), are 'schooled' there, as gen-dered and sexual beings. Sexual and other social identities, as possible ways of living, are produced in relation to the cultural repertoires and insti-tutional conditions of schooling. School-based identity production is never final, nor can it encompass the whole of (even sexual) life – but it can have lasting, ramifying consequences in individual lives none the less.

Over and again in our interviews and discussions and in 'found' auto/bio-graphical accounts on questions of sexual identity, memories of school-based episodes emerged with surprising vividness. The stories told involve different kinds of fun and sadness, attraction or repulsion, emulation or desire, by no means always explicitly sexual, yet rarely without some sexual content. Sometimes it is a teacher who offers new material for a pupil's making of identity, becomes an object of desire, or someone whom the pupil wishes to be, or to be like in some way. Sometimes the memories are about the sex-and-identity alliances of a group of school 'mates' defined against other groups or individuals. Stories are told about sex as subversion and as harassment, mobilized in pupil cultures as a way of disconcerting teachers or of taunting other (often unpopular) pupils, and used by teachers to control pupils. Very often, as we shall see, the sexual cultures of school students are articulated in opposition to the school and its overt and covert sexual regimes. Sometimes stories concern an intimate relationship with a school friend, a student or a teacher colleague. Sometimes they involve a deep sense of individual isolation and 'difference'; sometimes a slow gathering of information and self-composure around some new knowledge of the self. Two rather different examples, presented here without much analysis, may give a clearer anticipatory shape to the stories of this school-based level:

> The next clear memory I have of any kind of emotions was some time between 11 and 12 in my first year of high school. I started getting the same feelings [as I had had for the pop singer Julie Roger] about a girl in my class, and putting her into the same kind of day dreams. I knew enough by then to add a couple of kisses (no tongues!!) before the happy ever after bit. I found myself trying to get her attention, to like

me, showing off if I knew she was watching, I discovered I could make her laugh, so I became a court-jester for a while. Looking back I'm sure she was having the same kinds of feelings but didn't know what to do with them either . . . A couple of class mates passed by and one said, 'You know if I was a lez I'd go for M as well.' I didn't have any feelings about the phrase except curiosity – I'd never heard the word. I couldn't find 'lez' in the dictionary either. I went to C, the class know-all, to see if she knew. After carefully checking that no-one was listening she explained that 'lez' was short for lesbian and it meant women who went to bed with other women. I mulled this over for a whole – 'What? You mean girls fall in love with girls like with boys?' 'Yes', she said. I couldn't see anything wrong with it. It seemed perfectly natural. I thought, fine. I've got a name. I'm a lez . . .

(National Lesbian and Gay Survey n.d.)

This story, like many of those cited in the second half of this book, is quite explicitly about sexuality. The following story, analysed in detail by the author himself in a recent published text, is less explicitly sexual, yet is about the attractiveness of a particular kind of masculinity, lived as a form of heterosexual manliness which the author later calls 'muscular intellectual-ness':

It is morning, the double period before lunch time . . . The teacher, John Lefevre, stands at the front of the class. It is history A level, my subject, and he is debating with us . . . Something has happened in the news and Mr Lefevre, as usual, disagrees with the general opinion of the class. Richard, one of the boys, makes a point, and I wait to hear how Mr Lefevre will respond. However, deciding to get back to his teaching plan, Mr Lefevre terminates the argument.

'Believe me', he says, 'if I wanted to, I could make a very convincing case.'

'Go on then', Richard says, and we laugh. Mr Lefevre holds his ground.

'We don't have time, but believe me, I could make a very convincing case.'

This phrase hits me between the eyes. It's not an evasion. In fact, it seems more compelling than a full reply would have been and I am both intrigued and excited by it . . . 'Believe me, I could make a very convincing case' held out the promise of another world. I subsequently became similarly intrigued by a phrase in Malcolm Bradbury's *The History Man* which, of all things, we were reading for English A level. The phrase ran, 'About this time, Howard started pushing people around intellectually at parties.' You could push people around intellectually. I hadn't realised.

(Redman and Mac an Ghaill 1997: 162–3)

The liveliness of their telling testifies to the immediacy of both these memories; the energy with which they are (re)constructed in the present (prompted of course by particular inquiries) shows their subjective significance, then and now. In fact, because schooling is a universal experience in this kind of society, most people have stories of this kind, though some may be untellable.

Nationalities and sexualities

If schooling and sexuality make a difficult dyad to think about, the conjoining of questions about sexuality with those of nationality may seem almost wilfully contrived. Indeed, Richard has been asked, when he offered a four-day 'compact course' entitled 'Nationalities and Sexualities' at the Humboldt University, Berlin, how *can* sexuality, which is so private and personal a matter, be connected with the economic and diplomatic preoccupations which constitute the central agenda of states, nations and 'Big P' politics? One young man who attended Richard's course said that he had 'come off the street' because the course title seemed so novel. Of course, this opening question was a gift to any teacher of the topic: now the course could focus on the challenge to explore just how 'organic' (but also how 'constructed') such a connection can be. There was a productive tension, a 'point', a question embedded in the teaching and learning from the beginning.

But teaching and writing about 'Nationalities and Sexualities' is of course part of a larger struggle. The surprise at such a title[3] is testimony to the power of certain divisions, especially that between everyday personal, private, local lives and the universalizing categories and national and even global reach of 'public affairs' and 'international relations'. As many feminist critics have argued, formal politics and the state, while appearing universal within a given territory, are actually deeply gendered categories (see, for example, Pateman 1988; Anthias *et al.* 1992; Unterhalter 1996). The links between gender and sexuality have been explored extensively in writings, especially feminist writings, about sexuality. The debates about these links have taken many forms and covered many aspects of sexuality.[4] We have found Adrienne Rich's notion of 'compulsory heterosexuality' (Rich 1980) helpful, but particularly generative for us have been our readings of Judith Butler (1990, 1993). We have found Butler's work particularly useful for her idea that gender is performed and that it is inescapably linked to what she has called the 'heterosexual matrix', that is, the idea that gender is culturally understood through the notion of heterosexual attraction to those of the opposite gender/sex.

The sexual nature of the state, too, can be better understood when viewed through this lens. David Evans (1993), Davina Cooper (1994), Anna Marie Smith (1994) and others have argued that the state, national and local state policies and public discourses in general, though appearing asexual, always have sexual categories and preferences embedded in them. The state both has sexual foundations and regulates other sexual sites and practices and these are completely entwined with questions of gender. We need only think about the regulation of abortion and of new reproductive technologies to see how the state is involved in the regulation of women's bodies in and through their sexuality. Legislation about who may serve in the armed forces, about prostitution, about rape, or about the age of consent are also areas where the state intervenes to regulate or discipline gendered sexualities. Indeed, it is hard to conceive of a version of a nation that does not address its citizens in more or less explicitly sexualized and gendered terms, terms which are inflected, too, by other social differences like class and race.

Yet to say this still causes a certain frisson, an element of surprise, even outrage. The joining of sexualities and nationalities is far more likely to come from those who are interested first in sex and gender than it is from those who are interested first in the state, formal politics and nationalist histories and movements. In the explosion of work on national identity and nationalism since the early 1980s, most of it written by male historians, sociologists and political scientists, the majority of texts, from the classic to the contemporary, offer completely genderless accounts of these phenomena and rarely engage with questions of sex and sexual identity (e.g. Gellner 1983; Anderson 1991).

Nationalities and schooling

The introduction of the National Curriculum in the UK following the Education Reform Act 1988 has made it much easier to conceive of schooling and nationality as being related. Even before that, education (at least during the primary years) had been defined as a function of the state for over a century in the UK and other late capitalist countries, while in post-colonial countries it has been seen as one of the crucial responsibilities of government in the processes of nation-building. Indeed, in the run-up to the May 1997 General Election in the UK, it was striking that all three major political parties had identified education as a key priority area for the new government. So we are much more used to thinking about nationality and schooling together than about schooling and sexuality or about nationality and sexuality.

Even so, it sometimes comes as a shock to realize just how much of a part schooling is meant to play in the production of national identities. Thus, when Nick Tate, in his capacity as head of the Schools Curriculum and Assessment Authority (SCAA), or Secretaries of State for Education make statements about the kind of English that children are meant to speak, the canon of literature they are meant to read, or the kind of history they are meant to know, there is a kind of jarring, especially of liberal sensibilities.

Equally, when legislation about education specifies that school assemblies shall be of a broadly Christian character, it may even seem shocking in a multi-ethnic, multi-religious (and irreligious) society. In the UK education has been at the heart of highly contested versions of nation. Education, and the failures of education, have come to stand for what is desirable and what is amiss in the nation. There is, furthermore, a kind of moral fervour about the demands on schools to produce not only academically achieving young people, but also young people who are 'upright moral citizens', who refrain from taking drugs and from 'illicit' sexual practices (from teenage girls having babies through 'promiscuity', however defined, to same sex desire), which brings sexuality strongly into the picture.

State processes and formal politics are not the only ways in which national identities are formed. Important too are the publics which are constituted through the different media – through the national daily press, for instance, or through girls', women's and young men's magazines, or through the large and heterogeneous audiences for TV soap operas. We will be asking questions about how dominant versions of the sexual (as produced in the public domain of politics and the media and within the micro-politics of particular schools) affect sexualities in schools, about the part that public homophobias and sex education play in producing school-based sexualities.

Another pervasive theme of this book is the relationship between the margins and the centre. We will explore the ways in which the very fears held by the centre that those on the margins (for example, lesbians and gays) will disrupt and control the social fabric give the margins kinds of power, while at the same time punishing those who are marginalized.[5] As we shall see, marginalized categories turn out to be crucial in the self-production of the 'centred' ones (white, heterosexual, middle-class and so on), a process most noticeable (in relation to sexuality) in public displays of homophobia by politicians and in the media, but also important in the daily lives of those in schools. The significance of, and perceived danger from, stigmatized sexual categories (the 'homosexual', the 'promiscuous' young woman) is demonstrated in repeated moral panics which attend sexuality, education and sexuality and education.

The book will, therefore, focus on dominant, homophobic and heterosexist discourses in the public domain and on the experiences of lesbians and gays in schools. Connell (1995: 90), in his book on *Masculinities*, explains that:

> Rather than spread the research thin, I decided to concentrate on a few situations where the theoretical yield should be high ... I tried to identify groups of men for whom the construction or integration of masculinity was under pressure.

In exploring the experiences of lesbians and gays we are following a similar principle. Sexual identities, whether normatively heterosexual or seen as deviant, are strongly policed and produced in and through schooling and this places lesbian and gay teachers and students under particular pressures. For this reason, their situations are likely to help us understand sexualities more generally, encapsulating and focusing the ways they are played out in relation to other social differences (like class, ethnicity and gender) within school situations.

Auto/ biographical issues

It is commonplace, both in Women's Studies and in Cultural Studies (our 'disciplinary' areas), to acknowledge the role of autobiography in research and writing. Books are written from particular standpoints, and we believe that it is important for readers to understand where we are coming from, in terms of who we are as much as in terms of what we think. The research for and writing of this book (and other joint work on sexuality) has preoccupied us for so long now – it is nearly six years since we began to work together seriously – that it is quite difficult to remember what led up to our research partnership. The period of our working together has also been significant for both of us in our personal and professional lives.

For Debbie Epstein, the marginalization and stigmatization of particular groups has been an issue for as long as she can remember. Growing up as a Jewish, white South African opposed to apartheid, within a tradition of Jewish socialism, was key to her early identity formation. Being Jewish in apartheid South Africa brought with it the extensive privileges of whiteness, while remaining, in some ways, not quite white enough. Debbie well remembers, for example, lessons about 'race' as part of the South African national curriculum (entitled Christian National Education), the main point of which was to teach pupils about the inferiority of black South Africans, but which also included instruction on how to recognize a Jew. As a new immigrant to the UK in the 1960s and as a school teacher from the late 1960s through to the late 1980s she was immersed in and committed to feminist and anti-racist activism and approaches to teaching. These became the central foci of her PhD thesis (published as Epstein 1993) about anti-racist strategies in predominantly white primary schools. When she came out as a lesbian during the 'Stop the Clause' campaign,[6] it was, perhaps, inevitable that sooner or later her work would focus on issues of sexuality and schooling.

Richard Johnson has long been interested in the history and politics of education (see CCCS 1981; Education Group II (Cultural Studies Birmingham) 1990). For Richard, an interest in sexuality is, perhaps, less obviously key to his personal life, especially since, as a white, middle-class, heterosexual man his various identities are unmarked, usually unspoken and unnoticed. For Richard, then, concerns about sexuality and schooling arose in part from the experiences of his close gay and lesbian friends (one of which is detailed in Bartell 1994). He had also been influenced by his feminist friends and colleagues to begin to ask questions about heterosexuality. This was a process in which he was already deeply involved by the beginning of the 1990s, but after the death of his wife Jill in January 1992 he was forced to reflect, as part of the process of grieving, on the course of his own life with Jill. This included considering the effects on her of his involvement in a major heterosexual relationship outside their marriage. He has analysed this experience (both in personal and political terms) in poetry and in prose form in another book (Steinberg *et al.* 1997). Suffice it to say, here, that these experiences have significantly affected his analyses of sexuality in schooling and in the public domain.

The opportunity to work together on these issues arose out of a coincidence of interest in sexuality and schooling in 1991 when Debbie had just completed her PhD at, and was doing some part-time teaching for, the Department of Cultural Studies in Birmingham and while Richard was still on the staff there. Out of our joint interests, we formed a 'subgroup' of staff, graduate and undergraduate students associated with the Department of Cultural Studies, to read, discuss and investigate the Politics of Sexuality.[7] We were also fortunate to be able to carry out research in schools and with lesbian and gay students and teachers, using money from East Birmingham Health Authority and linking with Peter Redman's 'Young People and HIV' project. This book is the outcome of our research, discussions with each other and with others, as well as of our reading and thinking. We have both been asked, on occasion, about our collaboration. It seems strange to many that we, a woman who identifies as lesbian and a man who identifies as heterosexual, should wish to, or even be able to, work together in the kind of close collaboration required to produce a book. Indeed, the work has not been without its difficulties, but both of us have experienced our collaboration as among the most productive we have been involved in.

In writing this book, we have worked together in a variety of ways. We have discussed ideas, planned research, interpreted evidence together. We wrote Chapter 5 first, and we wrote it together, sitting at the word processor, fielding ideas off each other, arguing the merits of individual sentences, drafting and redrafting until we were both satisfied. We felt this was important as the chapter is, in some ways, the crux of the book, the point at which we turn our attention to the school as an institution and try to show how it is situated in the discursive frameworks we have developed in the earlier chapters. This introduction and the conclusion to the book were also written together, but right at the end of the process. Richard wrote the first drafts of Chapters 2, 3 and 4, while Debbie wrote the first drafts of Chapters 6, 7 and 8. At every point, we discussed what we were doing, shared our drafts and gave each other comments for redrafting. At the final stages, we spent time together in order to reach an agreed final draft, going through each chapter, changing some of the wording, ensuring that the two parts hung together as we wished them to. It has been a long and arduous process, but one which we would recommend to people as challenging and enriching. We hope that our readers will find this reflected in the book itself.

Using the book

We have written the book in two parts, each of which begins with a brief introduction on questions and methodologies. Part One, Sexualities in the Public Domain, explores the ways that a kind of 'national' public is constructed – through formal politics and government and through the media – which appears to be 'universal'. Like other identities, this version of the public and of nation (versions of who 'We' are) is defined in part by what it is not. Some identities are recognized and strengthened (for example, the 'normal' heterosexual identities of British subjects who marry, live together and have children), while others are not (for example, the heterosexual marriage between a British subject and someone from the Indian subcontinent, or lesbian and gay identities). Such discourses – versions of the nation – are closely connected with state power: with party, governmental and official 'policies', with legislation, administrative discretions and the law, with military and police powers and legitimized coercion. They do incite but they also repress; they do reward but they also punish; they do 'educate' but they also dominate; they do win the consent of some but they do coerce the rest. Often they are also organized around enabling other forces – the power of economic relations especially.

Part Two, Sexualities in Schools, looks closely and analytically at the production of sexual identities at this school-based level. Basically, we shall be arguing that sexuality is intrinsic to the formation of individual and group identities in schools and that schools are sites for the active making of such identities and of meanings around sexuality. In this regard, we are interested in exploring not only the formal sexual curriculum (in the form of sex education), but the sexual cultures of both teachers and students, which are intrinsic to the dynamics of schooling, for example in relation to control, resistance and 'discipline'.

We believe that both parts are essential to developing a full understanding of the complex and multiply-layered ways in which sexualities and schooling are connected and shape each other. It is, for example, necessary to know what the constraints on teachers are in order to be able to understand why they might teach as many do, especially in sex education, in ways which could be described as 'defensive'. Equally, we need to understand what the resources are for making sense of sexuality which young people in schools develop outside the school and bring with them into the school. The structures of dominance which are lived out by young people and teachers in schools are not those of the school alone. On the other hand, our understandings of the public discourses of politics and media in relation to schooling can be clarified by a close look at schooling as an important institution for the production of social identities, be they national, gendered, classed or sexualized.

We would, therefore, recommend that the book is read as a whole, but, for some readers, especially teachers, it may be more interesting to read Part Two before Part One. The final chapter, our conclusion, highlights the theoretical framework and political positions that have informed our study. Here we consider the implications of our analysis throughout the book for what might be termed 'sexuality and education otherwise'.

Postscript

The writing of this book was completed in April 1997; most of the research on which it is based was undertaken between one and five years before Labour's electoral victory of 1 May. We have not attempted to incorporate, into this account, our feelings (relief? hope? scepticism?) or our predictions around the Blairite victory. However, we had already paid some attention, in our analysis, to the limits of what we call 'social liberalism', and a cluster of discourses that are especially likely to frame Labour policies in the areas of sexuality and schooling (see, particularly, Chapter 3). We have also stressed the vulnerability of social liberalism to conservative assumptions and campaigning.

It is still too soon to predict the main lines of policy within the new government in an area that does not seem to have priority. It seems that many of the tyrannies and idiocies of Conservative rule are over, but what does this mean for sexual conservatism in a larger social sense? How far will emergent and oppositional elements within sexual culture influence the forms of regulation and social recognition under New Labour? It remains to be seen.

Notes

1 See Epstein (1997b) for a discussion of such games in primary schools.
2 For extended discussions of the dangers to children of notions of 'childhood innocence' connected to child sexual abuse, see Kitzinger (1988, 1990).
3 Not so unfamiliar in the academic literature, especially work on empire and sex/gender (Mosse 1985; Yuval-Davis and Anthias 1989; Parker *et al.* 1992). Even so, it is surprising in how many accounts of national identity and nationalism remain completely genderless.
4 For a representative selection of feminist writing about sexuality from many different perspectives see Jackson and Scott (1996) and Richardson (1996).

5 See hooks (1984) for a discussion of this in relation to 'race' and gender in the USA.
6 For an account of the role this campaign had in 'promoting homosexuality' see Stacey (1991).
7 Richard has written about the history of this group in Steinberg *et al.* (1997).

PART ONE

Sexualities in the public domain

In Chapter 1 we have argued that the connections between schooling and sexuality can be explored at two related levels. Schools themselves are places where sexual identities are produced on an everyday basis, but public culture – formal politics and the media for example – is also saturated with sexual representations. Sometimes these explicitly link sexuality and schooling; always, however, they provide the context in which sexualities are lived in the schools.

In this part of the book we focus on the ways in which sexuality and schooling are connected through public discourses. Because much public discourse occurs within a national frame, or constructs a national 'we', we have also to take seriously the ways in which both sexuality and schooling are 'nationalized' – given meaning in terms of 'the nation'. Schooling and sexuality are often linked through the nation: from a dominant point of view, for instance, schooling is often meant to underpin 'the family' as an aspect of 'the British way of life'.

This public or national level is important in our study, and inescapable for practitioners in and around the schools, for several different reasons. Most obviously, the schools themselves are subject to public scrutiny and regulation. Despite the delegation of control and finances to the school-based level, or perhaps because of it, schools have become increasingly subject to central state agencies. The labyrinthine regulation of sex education in British state schools by Act of Parliament and Department for Education and Employment (DfEE) Circulars is an obvious example. Practice in this area has to attend carefully to the state of the law. But school sexualities are also externally regulated through public media. One of the most powerful of sanctions for teachers and governors of schools is adverse publicity in the local or national media, especially if linked to parental complaints or political campaigning. Fear of publicity has itself an effect on school policies. Legislation itself not only works juridically but also forms opinions. It can convey a vague sense of prohibition which, in law, may not be strictly accurate. Section 28 of the Local Government Act of 1988, for example, is often understood as banning teaching about homosexualities in schools; actually it does no such thing. Rather it bans the 'promotion' of homosexuality by local authorities. Since local authorities have not been directly responsible for sex education since 1986, Section 28 does not limit the scope of sex education teaching in schools. It undoubtedly contributes to an atmosphere of intimidation however, a nightmare that includes scandals in the press, ministerial statements and the arrival of 'hit squads'.

A more diffused connection between public culture and schooling is through public representations of the sexual. There are particular forms of 'sexual news' in which schools or teachers are directly represented – sex education scandals for instance. But representing the sexual across the whole range of public media can be seen as a kind of sex(uality) education. Some sexual identities or behaviours are incited or rewarded, others attacked or punished. Some are regarded as 'normal' or thoroughly British, others dubious or 'alien'. Such constructions – which we will explore in detail – convey messages to adults and children alike, depending on their own positioning in sexual and national discourses. Moreover, public discourses of the sexual, especially those of commercial popular culture, furnish many of the raw materials from which young people fashion their identities and outlooks. When Peter Redman experienced the desire to be like his teacher 'John Lefevre', he connected the desirable aspect of his teacher with something said by a character in a novel he was reading. When the young woman in our first story was called 'lez' by a friend, she had immediate (and unsuccessful) recourse to a dictionary – that authoritative-seeming compendium of the dominant culture. Such processes are important for understanding the production of sexual identity in schools, but this is not all. Studying the ways young people appropriate, re-work or reject these versions also throws a retrospective light on the adult sexual world: its absences, its curiosities and its contradictions.

The different levels of contestation over the sexual constantly interact. Public debates about sexuality in general set parameters for what is possible or permissible in schools; school-based debates reconfirm the conservatism of the larger sexual culture or open up the contradictions within it, not least because school students have their own sources of sexual knowledge and culture. Schooling is a generative point for sexual life; a site where national–sexual culture is actually formed in a particular inter-generational dynamic. We want to study 'schooling sexualities' partly because we are concerned with educational issues and with state policies in this area; but we also want to study it because it is a generative point for sexual identities and culture more generally.

So far we have used some key terms – 'discourses' especially – without really explaining them. These terms may not be familiar – or they may be contentious. The term discourse as it has been used in cultural studies and in the social sciences brings into close association ideas of knowledge, power and identity. Human agents cannot stand outside culture and wield power precisely as they wish. Power is always limited and shaped by systems of knowledge which also shape the subjects and objects of power. Often, as the French philosopher and historian Michel Foucault argued, power actually inheres in forms of 'Power/Knowledge' (Foucault 1980). Classically, Foucault applied this term to systematic knowledges like medicine, criminology or psychology. These are systems of knowledge (of the body, of crime, of the human psyche) but they are also forms of power (of the doctor, of the law, of the psychiatrist). These forms of power/knowledge position us as subjects of particular kinds. They put pressure on us to adopt particular identities: the patient, the criminal, the 'unbalanced' or insane. In this particular sense, power and knowledge as discourse 'constructs' social identities. It is a kind of educative pressure, a kind of pedagogy or technology. Others would add that power is also accompanied by 'structures of feeling' (Williams 1977) or by fantasies of desire, enjoyment, fear, hatred, recognition, power and powerlessness (Fanon 1986; Zizek 1989; Benjamin 1990; Bhabha 1994). Most generally, we can say that terms like 'discourse' draw attention to the cultural forms and conditions of power. Obviously, discourse in this sense is not limited to state institutions; it is a medium of power across the whole social space.

This use of discourse is important to us today because of our approach to cultural studies, the intellectual–political perspective which we share. In our view, an important priority for today is to re-embed cultural analysis in an understanding of political and economic processes, and also to re-embed power relations and economic circuits in their own cultural conditions. In our vocabulary, 'discourse' is not just a description of culture or language as the more linguistic usages imply. Rather, it highlights the cultural *element* in social practices, without dividing meaning/feeling from the other forms of action in the world. On the other side, it does imply a criticism of simple or reductive economic arguments in politics: economic and political power cannot be reduced to some transparent working of 'interests' or the realistic pursuit of advantage. The question is advantage according to what criteria, agenda, priorities?

Discourse is used in two different ways in contemporary analysis. It is used strictly, in the singular, to describe a systematic disciplinary deployment of knowledge and power, especially of a 'scientific' kind.[1] This is useful sometimes for our own analysis if we want to highlight the importance of a particular strand of sexual discourse – for example the role of science or religion in conceptions of 'the normal' or 'natural'. Alternatively, discourse can be used more loosely – adjectivally as in 'discursive formation' or 'discursive strategy'.[2] 'Discursive formation' draws attention to *combinations* of discourses and gestures to the dynamics of larger social changes. This version of discourse draws Foucaultian analysis closer to a culturally rich materialism, which is concerned with the history of unequal social relationships and the forms of consciousness which challenge or support them.[3]

Grasping our topic at all would be hopeless did not regularities of meaning congeal around both 'sex 'and 'education'. These meanings are tangible – as we discover if we transgress them – but they are also moveable. 'Formation' implies both the pattern and its historicity or transience. Some elements in a formation may be relatively old, residual or revived; others may be currently dominant – they define where all the other elements belong; others are new or emergent, capable in potential of redefining the whole area. There may be very strong contradictions within or between these elements, inhibiting and enabling new practices. It is these contradictions that block a formation – or move it along.

By 'discursive formation', then, we mean a particular historical combination of discourses or discursive strategies with different histories, but combined in particular relations of force, in process in the same place and time. Discursive formation in this sense is close to the idea of a sexual culture, understanding this as something which is always being produced, always changing and internally very diverse. 'Discursive strategy' refers to a subset of this formation, itself a combination, unified around its practical/political tendency. Strategies often link different nodes or sites: the family, school and state for instance. 'Strategy' in this sense is broader than political party. Strategy may include intentionality and planning, but also indicates forms of power and culture with logics of their own. It is one element in a struggle of many elements in a historical formation. In contemporary sexual culture in Britain and the USA for instance, 'moral traditionalism' – the insistence on the importance of 'family values' and conservative gender relations – is a good example of a strategy.

Discursive formations always involve the internal contestation of strategies: moral traditionalisms versus sexual radicalisms for instance. We always need to ask: what are the relative positions of different discursive and political strategies? How does one strategy contain or disorganize another? How is another emerging? Is it potentially counter-hegemonic? These terms – dominant, hegemonic, subordinate and emergent – describe the relative positions and potentials of strategies.

We can now formulate the purposes of Part One more clearly. In our first three chapters we seek to identify the discursive strategies which make up the contemporary cultural formation around the sexual. This is the context of power and meanings within which the work of sexual identity in schools takes place, though schooling also plays a part in constituting and changing the formation. In addition we want to look at some of the more particular ways in which public sexual discourse impacts upon the school, regulating, constraining and disorganizing its practices.

In Chapter 2 the focus is on the national dimensions of schooling and sexuality. We address the sceptic's question: how can sexuality and nationality be so closely connected? And what is the place of schooling in making this connection? We are especially concerned in this chapter with the construction of sexual hierarchies, in which some forms and aspects of the sexual are recognized and supported as exemplary of Britishness or Englishness and others are rendered marginal – or worse. We are also concerned to identify what is specific about the sexual politics of the 1980s and 1990s compared with earlier periods.

Chapter 3 looks more closely at the range of sexual discourses deployed at the formal political level in Britain today and at the state of play between different discursive strategies. This is important for understanding the directions and ambiguities of state regulation of sexuality in and around the schools. It is also linked to our exploration of emergent and potentially counter-hegemonic strategies in Chapter 8. Though our focus in Chapter 3 is on the dominant discourses, our aim is also to show their contradictoriness and instability.

Chapter 4 shifts attention from formal politics and the state to the other major regulative force – the public media. The roles of the media in relation to sexuality are diverse, but our case studies concern the role of sexual scandal in the daily and Sunday national press. We argue that 'the scandalous' is one of the key ways in which the sexual figures in the national sexual culture, that it is deeply problematic, and that it disorganizes a more educative and egalitarian practice. We end the chapter with discussion of the ways in which schools, children and teachers have figured in recent sexual scandals.

Notes

1 Foucault, for example, was especially interested in the emergence of the social sciences but often in their 'applied' aspects (e.g. Foucault 1977).
2 For Foucault's use of 'strategy' see Foucault (1978: 99–114). Strategy is always a discursive combination.
3 Historically too 'discursive formation' seems to arise as a category at the point where Marxist theory, especially the Gramscianism of the 1970s, takes on board some elements of Foucauldian discourse theory and poststructuralism more generally, e.g. in the work of Stuart Hall and other Birmingham writers and Ernesto Lacau and Chantal Mouffe (1985). See for example Hall (1988: 51).

CHAPTER 2

Sexualities, nationalities and schooling

Our first task in this chapter is to understand how the links (so surprising and scandalous, it seems) are made between sexuality, the nation and the school. Our second task is to describe in outline the dominant national–sexual formations. Which sexual and gendered identities are privileged in constructions of Britishness and which marginalized or rendered Other? Our final task is to identify some typical features of the national–sexual politics of our own times and the ways schooling is positioned within this nexus.

Constructing the (sexual) nation

We want to argue that national identity, in general, can best be understood as a 'nationalization' of other social identities. National identity works in and through everyday social identities and experiences. It depends on everyday experiences and influences the ways they are lived. Practices of the state, or of other institutions that take the national voice, continuously regulate other social identities, differentially representing or recognizing them. In this sense nationality functions as a kind of meta-narrative of identity. It puts all the citizens in their places; it defines who belongs and who doesn't. It 'nationalizes' – names and rewards as national – some groups; excludes and punishes others as foreign or alien. We can analyse any version of the nation – a political speech, a television situation comedy, a package of legislative policies or indeed a National Curriculum or a subject area within it – as a structure of recognitions of this kind.[1]

In any representation of the nation, some social groups and identities find themselves plentifully recognized and endorsed, others marginalized or stigmatized. In the controversies over the National Curriculum in history, for example, debate centred upon what we might call differential remembering and forgetting. Was the curriculum mainly to be about Britain and Britishness and how was Britishness to be defined? How far was the formation of Britain in a wider world of Others to be recognized? The questions gained urgency because of the settled presence of people from the old imperial 'peripheries' in the British Isles today. Were these long relationships to be honoured in memory, concretized historically, and what did that mean for the whole national framework as a way of doing history, of publicly remembering? What implications did the inclusion and exclusion of a 'national' history have for identities in Britain today? Would young people of Asian or African–Caribbean or Hong-Kong Chinese heritage recognize themselves in this version of Britishness? How indeed would white Anglo-British schoolchildren understand themselves in relation to their black friends and neighbours and their own white imperial past? (For some of these debates see History Workshop 1990.)

These processes of remembering and recognizing are important because they affect the powers of different groups to define themselves and become active, collectively. They shape individual identity too. Non-recognition or mis-recognition makes it hard to develop or elaborate a recognizable identity, to put into circulation an acceptable story about yourself. Public stigmatization threatens to disorganize identities, especially at their points of emergence. When recognition structures are linked to state power, they affect material security, at individual and communal levels. The state may punish certain social identities (single parents for example) and reward others (for example married men). It wields a wide range of powerful ways and means: from direct criminalization to taxation and 'benefits' policies.

An example may focus this argument more clearly. In June 1996 there was a controversy in Britain about the destination of money from the National Lottery, a proportion of which is donated to various charitable causes. The Prime Minister attacked awards to sexual minority groups as 'ill-founded and ill-judged'. Four or five awards (out of more than 2000) were given to lesbian and gay support groups (a community centre, an outreach project, a youth group), and one each to an anti-deportation group supporting asylum seekers and a charity offering education, health provision, welfare and legal advice to prostitutes and rent boys (*The Guardian*, 12 June 1996). On the same day, Major's attack was given prominent, often front page/double spread attention in the Conservative national press under headlines like 'Lottery Bonanza for the Bizarre' (*Daily Mail*), 'Jackpot They Do Not Deserve' (*Daily Express*), 'Lotta Waste: Handouts to Hookers and Mums who Drum' (*Sun*), 'Major Hits at Lottery Cash for Vice Girls' (*Daily Telegraph*). In four papers, including the Labourite *Daily Mirror*, this story was juxtaposed to another: a story of a young woman who had disappeared from a nightclub when separated from her friends. Pictured smiling to camera in her graduation outfit, with mortar board, gown and degree certificate, she was described as a model young woman – as '[a] doctor's missing girlfriend' (*Express*), 'our loving daughter [who] would never run away' (*Mail*) and 'my perfect daughter' with 'everything to live for' (*Mirror*).

Such juxtaposition is a common rhetorical device in the British press: idealized examples of the 'normal' sexual categories, associated with heterosexual marriage and coupledom, are placed alongside images of other sexualities, especially of homosexual desire or of sex workers. The 'perfect' figures, often young women, are, however, often presented as threatened and vulnerable; the Others are constructed as marginal, bizarre, worthless or threatening, threatening especially to children and to other 'innocents'. As the *Sun* leader put it, speaking as usual for a (populist, masculine) 'everyone':

> The people who buy the [lottery] tickets are sick of seeing their cash given to lesbians, gays, prostitutes, rent boys, junkies and asylum seekers . . . The lottery needs what the balls get every Saturday . . . *A darned good shake-up* (original emphasis).
>
> (*Sun*, 12 June 1996)

Such constructions convey messages which are read by young people in many different contexts. The proceeds of a lottery which is termed national, and which is contributed to by more than 90 per cent of the population should not be used to support, in any way it seems, young sex workers or lesbians and gay men. Such groups are deemed socially worthless; they are to be denied any kind of recognition; they don't count at all. Indeed, since a main purpose of one stigmatized organization – that for the education of prostitutes – was to prevent the spread of HIV and AIDS, the implication of banning such help is to deny the right to life to stigmatized groups. Such groups, despite their not-unheard connections with the private lives of public men, simply should not exist. On the other hand, positive recognition – backed in this case by lottery money – can do wonders for a local organization, battling against prejudice and shortage of cash.[2] Nor is it clear that those who can identify with the preferred sexual categories are well served by them. Idealization makes it difficult to discuss the more problematic aspects of being seen, for instance, as 'a good girl'. Similarly, to erect marriage as an (impossible?) ideal is to feed its failures.

The regulation of local social identities by public discourses is only one side of the relation of nationalities and sexualities. National identity is also dependent on other social identities. Particular versions only work politically if they connect up with everyday life experiences. Versions of the nation are always (as a minimum list) gendered, classed, racialized or ethnicized, and sexualized in particular ways. They address these differences through ordinary, everyday, private practices like the production and consumption of food, patterns of family life, seasonal celebrations, sport and leisure. There is no clear division between state and civil society, or between public and private domains. These boundaries are shifting, mobile, uneven, contradictorily defined and fought over. Yet forms of the public/private division are central, for example, in struggles over sexual regulation and freedom: they are not only imposed; they may also be fought for. They are indeed the product of power *relations*. Nationalism therefore 'works' – it becomes a 'material force' – to the degree that it crosses into the local and everyday, connects itself with existing social identities and reconstructs agenda for living. It must be naturalized as 'common sense' or, in Billig's useful term, 'banal' (Billig 1995).

So every version of the nation is also a social politics. Different patterns of recognition and non-recognition shape civil society in different ways. In the era of Thatcherism, dominant political discourse insistently preferred the identities of entrepreneurs and managers over those of workers and professionals, married men and women over single mothers. New social identities were also invented and evaluated: 'the job-seeker', for instance, or the 'failed' teacher or school, or 'the parent-consumer-who-chooses-for-the-child'.

It follows also that national identity is always complex, composite, plural – 'national identities'. 'Making differences' is a key function of nationalist discourse, differences 'externally' of course, but also inside the nation. Most approaches to nationalism and national identity, even those that see it as a construction, stress the production of unity, community and relative cultural homogeneity – 'one nation, one culture' (Gellner 1983; Anderson 1991; Smith 1994; see Schlesinger 1991 for a critique). The analysis here suggests that it is more revealing to understand the nation as an accentuation of differences.

Finally, national identities are constructions or productions. Even the nation's traditions must be invented (Hobsbawm and Ranger 1983). In this production, mass schooling has always been an important aspect since its nineteenth-century origins (Gellner 1983). Historically, universal schooling and nation-building have gone hand in hand. As in Britain today, control of schooling has always been important to nationalist politicians (Avis *et al.* 1996).

That the nation must be produced is clear if we compare the diversity of sexual practices in contemporary Britain with what counts as British in a particular version. If we try to encompass all the different ways that lives are led with some erotic content or meaning in Britain today, we find an incredible, chaotic diversity: differences in erotic and bodily preferences, in the objects and intensities of desire, in 'dating', in patterns of marriage or partnership, and in public custom and ritual around these things. Not all of these differences are easily 'ethnicized'. There are diversities within 'communities' too, including the class and regional communities of Anglo-English 'natives'.

In 'nationalizing' such chaotic patterns, however, we must make a selection, which is also an evaluation, from the whole range. We transform the scene: we make some practices visible; we make others disappear. There is a world of difference between speaking of 'ways of life in Britain' and of 'the British way of life'. The difference, the transformations, testify to the work involved in producing a nation.

Nationalizing identities: some transformations

Production requires producers. Of course, we are all producers of sexual and national identities in our daily life. We produce national and sexual identities and connect them, for instance, if we introduce ourselves as 'an Englishman' or 'Englishwoman'. Any elaborated or powerful version, however, requires the work of specialized cultural producers with access to the larger publics. These agents may be individuals ('intellectuals' of different kinds including academic researchers) or institutions (e.g. particular media, political parties, education systems, schools). They produce, make public and circulate particular versions of what it is to be British.

It is useful to work through one such version to make this argument more concretely. Our example is chosen from a nation at war, a classical location of the making of sex–gender differences, often in exaggerated forms.

British television news in 1982 was dominated by the Falklands/Malvinas conflict.[3] So too were the reviews in which the BBC and ITN produce, between Christmas and the beginning of January, their condensed retrospects of the year. Though new forms of television and neo-television (satellite, cable, video) are eroding this post-Christmas holiday nation, broadcast television, especially in its entertainment forms, remains a powerful source of nation construction. Of the two reviews of December 1982, the Independent Television News (ITN) version was the most 'popular' and closest to entertainment narratives – it was a racy adventure story, with little room for critical reflection and with the more tragic aspects of the war suppressed. Most striking, perhaps, were the emotional scenes as returning soldiers disembarked and were greeted by crowds of friends and relatives. These scenes 'worked' as popular television and as patriotic display because they connected up private everyday identities and feelings about them with the celebrating of a 'glorious national victory'. On the public side were familiar national symbols: monarchy, union jack, Land of Hope and Glory. On the private side was 'the family' – 'the men' (not boys now, but men) returning home alive, survivors, heroes, and the fathers, mothers, brothers, sisters, but especially girlfriends, wives and children who welcomed them home. In ITN's version, personal, familial and sexual relations were accentuated by the editing together of a sequence of hugs and kisses, each on a beat of patriotic music. The sequence closed with a soldier and (we are to assume?) his wife and young son walking away from camera along the quayside, arms wrapped around each other, carrying a union jack: the family 'nationalized'.

Most obviously there is a process of *selection* going on here, producing patterned presences and absences. Absent (though sometimes mentioned afterwards, at the margin) were sons, husbands or lovers who did not return, or returned wounded, scarred or maddened, those who waited in vain, or greeted their loved ones in pain or anger. Absent too were those whose intimate relationships departed from the dominant sexual norm. No homosexual lovers could have a place here. Rather the representations were hysterically heterosexual – 'Lock Up Your Daughters – The Bootnecks are Back' threatened one ship-side banner. Though members of the forces were central to the narrative, many of their experiences too were absent or misrecognized. Later some soldiers spoke of the horror they had been through, unrecognized and unrecognizable in the terms imposed by the civilian nation and its media war (e.g. 'The Falklands War: The Untold Story', Yorkshire TV, April 1987).

Selection is accompanied by *evaluation*. This was clearest in Mrs Thatcher's own versions of rejoicing over victory, in her interventions during the war and in her triumphal post-Falklands speeches. The Task Force and its victory was made into 'an object lesson' representing 'the real spirit of Britain' that could be recaptured in other ways, notably in economic successes. Soldier heroes (and especially their officer–managers) were exalted to the status of exemplary citizens. Those who had opposed the war were 'the waverers and the fainthearts'. The leaders of strikes on the railways or in the National Health Service were obstructing 'Britain's recovery, which all our people long to see'. Reinventing her own traditions, Mrs Thatcher insisted:

> We have not changed. When the demands of war and the dangers to our own people call us to arms – then we British are as we have always been – competent, courageous and resolute.
>
> (Thatcher 1989: 161)

As in Thatcher's speech, evaluation can take the form of a simple polarization of good and bad: the exemplary versus the deviant; the socially central versus the marginal. But there are more complex postionings even in apparently simple texts. We, the ideal viewers or listeners, are neither heroes nor villains: rather we are addressed as potential heroes or warned against excluding ourselves from the triumphal scene. If we cannot wear the ideal categories, it is up to us to measure up to them, even to cut or stretch ourselves to fit. Such representations do not merely recognize or refuse recognition – they also mis-recognize, or recognize conditionally. Their effect is to put pressure on the reader to change or to conform: you can be recognized, but only if are like 'us'. You must assimilate to the dominant Englishness or ethnicity – especially if you are black or a militant trade unionist or otherwise appear as a stranger.

Sexual identities take the weight of these pressures in a particular way, partly because invisibility is an available strategy, partly because sexuality, in contemporary discourse, is seen to go to the heart of personal identity (Heath 1982; Weeks 1986). The dilemmas of mis-recognition – whether to conform or to stay silent and be 'true to yourself' – are experienced clearly and collectively discussed. Strategies of 'coming out' or 'staying in the closet' are central to histories of personal and collective politics among lesbians and gay men (Weeks 1977; D'Emilio 1992). Heterosexual scandals concerning public men also depend on secrecy and disclosure, a 'veiling' that rests upon the public lie.

Such dynamics are well illustrated by the different treatments meted out by national media to 'out' gay men. Nigel Hawthorne is a British actor who is well-known for his role as the civil servant Sir Humphrey in the successful situation comedy 'Yes Minister'. He also recently took the lead part in 'The Madness of King George', a film, interestingly, about the traumatic personal pressures of mis-recognition. In March 1995, he gave an interview to the well-established radical US gay magazine, the *Advocate*. The interview was construed as a promise to come out as gay at the award ceremony for which he had been nominated as 'Best Actor'. In the national press coverage in Britain, Hawthorne and his partner were presented relatively sympathetically, but as victims, not of heterosexual discrimination, but of 'American' radical gay activism. 'Outing' had 'soured' the couple's pleasure in a possible award. As the *Daily Mail*, assiduous in its pursuit of gay activism, put it:

> Everybody who's anybody has always known that Nigel Hawthorne was gay. And nobody with any sense much cared. After all, Mr Hawthorne never made a big deal about his sexuality; he just got on with his career of being a superb actor, entertaining and enriching the lives of millions in the process.
>
> (*Daily Mail*, 23 March 1995)

The two men were presented (and presented themselves) as 'an old married couple', living quiet, country-loving and very 'English' lives, complete with dogs, cats, gardening, tennis and evenings out (a concession to urbanity this?) at a local restaurant.

> Nigel has played gay people but he's not into this banner-waving thing. We don't go screaming around in leather trousers and go to gay bars. We are not interested in that, not remotely.
>
> (Trevor Bentham, quoted in the *Daily Mail*, 23 March 1995)

The couple's 'quiet' homosexuality was juxtaposed to noisy kinds: gay rights activism, the (urban) gay scene, the strategy of outing public men, anything that 'flaunts' homosexuality in the public domain, anything militant or

'American'. The much mythicized figure of Peter Tatchell and OutRage! condensed many of these negative oppositions:

> Win or lose, homosexual or heterosexual, this actor represents the best of Britain. And in the quiet dignity in which he has conducted his private life has shown himself to be light years from the brutal McCarthyism of the odious Peter Tatchell and his evil campaign to 'out' those whose sexuality is nobody's business but their own.
>
> (*Daily Mail*, Leader, 23 March 1995)

What disappears here is the daily harassment of lesbians and gay men because of their sexuality. The use of the term 'McCarthyism' to brand a gay group as inquisitorial and persecutory takes this further by forgetting or inverting the relations of power involved in a past episode. McCarthyism, of course, was a campaign not only to persecute leftists in post-World War II USA, but also to 'out' homosexuals and throw them out of public office (D'Emilio 1992). In Britain today, indeed, the press itself uses oppressive sexual publicity almost daily. The Tatchell/Hawthorne opposition was constructed, as we shall see, in the middle of one periodic glut of sexual news – in the same month the press ran detailed stories about a governor of the Bank of England who had resigned because of a heterosexual affair and about a comedian, Freddie Starr, accused of homosexual acts with his gardener. It is possible – just – to be gay, 'out' and publicly approved of in Britain. This approval, however, is conditional, if not on a certain quietude, certainly on otherwise exemplary behaviour. A homosexual life or act must leave unchallenged the dominant sexual and other categories – heterosexuality, marriage, coupledom and the great law of quiet private life, all components of a complexly constructed cultural Englishness. Where these *are* challenged – as in the Jane Brown case – retribution is likely to follow (Epstein 1997c and Chapter 4, below).

Within this framework the most fervent militants on behalf of heterosexual conformity can campaign against sexual difference and yet 'tolerate' homosexuality as such. Such conditional toleration can involve particularly nasty discrimination:

> I've known a good many homosexuals in my time. Like heterosexuals I know, I thought some were nasty creeps, or devious twisters . . . Others I liked, trusted and admired . . . I do not like nor approve their sexual practices. But provided they behave decently and discreetly, and do not flaunt their life style that offends people of normal habits, I see no reason to discriminate against them . . . Forget about Mr Tatchell's sex life. Look at him as you would any other man and you will see a nasty vicious rat, who is making the often sad and difficult lives of homosexuals more sad and difficult.
>
> (Norman Tebbit, *Sun*, 23 March 1995)

Here it is homosexuals (of a particular kind) who bring discrimination upon themselves. Yet, while Tebbit expresses tolerance for his gay friends, he reserves the right to discriminate against those he chooses as his enemies and adjudges evil. Despite the appearance of even-handedness ('like heterosexuals I know'), there is a *particular* onus on gay men to *prove* themselves acceptable. The reality of this pressure is clear in the work which journalists themselves must do to 'nationalize' or 'domesticate' gay figures they approve of. This highlights the task of normalization which potentially stigmatized individuals and groups must themselves perform. This explains the piling up of positive signs of normality (and of negative disavowals of 'looniness') in the descriptions and self-ascriptions of Nigel Hawthorne and his partner.

To return to the general argument, representations of the nation do not only produce exemplary figures of belonging or exclusion; they also put pressure on all of us, some more than others, to conform. They mis-recognize, then offer recognition, but only conditionally.

Much recent work on the process of identity – in relation to nation but also class, gender, sexuality, ethnicity and 'race' – has stressed how exclusion is by no means the end of the story. Excluded categories remain very active; they become the Other against which the Us is defined. In other words, they remain indispensable (e.g. Said 1978; Stallybrass and White 1986; Bhabha 1994; Redman 1997). The splitting of acceptable/unacceptable gay male identities in the dominant discourse requires someone to play the (Other) part of Peter Tatchell. Someone must represent the quintessentially British; someone the appropriate national Other, in this case the sickeningly upfront (gay) sexuality of the United States. Inversely, the categories which John Major and the Conservative press stigmatized in the National Lottery controversy requires *their* exemplary (good) Other in the shape of an idealized young heterosexual woman. The terms in which both poles are described suggests not only the strenuousness of attempts to anchor slipping moral values, but also the strongly imaginary character of constructions of this kind. They must be good or bad enough to be *believed in* – even if they are just too 'good' or too 'bad' to be believed![4]

This exaggeration of differences, a key moment of identity, will concern us later. For the moment we want to stress how Othering both disciplines 'internal' categories and draws boundaries around the nation. These two moments – putting the citizens in their places, but also identifying the boundaries of (national) citizenship – are often intertwined. Referring to the United States as a place where gay militancy is 'rampant' is intrinsic to the hierarchization of forms of English gay identity. 'The Activist Gay Man' is not (culturally) English at all: he belongs, if anywhere, to the 'McArthyite' USA. Images of the nation are almost always also images of international relations.

The work of producing the nation is frequently disguised, denied or *naturalized*. This is one reason why critical analysis is needed to recover it.

A common figure is 'national character', seen as something that is inborn, or perhaps regularly produced through some enduring relation to the land, the landscape, the weather, the island's isolation, or an original racial mix. Mrs Thatcher's 'Spirit of Britain' recovered through 'the Falklands Factor' is an essence of this kind. Forms of racism – where national identity is anchored through explicitly racial identifications or through some alignment of culture and territorial belonging with an unspoken racial theory – are perhaps the most pervasive forms of this naturalization in contemporary Western Europe. The nation is natural, in this way of thinking, because it corresponds to a given ethnicity (more openly nowadays 'a race') which itself belongs also to this territory, settled it aeons ago, and has cultivated, nurtured and possessively loved it ever since. This gives to questions of race and (gendered) ethnicities a particular contemporary salience for processes of inclusion and exclusion (Barker 1981; Gilroy 1987; Anthias *et al.* 1992). Such naturalizations operate most invisibly in their most 'innocent' moments. Here, for example, is Mrs Thatcher again, a very knowing nation-constructor, on the subject of 'courtesy', a category long naturalized as distinctively British (English?) and resonating with nostalgia for 'gentlemanly' sexual behaviour:

> The culture of courtesy could be re-introduced, and it should begin in the homes and go on through the schools and into university life and then business. It could become ingrained and there were still plenty of societies in the world where it was. And she repeated it was *natural to the British*.
>
> (Thatcher Interview, *Daily Mail*, 29 April 1988, emphasis added)

This is an interesting passage. There is a marked contradiction between the promotion of 'courtesy' implied in the first two sentences and its naturalization as 'British' in the third. Also interesting is the deletion of agency throughout the passage. Courtesy became British (again?) all by itself. It was always really there. Or it just got into homes and went on from there. In these ways Mrs Thatcher's own cultural 'promotion' is at once most active – and veiled. More specifically what is hidden here is the whole cultural politics of the New Right which is concerned precisely to use schools and other institutions to inculcate a particular moral order. It is interesting that this project is veiled in Thatcher's public stance. In other contexts, the use of state agencies to 'promote' a particular view of sexuality, or to 'indoctrinate', has actually been banned, most notoriously by Section 28.

In sexual matters, arguments from national character gain further support from 'nature' itself, since sexuality is seen as being rooted in biological propensities. Here, for example, is the former Chief Rabbi, Lord Jacobowitz, puzzling over the spate of political sex scandals, the furore over

OutRage!'s 'outing' threats, and statements from the Catholic hierarchy in Britain tolerating homosexuality, short of physical acts:

> The laws of nature cannot be adjusted to match the fads of the day. They are bound to be permanent. And it is the duty of moral leaders to say so, as loudly and clearly as they can.
>
> (*Daily Mail,* 8 March 1995)

In contemporary sexual discourses, sexual patterns are as often fixed by science as by religion; 'natural' – as in 'the laws of nature' – can convey the gravity of both. The appeal to 'nature' can also be naturalizing in a third sense: an appeal to common sense and the taken-for-granted – 'it's only natural that . . .'

'Nationalizing our schools': vicious circuits

We can now understand public debates about education and about sexuality more fully. They function as structures of recognition; they are, among other things, an action upon social identities already formed or forming. This argument has a particular relevance to schooling. Schooling is about forming the identities of the young (though it forms adult identities too). Because it is about the young, it is about forming the nation of the future. Because it is about education, there is permission (in some models) for adults to teach, preach and generally know best. Both public debates about schooling and sexuality and school-based activity are pre-eminently about cultural regulation, identity formation and, more covertly, self-production. It isn't only pupils who produce themselves in schools, but also teachers, parents and other participants. In producing appropriate behaviours and cultural identities on the different sides of power relations, the whole process also produces the social relations themselves, especially between children and adults, parents and children, teachers and pupils, and parents and educational professionals. Moreover in debating policies for sexuality and schooling, the nation is also being produced as a sexualized collective identity: this is a prime opportunity to elaborate some ideals on, so it is hoped, the unprotesting bodies of the children.

This helps to explain the intense preoccupation of New Right movements and Conservative governments with the education system throughout the later 1970s, 1980s and early 1990s. There are many ways of describing the Thatcherite restructuring of the education system which is still continuing (e.g. Jones 1989; Education Group II (Cultural Studies Birmingham) 1990). Our interest here is in one side, especially, of a very contradictory process. We are less interested in the attempt to take education to the market place though this has been an important source of disorganization, deepening inequalities, defeating hopes and changing identities. More interesting here is what the Conservative Educational Association, which represents Conservative LEAs, has called disapprovingly 'nationalizing our schools' (Ann Taylor, *Hansard*, 9 November 1992: col. 649). Nationalization is partly a matter of state organization. In the 1960s and 1970s, educational institutions acquired a degree of autonomy both from the central state and from the immediate needs of capitalist business, or these needs were defined loosely enough to leave room for other aspirations including critiques of 'the knowledge factory'. This process was reversed from the later 1970s. Intervention cut down the powers of local authorities, for long an effective counterweight to central state power, and one space for socialist and other radical influences. Most dramatically the Conservative government used its central power to abolish the Greater London Council (GLC) and the Inner London Education Authority (ILEA), both centres of socialist influence and the latter an important centre of educational innovation. Centralization was associated with the apparent empowerment of the schools themselves, freed from the control, but also the support, of the local state. Successive Conservative Education Acts have massively increased the direct powers of the Secretary of State for Education and the Department for Education and Employment. These new powers have been used, moreover, in interventionist ways, especially on matters of the curriculum and the supposed 'failure' of school managements. As we noted in Chapter 1, the National Curriculum is the most conspicuous example of this nationalization of schooling, but we would have to add the power of adjudicatory inspection, the enforcement of tests and competitive league tables, the power of government-appointed quangos in the curriculum area, the control of teacher education and the deprofessionalization and deskilling of the activity of teaching itself. As Geoff Esland has put it:

> Of all the areas of social policy subjected to the New Right's 'cultural revolution', the reform of education has arguably been the most central to its moral and political project. As with certain other policy areas, the education system has seen longstanding organisational practices overturned and been forced to operate as a quasi-market for the delivery of its services . . . However, where education differs from other areas of social policy is as its significance as the prime cultural agency in the formation of identity and the reproduction of social values and moral principles – especially those of nationality and citizenship.
>
> (Esland 1996: 26)

Conservative educational policies have also linked schooling, nationality and sexuality in a particular way. New Right discourses have constructed a crisis in national sexual mores to which education generally and schooling in particular are related, both as cause and solution. This ongoing, long-term and unrolling moral panic, in which teachers are derided, is one of the ways in which moral traditionalist discourses are refurbished and connected to arguments about the market and parental choice. Poor schooling is a cause of moral decay. Teachers have lost their way, morally, influenced by an unthinking progressivism which has undermined basic beliefs. It is not only teachers who are attacked. Parents (especially single and working-class mothers) are blamed for not exercising proper parental control. Pupils in state or local authority schools are accused of being violent, disorderly, even criminal. These attacks are more than figurative: Conservative policies have palpably worsened the lives of these groups. On the other hand, pressure is put on educational agents to act as the moral saviours of the nation. Conservative press and politicians construct schools as scandals, but they can also construct educators as moral heroes and heroines. From the days of the Black Papers in the late 1960s to Mr Major's ill-fated fundamentalist Conference speech of October 1993, the New Right moral agenda has been underpinned by the belief that the schools should and can lead the return 'Back to Basics'.

These terms of recognition, non-recognition and conditional recognition do impact upon the schools. Centralization has produced much tighter relays between the hegemonic state definitions and school practices. More subtly, school policies are shaped by the hopes, fears and expectations set up by the dominant terms of discourse in the public sphere, the promotion, for instance, of moral panics about the use of sexually explicit language, or about (otherwise) undisciplined children in school. Responsible school policy-making has to attend very carefully to formal and informal controls of this kind. In sex education, it is important to be familiar with the contradictory state regulations, but also to walk carefully around deliberately nurtured parental sensitivities and inquisitorial media.

So public discourses today do set many of the terms of experience in schools. They affect material resources but also personal energies and levels of commitment. In January 1997 the *Times Educational Supplement* could report detailed and extensive research on the massive discontent and unhappiness of the teaching profession in England, Wales and Scotland (*Times Educational Supplement* (TES), 10 January 1997). This is not surprising given the derision poured on teachers (Kenway 1987; Ball 1990). The whole material *and psychic* economy of the education system, including, centrally, rates of pay as an important index of 'worth', has been undermined. Like many public or state professions, the job has become almost impossible.

Paradoxically, one effect of intensified control is to increase the distance between public policy and everyday life. There has been a determined minority attempt to narrow the terms of sexual recognition (Chapter 3) while at the everyday level and in entertainment and youth-related media (Chapter 8) sexual categories have become more diverse and more fluid. In schools, this distance is expressed as an alignment of pupil identities with the forms of commercial popular culture in opposition to the official sexual culture of the school and the dominant *political* discourses of the sexual. Once more, however, schools find themselves under fierce pressures, caught between the moral traditionalism and sexual hypocrisy of political elites and the incitements of capital's colonizations of the sexual, between the straight and narrow of 'the family' and the evidence of sexual difference all round.

We hope that it is obvious from our analysis so far that there is no easy escape from the vicious circuits. Even the processes which conservative critics define as problems rarely have their point of origin in the schools. Every key social institution is throwing up scandals of its own: the churches, the armed forces, Parliament, the monarchy, the law, the police and mainstream media themselves. From our own point of view, schools may have better or worse policies in the sexual and other domains; good practice makes a difference. But the worst problems of the sexual culture, as we define them, have little to do with formal education. They have much more to do with social and political conditions and with the attempt to impose very narrow terms of sexual recognition on a sexually diverse society. Certainly the causes of the problems which schools themselves are facing are much more complex than their conservative critics imply.

It is important to add that schools, teachers or groups of pupils or parents who are attacked are not powerless victims. The last few years have seen several fightbacks by schools and their communities. Campaigning by parents, governors and local activists saved the job of Jane Brown, the primary school headmistress who was attacked for being a lesbian and for her gall in calling the ballet Romeo and Juliet 'exclusively heterosexual'. In several of the causes célèbres around sex education, sex educators have been supported by colleagues, parents and school governors. The Dunblane parents' campaign for the banning of private ownership of handguns is a related example. National teacher union policies over testing, class sizes and other issues have been supported by parent groups. Such campaigns are easily re-scripted by more powerful 'voices over' in media and in politics. None the less, one of the less intended effects of Conservative policy has been to create a network of knowledgeable school supporters in local communities, people who are committed to a school and directly experience attacks on public education, including those of governments. Our analysis of the policing of schools shows how important it is to secure the support of this local public, especially on controversial matters like sexuality policy.

The nation and sexual hierarchies

Circuits of representation, recognition and material reward and punishment do create, over time, more stable social configurations. These are not permanent structures, but they change according to a different rhythm than that of state policy or media representation. Sexual formations are established, both as states of sexual law and as a hegemonic sexual culture. In 1984 in the middle of 'sex wars' in the United States, Gayle Rubin wrote a classic essay on sexual politics. She described such hegemonic formations as 'The Charmed Circle' and 'The Outer Limits', inscribing both in a neat circular diagram:

> According to this system, sexuality that is 'good', 'normal' and 'natural' should ideally be heterosexual, marital, monogamous, reproductive, and non-commercial. It should be coupled, relational, within the same generation, and occur at home. It should not involve pornography, fetish objects, sex toys of any sort, or roles other than male or female. Any sex that violates these rules is 'bad', 'abnormal' or 'unnatural'. Bad sex may be homosexual, unmarried, promiscuous, non-procreative, or commercial. It may be masturbatory or take place at orgies, may be casual, may cross generational lines, or may take place in 'public', at least in the bushes or the baths. It may also involve the use of pornography, fetish objects, sex toys, or unusual roles.
>
> (Rubin 1984: 13–14)

Later in the same article she noted how 1980s conflicts had somewhat moved 'the line' dividing respectable from non-respectable sex:

> Unmarried couples living together, masturbation, and some forms of homosexuality are moving in the direction of respectability. Most homosexuality is still on the bad side of the line. But if it is coupled and monogamous, the society is beginning to recognise that it includes the full range of human interaction . . .
>
> (Rubin 1984: 15)

In a footnote to a later version, she added that her diagrams were oversimplified to make a point, that 'the point remains valid', but that 'the actual power relationships of sexual variation are considerably more complicated' (1992 footnote, Rubin 1984: 14).

Rubin's scheme lacked a sustained historical or cross-cultural dimension. The article dealt with the contemporary history of sexual conflicts in the USA, increasingly dominated by New Right campaigning. Thanks to the extensive work of historians of sexuality, many of them lesbian and gay activists, it is possible, today, to provide a more historical account of sexual formations, ancient and modern (e.g. the collection in Duberman *et al.* 1990). This is relevant here, however, only to help in defining what is particular to contemporary sexual formations.

We had two hunches about this when we started writing this chapter. The first was the persistence through the modern period of particular sexual formations connected with the modern Western nation-state. This formation is often hegemonic, across nation-state boundaries, in the propagation of (some) Western ways of life. Similar formations, for example, have figured in Third World nationalist movements (e.g. Radhakrishnan 1992). The second hunch was that this formation has developed, in Bob Connell's phrase, marked 'crisis tendencies'. In borrowing this term from Jurgen Habermas, Connell warns against too easy an ascription of crisis (Connell 1995: 84; and see also Connell 1987: 158–63). It implies previously fixed structures for instance. We might add that 'the family' has often been 'in crisis' historically, certainly, in Britain, in the 1960s, 1970s and 1980s, but also in the late nineteenth century, in the inter-war period and during two World Wars! There are dangers too in taking over the figure of sexual crisis uncritically from New Right theory. More generally, recent theories of sexuality have been exceptionally persuasive about the instabilities of *all* sexual categories and boundaries, especially the strategically critical border between homo- and hetero-sexualities (e.g. Butler 1990, 1993; Dollimore 1991; Sedgwick 1994; Steinberg 1997). Has this always been so? Is it something about the nature of identity and desire as such? Or are such instabilities peculiar to a particular 'postmodern' phase?

The persistence of the dominant sexual model is the easier hunch to explore. The configurations which Rubin identified in the mid-1980s are not so dissimilar to those discussed in Michel Foucault's *History of Sexuality Vol. 1*, which summed up sexual formations in Western Europe during the nineteenth and early twentieth centuries. *The History of Sexuality* is also a classic text of contemporary sexual debate (Foucault 1978). It helped to form much recent history-writing, including its controversies. Foucault's crucial insight is that sexuality is not 'a stubborn drive' but:

> an especially dense transfer point for relations of power: between men and women, young people and old people, parents and offspring, teachers and students, priests and laity, an administration and a population.
>
> (Foucault 1978: 103)

Modern sexuality is the product of particular discourses which in turn have produced key social identities. Foucault was especially interested in the ways in which medical and other discourses sexualized the very body and being of woman, producing her as 'hysterical', dominated by the womb. He also centred, as Rubin does, on the pivotal place of the conjugal couple, or what, drawing attention to the politics of population, Foucault calls 'the Malthusian couple'. More marginal but massively incited in nineteenth-century discourse were two further figures – 'the pervert' and 'the masturbating child' (Foucault 1978: 105–14).

Foucault's account has been criticized for his relative neglect of gender relations (cf. Hartsock 1987; Fuss 1989; Ramazanoglu 1993) and for his argument that homosexuality as a category was 'invented' only in the later nineteenth century (cf. Boswell 1990; and Halperin 1990). Especially interesting for us, however, is the centrality he gives to the child, child–adult relations and sexual pedagogies in the configuration of 'modern' sexualities. In the family, it is not only 'the husband–wife axis' but also 'the parent–children axis' that is central to the social construction of sexuality and its forms of power in the modern period. This is a more double-edged view of the family than that of contemporary religious traditionalism. The family is not only a place where sexuality is to be controlled or rendered safe or holy: it does not repress or restrain modern sexualities merely; rather it produces them. As Foucault puts it:

> What has taken place since the seventeenth century can be interpreted in the following manner: the deployment of sexuality which first developed on the fringes of familial institutions . . . gradually became focused on the family . . . In the family, parents and relatives became the chief agents of a deployment of sexuality which drew its outside support from doctors, educators, and later psychiatrists . . . Then these new personages made their appearance: the nervous woman, the frigid wife, the indifferent mother . . . the impotent, sadistic, perverse husband, the hysterical or neurasthenic girl, the precocious and already exhausted child, and the young homosexual who rejects marriage or neglects his wife . . . It was as if it [the family] had suddenly discovered the dreadful secret of what had always been hinted at . . . the family, the keystone of alliance, was the germ of all the misfortunes of sex.
>
> (Foucault 1978: 110)

The family and the heterosexual married couple are certainly central here, uniquely privileged by regulative discourses and the state. But Foucault adds that the family also bears the weight of the sexual *problems* of the modern period and that the child, far from being outside the sexual domain, is a key figure in its construction and crisis.

Later work on modern sexual hierarchies, especially in relation to nation/ nationalism, allows us to elaborate this sexual formation of Western modernity. Recognized (and regulated) are the central features of heterosexual monogamy: marriage, the conventional gendered division of labour and the separation of spheres. In nationalist versions, women are reproducers of the nation or 'race', of labour power, of a national or imperial citizenry, and of ethnic or racial purity (Yuval-Davis 1989; Anthias 1992; Brah 1996). Women as mothers or agents of 'civilization' have a particular responsibility for the reproduction of national or imperial identities (Davin 1978; Ware 1992). In widely different historical nationalisms, women, or the mother–child dyad, symbolize the nation, its heart, spirit or essence (Koonz 1988; Radhakrishnan 1992). Women's bodies mark national boundaries, as in the racial theories of National Socialism or the systematic use of rape by Serbian nationalists in the forced ethnicization of Bosnia (Zarkov 1995). Men, on the other hand, dominate what Connell has called 'heavily masculinised core institutions', including public politics, the state and the military (Connell

1987, 1995). They also constitute the armies of younger men who 'go out and fight and die' for their countries. Nationalisms accentuate the gender divide, especially (and with great contradictions) in times of war. In the early 1980s, for example, the conservative reconstitution of gender roles was aided by Wars and Weddings, especially the Falklands/Malvinas conflict and the celebrated and disastrous marriage of Princess Diana and Prince Charles.

Male dominance of the public sphere has been accompanied by forms of 'homosocial' male bonding and masculine exclusivity. In a classic study of sexuality and German national identity, George Mosse has shown how the emergence of authoritarian regimes, and ultimately of National Socialism, was accompanied by distinctive forms of *männerbund* (or male bonding), from the friendships and homo-erotic attachments of the romantic period to the murderous policing of homosexualities and heightened misogyny of Nazism (Mosse 1985; Sedgwick 1985; Theweleit 1987).

'The family' has been the key figure in this conventional gender order. It is a very condensed category indeed: it fuses a version of heterosexual relations (love 'n marriage), conventional gender divisions and relations of a patriarchal kind, a stable legally-regulated procreative unit of two oppo-site-sex biological parents, a nurturing 'moral' environment for children, the regulation of both adult sexualities and child–adult relations, including the prohibitions against incest and cross-generational sex. To this we might add from a list compiled by Eve Sedgwick: 'a surname', 'a circuit of blood relations', 'a system of companionship and succor', 'a building', 'an econ-omic unit of earning and taxation', 'a prime site of economic and cultural consumption', 'a mechanism for accumulating material goods over several generations', 'a daily routine', a 'unit in a community of worship' and, to return to the nation again, 'a site of patriotic formation'. In a 'proper' family, all these functions 'are meant to line up perfectly with each other' (Sedgwick 1994: 6).

The specificity of these arrangements becomes clear if we take them apart in the imagination, or attend to those who consciously choose to live differ-ently:

> Looking at my own life, I see that – probably like most people – I have valued and pursued these various elements of family identity to quite differing degrees . . . But what's been consistent in this particular life is an interest in not letting very many of these dimensions line up directly with each other at one time. I see it's been a ruling intuition for me that the most productive strategy (intellectually, emotionally) might be, whenever possible, to *dis*articulate them one from another, to *dis*en-gage them – the bonds of blood, of law, of habitation, of privacy, of companionship and succor – from the lockstep of their unanimity in the system called 'family'.
>
> (Sedgwick 1994: 6)

She notes similar alignments in relation to individual sexual identity: bio-logical sex, gender assignment, predominant traits of masculinity or femi-ninity, gender assignment of partner, masculinity or femininity of partner, self-perception as gay or straight, self-perception of partner, choice whether to procreate or not, the most eroticized sexual organs, sexual fantasies, the main emotional bonds, the enjoyment of power in sexual relations and 'your community of cultural and political identification' are all supposed to be aligned (Sedgwick 1994: 7). The 'queer' possibilities that you might be straight in one aspect and gay in another, choose to procreate outside of heterosexually organized living arrangements, enjoy non-procreative or non-penetrative forms of sex as an (otherwise) 'masculine man', or depend for emotional succour not on a single partner but on a network of more or less eroticized friendships, are eventualities hard to grasp within the domi-nant alignments. They are, however, possible and viable ways of living sexual identities (more than one) at different moments in the life process. It is probable that rather few lives exhibit the perfect alignments which the dominant model suggests.

Even so, today, the dominant model remains both recognizable and the predominant source of recognitions. Sexual categories which are outside 'the charmed circle' of the heterosexual married couple-with-biological-children are still unrecognized, mis-recognized or othered. Even minor departures from the model – having adoptive rather than 'natural' children for instance – continue to be (re)marked. The sexual border wars continue to rage: especially in Britain today around the full acceptance of lesbian and gay identities, and more or less acceptable heterosexual relationships. Common readings of the current situation are those of 'slow motion' (especially in masculine roles or identities) or of 'backlash' (Segal 1990; Faludi 1992). The 'marginal' categories of the modern national sexual formation remain as active as ever, not least in defining what goes on in the 'centre'. Increasingly the most persuasive approaches to identity see margin and centre not as external opposites, but rather as internally related and in some sense linked and dependent (e.g. Stallybrass and White 1986; Hall 1996a). As we shall see, insights like these help to make sense of the double focus of contemporary public discourse: on the problems of heterosexuali-ties and the legitimacy – or not – of lesbian and gay and other marginalized identities. As we have noted, children have been involved in these dis-courses from their modern beginnings; they are constituted as deviant sexual categories of their own. Once again today the (sexual) security and (sexual) nature of children – girls and boys often differently – are centre stage: children are both threatened and dangerous. They *know* and prob-ably *do* too much, too soon, too young. Sexually, they are not childish enough.

There certainly are continuities in the modern history of national–sexual formations. So what's new?

Some features of the contemporary

The first feature that seems new is a heightened and open contestation over sexual categories and boundaries. Of course there have always been struggles around the sex/gender order. Sometimes the contestation has been particularly acute, when sexual taboos were broken, when radical movements made a virtue of 'speaking out' – in the late nineteenth century for example. The dynamics of this phase created many of the sexual ideologies of today, especially the idea that sexuality is not so much an act, more an 'identity' with a bodily or medico-constitutional basis (Weeks 1981; Langan and Schwarz 1985; Mort 1987; Bland 1995).

Today's sexual struggles are, arguably, still more overt and have certainly been more sustained. Much of our sexual politics is driven by the conflicts of social movements, and especially the confrontations between radical movements of sex and gender and sexual traditionalism. Under 'radical movements of sex and gender' we include currents which have declared themselves as 'movements': the different phases and kinds of feminism, lesbian and gay movements, 'queer politics', some kinds of men's groups, the representation of professional sex workers or of single mothers or of women who have been abused by partners, the extensive networks of support and agitation around the AIDS and HIV epidemics, and many other specific campaigns. We also include cultural currents without a name: struggles against oppressive forms of masculinity in different ethnic (including Anglo) communities, the much greater cultural visibility and variety of lesbian and gay identities, the increased public visibility of child sexual abuse as a widespread social problem, the recognition and public representation of female sexual desire, not always as a masculine production. Such currents have often fed into voluntary associations and organizations of different kinds and vintages – in our areas for instance, the Terrence Higgins Trust, the Family Planning Association, the Brook Advisory Clinics and the Sex Education Forum.

What links these agitations today is a double play around difference and inequality. Movements are concerned first to remove some of the most obvious inequalities around traditional gender positions, women's lack of power over their own reproductive capacities for instance, or the long-running battles over equal pay, or over the persistent heterosexism of official institutions, the armed forces or the churches for example. But, secondly, often latterly, they have been concerned to challenge the rigidities of sex/gender boundaries themselves, especially of the divides between men/women, masculinities/femininities, and homo-erotic and heterosexual desire. The movements themselves, their power and experience in struggle, have also generated shifts in critical theories. Theoretical agenda have moved from analysing inequalities and power relations between relatively given or fixed social categories (men and women; gay and straight) towards a questioning of the categories themselves – their fixity, separateness or boundedness – and towards seeing the play of power around them as less binary and less uni-directional.[5]

Opposed to these currents are movements which seek to renaturalize and to reinstate ideal or necessary forms of the family, to shore up the dominant elements in modern national–sexual formations. Sexual traditionalism is new, not in the content of the message, but in the historical context of its articulation. Part of this context is the rise of contemporary sexual radicalisms themselves. This *dynamic between movements* creates many contemporary specificities.

The dynamic can be illustrated in different ways. Most obviously, traditionalist campaigning, where it gains power, can change the legal and legislative terms of struggles to its own advantage. We will argue later that moral traditionalist movements have had increasing successes at a legislative level from the mid-1980s. The ideological effects of traditionalist campaigning, both for movements and individuals, can also be disorganizing and disempowering. In sexual matters exposure in the press can, as we shall see, have serious personal consequences for individuals, their friends, partners and families. Yet apparent successes also stimulate radical activism. As many have argued, Clause 28*, which banned 'the promotion of homosexuality' by local authorities in Britain, stimulated campaigns for lesbian and gay rights: Section 28* was 'Thatcherism's promotion of homosexuality' (Stacey 1991; Smith 1994). It also, together with the preceding experience of anti-discriminatory policies themselves, provided object lessons from which activists could learn. In particular the relative vulnerability of local authority policies provided much fuel for re-theorizing radical strategies (Cooper 1994; Smith 1994).

The influence of radical movements on sexual traditionalism is more hidden, yet arguably more profound. Sexual radicalism (and the historical conditions that gave it birth) underlie the emergence of traditionalism. The emergence of the lesbian and gay movements from the early 1970s destabilized the unequal settlement struck, in Britain, around the work of the Homosexual Law Reform Society and the still harshly restrictive Sexual Offences Act of 1967 (Weeks 1977). The somewhat earlier mobilizations in the United States also disrupted the relatively incorporated legacies of an earlier period of homosexual organization, as John D'Emilio has shown (1992). In most Western countries the increasing visibility of gay and lesbian identities – in movement and self-help politics and in commercial popular culture – threatened defences, in law and in public culture, against a fuller recognition of homosexual identity and desire.

Similarly, it is important not to underestimate the major impacts of

* The term 'Clause' is used when referring to a Parliamentary Bill. 'Section' refers to an Act of Parliament.

feminism. The women's movements of the post-war period have been a major disturbance to the gender order across the whole range of practices and institutions. They premised an organic shift in gender relationships and forms of consciousness. From the beginning sexuality was a major theme within the 1970s movements, centring on the relationships between men's power and heterosexual sex (e.g. Mitchell 1966; Firestone 1970; Millett 1970). But the challenge was wide as well as intimate. To the extent that the dominant definitions rest on a very restrictive view of women's role and appropriate aspirations, feminists of all kinds, even those that sought 'equal opportunities' within a liberal framework, put a land mine under the old gender order that would fracture it further. How could the (ideal) family ever be the same, once women claimed some parity with men?

It is easy to see how one response to such a threat was to try to re-naturalize 'the family' – make it natural-seeming again – and invest it further with positive social values. This re(in)statement of 'family values' involved an insistent 'nationalization' of the family, a re-inscribing of the modern configuration of nation, conventional gender relations and the idealized family form – almost as if for a new war. In an important article Susan Reinhold has shown how in the struggles around 'positive images' that led up to the introduction of Clause 28, 'the family' was seen as threatened by gay families and households. One response was to distinguish between 'real' and 'pretended family relationships' and to prohibit the promotion of the latter. Another was to insist, once more, on the centrality of 'the family' to the nation, even the identity or fusion of the two categories. As Mrs Thatcher put it, drawing in a most paradoxical way on liberal discourse: 'A nation of free people will only continue to be great if family life continues and the structure of that nation is a family one' (*Woman's Own*, 31 October 1987, quoted in Reinhold 1994).

As many authors have argued, there is a strongly imaginary or 'wishful' side to this project (Barrett and McIntosh 1982; Franklin, Lury and Stacey 1991). Yet the family in the form in which it is now idealized is really rather recent and perhaps rather short-lived. Some elements of the ideal existed in the earlier history of the middle class – a version of separate gender spheres from early nineteenth-century Britain for instance (Davidoff and Hall 1987). Others, however, are much newer – the idea of heterosexual marriage as the legitimate centre for sexual satisfaction for *both* partners for instance. Before the inter-war years, it is hard to find a popular version of female sexual enjoyment, available to most women.[6] Similarly, the specific family ideal, in which nuclearity and quality of life including emotional intimacy and companionship is most valued, is based on the possibility of effective birth control and, perhaps, on the era of mass domestic consumption (including 'a home of your own') (Gittins 1982).

This family flourished in Britain, at least as an ideal, from, say, the 1920s to the early 1960s. Yet by the later 1960s, perhaps earlier, the ideal was being undermined by the contradictions of post-war affluence, especially as they impacted on the aspirations and the work of women. Women's primary role in the domestic sphere was undercut by the large-scale entry of women into waged work, a process accelerating today with the decline of skilled manual (male) labour. At the same time, the development of high mass consumption provided an incitement and an arena for the elaboration of female sexualities and femininities, often of a strongly aspirational and desiring kind and not always limited to the familial context (Winship 1985, 1987; McRobbie 1991; *Feminist Review* 1997). It is arguable that the contemporary decline of well-paid employment for men (and so of 'the family wage' and the identity of 'breadwinner') produces crisis tendencies in masculinities as generative as the contradictions which first precipitated the women's movement (Segal 1990; Connell 1995).

The radicals of sex and gender of the 1970s and 1980s further relativized the older formation. Feminists insisted that heterosexual relations were a site of male power and women's subordination and that sexual practices themselves, whether matrimonial or 'permissive', were often at the centre of this oppression (e.g. McKinnon 1982, 1987). Lesbian and gay activists, by asserting the value of homosexualities, stressed the oppressive nature of the assumption that everyone was or should be heterosexual (e.g. Rich 1980). Queer theory and later feminist interventions have started to unpick the connections between gender difference and power and the heterosexual norm (e.g. Butler 1990). Critical voices from within non-Anglo populations have pointed out the ethnic specificity, and the oppressive 'whiteness', of the family ideal and of its critics (e.g. Lawrence 1982). The constructed nature of the connection between a version of the family and a version of the nation – of Englishness especially – became more visible.

From the 1970s onwards, the contradictions of 'the family' have become intrusively visible on the surface of public culture and within the political elite. They were played out, as we shall see, in the media scandals prompted by John Major's 'Back to Basics' speech in October 1993 (Chapter 4). At the same time, however, 'the family' continues to operate powerfully as an ideal, and not only among social conservatives. It remains dominant, in the sense that in public culture other forms are judged against it. This reproduction of the ideal owes most of all perhaps to the active exclusion from public discussion of emergent alternative family forms which would provide other lodging places for security and intimacy. What is certain is that 'the family' will never be the same again – if, indeed, it ever 'was'.

This 'revivalism' of 'the family', then, is a further particular characteristic of the contemporary period. This is a post-permissive, post-feminist, post-gay liberation, post-'queer nation' version of the family, a family which thrives as an ideological figure, an ideal that functions by being under continuous threat. This helps to explain the characteristic and puzzling double movement of sexual traditionalism, harping on its own ideal, but also endlessly reiterating, drawing attention to, and reproducing the sources that are held to threaten it.

Again, images of the sexual other, especially of gay men, say a lot about social orthodoxies. When Lord Halsbury introduced his Bill, the predecessor of Clause 28, he made the usual distinction between acceptable and unacceptable homosexualities. The unacceptable homosexual, Halsbury declaimed, suffers 'from a psychological syndrome', the three key features of which are:

'exhibitionism: they want the world to know all about them';

'proselytizing: they want to persuade other people that their way of life is the good one';

'boasting of homosexual achievements as if they were due to and not in spite of sexual inversion'.

(Hansard, 18 December 1986: 310)

All three features are directly related to cultural and political assertion. This is what disturbs Lord Halsbury. This homophobia is historically specific. It is posited on the existence of highly visible forms of gay politics and culture and testifies to their impacts. A similar case can be made in relation to the impacts of feminism, without which many forms of hyper-masculinity, 'new laddism' and revived misogyny, many campaigns for the rights of men, foetuses and other members of the 'new oppressed', as well as, obviously, the politics of pro-feminist men, would be inconceivable (McNeil 1991; Science and Technology Subgroup 1991).

The contemporary accentuation of sexual identities (gay, straight, masculine, feminine, queer, transgender and transgeneration) owes much to the salience of the sexual in the advertisement, retailing and consumption of commodities of all kinds. Studies of popular and especially of youth styles have shown us how sexuality and commerce are imbricated, though neither is reducible to the other (Coward 1984; McRobbie 1989, 1991; Mort 1996; *Feminist Review* 1997). It may indeed be that it is the level of development of the commercialization of sexual identity, the dynamic between the use values of personal and group sexual life and the search for markets and profits of the cultural industries that together mark off today's sexual politics from all previous periods (Evans 1993).

One final feature of the contemporary is the repositioning of the national frame itself. The national is no longer the only 'universalizing' framework for social recognitions and institutionalized power. Transnational and global processes are repositioning the nation as the adjudicator of other social identities. They include the development of new means of communication and the growth of supranational organizations. Important for our topic is the post-colonial dialectic of national and ethnic identities in and around the metropolitan core. This involves migrant and settler populations from ex-colonial countries. The presence of these 'translated' communities extends and makes more visible all the differences of actual ways of living within the British Isles, including forms of family and sexual life. Globalization also extends the range of transnational influences and comparisons, creating new cultural propinquities. All this affects the terms on which versions of British-ness are constructed and bounded (Hall 1991).

Crucially, contemporary globalization is no mere enlargement of metro-politan nations but promises transformations. The contemporary French philosopher Jacques Derrida has an interesting discussion in his *Of Gram-matology* on what he calls 'the supplement'. He distinguishes 'two significa-tions' of the supplement, 'whose cohabitation is as strange as it is necessary': on the one side a supplement is a self-addition, an enlargement, a surplus, 'a plenitude enriching another plenitude, the *fullest measure* of presence' (Derrida 1976: 144). It accumulates, extends, still more of the same. At the same time, the supplement also 'insinuates itself in-the-place-of', showing up and supplying a lack or need, threatening substitution, promising change (Derrida 1976: 145). Derrida distinguishes this second signification from the first by calling it 'that dangerous supplement'. The distinction is helpful for thinking through a range of questions associated with nation, culture, sexu-ality and schooling in a period of globalization: the ways in which ethnic diversity modifies British national identities for example, or the likely impacts of a fuller recognition of lesbian and gay identities under 'European' pressures.

Notes

1 This account is based in part on the work of the Popular Memory Group which Richard worked with in Birmingham in the mid-1980s. For an account of the work of the group see Clare and Johnson (1997 forthcoming). For applications of these ideas to issues of national identity and of empire see Johnson (1993a, 1993b); Dawson (1994). For some parallel arguments in the sexual domain see Plummer (1995). Benjamin (1990) was important for the Popular Memory Group's account of recognition.

2 The fortunes of one group in this controversy can be traced in the magazine *Out-Write* (Leicester). I am grateful to Bob Bennett for discussions of the lottery con-troversy and the local impacts of the grant. See also the useful comment by Suzannne Moore, *The Guardian*, 13 June 1996.

3 This analysis follows closely the original discussion summarized in Clare and Johnson (1997 forthcoming) and based on the Popular Memory work. On nation and media compare also Schlesinger (1991) which, however, lacks the gender dimension.

4 Our discussion of splitting – particularly between the idealized good and the

denigrated bad here – depends on our reading of the work of Melanie Klein (see especially Mitchell, 1986).

5 This shift has been understood in many different ways: from materialist to post-modernist theory; from humanist to anti-humanist approaches; from essentialism to constructivism; and in the sexual domain from lesbian and/or gay theory to 'queer theory'. The literatures here are vast. For one recent outline discussion in relation to sexual theories see Steinberg, Epstein and Johnson (1997: 8–16); for especially acute and subtle readings of some differences see Fuss (1989).

6 For feminist dilemmas around this see Bland (1995). For an example of working women's sexual experiences in the period of suffragism see Women's Co-operative Guild (1978).

CHAPTER 3

'Giving out a message from this house': political discourses of sexuality

The focus of this chapter is on political discourses of sexuality. We mean 'political' here in the most limited sense. While power is diffused throughout civil society, it is also condensed in the state and articulated through formal politics. Much recent writing (including that on sexual politics) has returned to an earlier emphasis on the state as the locus of power (e.g. Evans 1993; Cooper 1994; *Feminist Review* 1994). This is not surprising given the 'strong state' aspects of contemporary Conservatism in Britain.

In this chapter we first identify some of the main events, phases and dynamics of the contemporary period – in effect the last 10 years. This provides the setting for our closer reading of parliamentary debates, legislation and departmental regulations produced in four particular episodes. It also provides some justification for our choices.

Second, we identify and map the main discursive strategies in play in the public domain, and, to some extent, the relations of force between them. Dominant discourses are often embedded in state policies, so act directly on schools. In any case they produce part of the field of power relations and meanings in relation to which educational agents must act.

Our reading is a critical reading. It is attentive to absences and silences and to what Richard Hoggart (without benefit of psychoanalysis) called 'the differing pressures of emotion behind idiomatic phrases and ritualistic observances' (Hoggart 1957: 18). It is important, throughout, to remember what a very particular world the political elite inhabits, as particular in its way as the school. As we read our way into the sources, what interested us most were the contradictions and ambivalences, lapses and limits, confusions and double binds in these very particular dominant moments in a larger sexual culture.

'The new politics of sex and state' 1984–96?

We have been close watchers of sexual representations – news, theories, fictions – since our project began in 1990. Like other commentators, we identify a shift in public sexual politics in the mid-to-late 1980s (cf. *Feminist Review* 1994).

One way of understanding this shift is in terms of the successes of moral traditionalist and New Right campaigning on sexual and educational issues. Increasingly these campaigns set the terms of public debate. Such campaigning dates from the early 1970s though with different configurations. It was only from the mid-1980s, however, that Conservative governments responded – in legislative terms – to these pressures. This was part of a larger movement in which, first, the Conservative repertoire shifted further in a moral traditionalist direction, but, second, moralist initiatives came to define much of the ground of national politics in 'social' matters, including the politics of New Labour. Overall this marks a further moment in the transformation of politics itself. First, politics was reduced to economics or to the 'free' play of private interests, public institutions coming under privatizing pressure. Then political and social–ethical issues were further reduced to matters of individual morality and responsibility (for early emphasis on Thatcherism's 'moral' themes see Edgar 1988).

By the mid-1970s, a distinctive New Right platform in educational policy had developed around 'parental choice' and educational 'standards' [for this and most of what follows see Johnson (1991)]. Parental choice offered a way to elaborate the economistic, free-market side of Thatcherite discourse, though embedded in this strategy was also a traditionalist conception of nation, family and parenthood. The slogan of 'standards' (eventually a 'National Curriculum', testing and league tables) corresponded to a state-enhancing authoritarianism, and was underpinned by nostalgia for the traditional curriculum of the grammar school. New Right campaigning shifted the terms of debate on educational policy as early as the mid-1970s (CCCS 1981). However, direct legislative influence from either New Right pole was limited under the first two Thatcher governments. This can be seen in an early and unavailing attachment to educational vouchers, in splits between educational traditionalists and free marketeers, and in the resistance of key New Right figures like Sir Keith Joseph to 'nationalizing' the curriculum from the centre. It wasn't until voucher schemes were desegregated into their components to be applied piecemeal as elements of an educational market and a National Curriculum was accepted that a distinctive policy emerged – the Education Reform Act of 1988.

A similar pattern emerges in sexual politics, though the profile of movements is different. Many moral traditionalists are not members of the political New Right – however it is defined. Moral traditionalism does have one political focus in neo-Conservatism, a component in the Thatcherite mix, but it has another in religious currents and tendencies, especially in conservative Catholicism and fundamentalist evangelicalism. As Martin Durham has argued, there is not so close a fit between the New Right and religious moralism in Britain as in the United States (Durham 1991). Some clerics who are conservatives on sexual matters have been critical of Conservative governments on social policy. Moral traditionalism is a strand in some New Right programmes, but not in others. Some New Right figures are liberal, even libertarian, on sexual issues, resisting state intervention in a 'private' domain.

The recent history of traditionalist moral campaigning can be traced to the early 1970s. Campaigns have focused on abortion and on embryo research, on liberal sex education, on sex, violence and 'blasphemy' on television and other media, on the availability of birth control advice to young people, and on pornography. Formal parliamentary connections, mainly with the Conservative Party, were made early, with the formation of the Lords and Commons Family and Child Protection Group in 1979. As Martin Durham has shown, however, sexual traditionalism scored few legislative victories before the later 1980s, with major disappointments over abortion (Durham 1991). In his careful, sceptical account, Durham stresses the distance between political Thatcherism and 'moral movements' and the failure to influence Conservative governments despite Thatcher's antipermissive rhetoric. The early 1980s were littered with private members' initiatives pursuing moral traditionalist causes, usually without government support. As late as October 1985, Victoria Gillick and her supporters were locked in battle against a Conservative Department of Health and Social Security (DHSS), the government and the House of Lords over parental control over contraception for minors.

There were, however, deeper correspondences between moral and religious movements and Thatcherism. The stress on individual morality at the cost of a more social ethic is one such convergence. There are similarities too, notably a moral and ethnic absolutism, between the theocratic moral regulation of society and the neo-Conservative belief in One National Culture. The moral agitations of the 1970s and early 1980s should be read for their symbolic effects, not only for legislative failures. They amplified outrage and disbelief at sexual radicalisms. They provided the tone of New Right activism, including Mrs Thatcher's own missionariness. They linked nation and family, politics and sex. As David Wilshire, the Conservative MP who introduced Clause 28, put it in an interview with Richard Johnson:

'I'm a Thatcherite, I sometimes wonder if I'm a Conservative' is the sort of flippant comment I give to people . . . I would draw your attention to the fact that Mrs Thatcher was brought up in a strict Victorian Methodist household just as I was . . . with very clear views about behaviour . . . I know exactly what she means because I was the same

... I've always developed a thesis to anyone who would listen that you will never understand Margaret Thatcher if you don't understand that period of Methodism and its values. So they shriek at me and it's therefore no surprise, I hope, that because we share the same background that we probably think in similar ways, and therefore that I should consider myself a Thatcherite.

(Wilshire, Interview with Richard Johnson, 16 May 1995)

The sexual and educational movements converged in several critical areas. In sex education, New Right suspicions of the local state and public professionals converged with traditionalist protests against sexual liberalism producing key demands: parental right to withdraw children from sex education lessons, insistence on 'the value of family life' and of marriage in any programme, and a shift of control from LEAs to schools and parents. A similar convergence underlay the campaigns against LEA anti-discriminatory policies which led to Section 28 (Cooper 1994; Smith 1994). Traditionalists have also campaigned to tighten the 'Christian' character of worship in schools, a cause that converges with more narrowly ecclesiastical concerns. They have been active too around attempts to devise a consensual, multi-faith, multi-ethnic moral code for schools and schoolchildren.

Again patterns changed in the mid-1980s. Governments seemed readier to take over the minority amendments of activists. They were modified in the process, but concessions were made. In response to traditionalist demands for *general* right of parental withdrawal and to control sex education legislatively through the category of 'obscenity', the Education [No. 2] Act (1986) took powers over sex education away from LEAs and gave them over to school governors, including the right to decide whether sex education should be taught at all, the obligation to inform and consult with parents, and the power to allow individual parents to withdraw their children. It also gave legislative expression to the prioritization of 'the family': where sex education was taught, it should be 'in such a manner as to encourage those pupils to have due regard to moral considerations and the value of family life'(Education [No. 2] Act 1986: Section 46). The 1993 Act finally granted the *general* right of withdrawal and made adjustments to sex education in the National Curriculum to allow this (Education Act 1993: Section 241). Sex education in the National Curriculum was narrowed, significantly, to 'biological aspects'. Discussion of AIDS, HIV and venereal diseases and of all other aspects of 'human sexual behaviour' were explicitly excluded. The governing bodies of all secondary schools, however, were required to make sex education provision (*outside* the National Curriculum) for all pupils. In the following year, during scares over sex education in primary schools (permitted but not required under the Act) there was further censorship of sex education texts recommended by the Health Education Authority (Chapter 4). The conservative Catholic Minister of Education, John Patten, also

rewrote the DfEE's circular on sex education in a moralist direction, eroding pastoral confidentiality. Some part of the parental control which Gillick
and others were demanding was secured, in schools at least, through the
breach of the confidential relations between adolescent pupils and their sex
education teachers and pastoral advisors (DfEE 1994: Sections 38–42). Subsequently there has been extensive debate and some 'tightening up' around
the forms of worship in state schools and, as we have noted, attempts at a
cross-religious statement of values for schools, the subject of much traditionalist pressure.

The ten years which began with the introduction of Section 28 (1986) and
ended with parliamentary struggles around a new Divorce Act (1996) were
marked by a dense cluster of public sexual issues, many intersecting with
schooling, all helping to form a public sense of sexual anxiety and confusion.[1] The late 1980s and early 1990s saw heightened campaigning
around Health Education and other aspects of the AIDS and HIV epidemics;
battles over artificial insemination and so-called 'virgin births'; new legislation around the age of consent for gay men; attempts to legalize homosexuality in the armed forces and to gain compensation for sexism, sexual
harassment and sexually discriminatory dismissals; struggles over the ordi-
nation of women, the position of gay men, child sexual abuse, and heterosexual misdemeanours in the Anglican, Catholic and other churches;
continued battles over the adequacy of police and judicial responses to rape,
sexual harassment, 'stalking' and domestic violence; many-sided battles over
the government's policy of cutting social security payments to single mothers
by enforcing maintenance payments through the Child Support Agency;
and, of course, the major struggles over the 'promotion of homosexuality'
by local authorities which led to Section 28 of the Local Government Act
1986. These themes were highlighted, from October 1993, or earlier, by the
adoption of 'moral crusading' or 'Back to Basics' stances by politicians,
churchmen and other public figures. The most famous and ill-fated of these
declarations was John Major's speech at the Conservative Party Conference
of October 1993. This was followed by gleeful press exposure of a flood of
financial and sexual scandals in the ranks of his government and party.
Meanwhile the long-running sexual sagas of the Royal Family continued,
especially the bitter deconstruction of the Charles and Diana romance and
the parting of the Duke and Duchess of York. Indeed, every official institution, every moral pillar – the monarchy, the churches, the military, the
police, the judiciary, the governing party, Parliament, the independent
schools, not to mention the Bank of England, the City and the national
media themselves – has been shaken by sexual scandals and conflicts. LEA
schools, especially before the mid-1990s, were a relatively minor item in the
sexual disturbance. Unsurprisingly, new forms of fictional entertainment
sprang up, pulling together themes of political machination, financial
corruption, cover-ups and sexual scandals. These included the television

detective series *Prime Suspect III* and *IV*, the television drama series *Our Friends in the North*, the political melodramas adapted from novels written by Michael Dobbs, a Conservative MP, *The House of Cards* and *To Play the King*, the one-off TV drama, *The Politician's Wife*, and the novel of another Conservative MP, Edwina Currie, *A Parliamentary Affair* (1994).

It is misleading to see this period in terms of unrelieved anti-feminist 'backlash' or a new sexual puritanism. As we shall see in Chapter 4, scandals are a sexual incitement as much as a punishment. Commercial agencies of all kinds, from pornographers and pimps to advertisers and gurus of fashion and 'style', continue to work on the heightened tensions between sexual categories: crossing gender categories for instance, or sexualizing childish femininities. New/old sexual categories emerge and are publicly named: 'baby dykes' (see Chapter 7), 'men behaving badly', 'new ladettes', 'scarfing', pornography on the Internet, Satanic abuse, sex tourism etc. By the later 1990s, paedophilia in particular had become a huge and deeply threatening media presence.

In the same period, radical movements have continued to make challenges and some gains and to work out their own moralities (e.g. Weeks 1991). From this point of view (which is our own) the contemporary scene is deeply confusing too. It is marked by paradox, contradiction, great unevenness between sites and large difference between social groups. Again, the interactions of moral traditionalism and sexual radicalism seem central – and recognized as such on both sides (returning to the Wilshire interview):

RJ: Why in the mid-'80s should issues that have been boiling away and being campaigned around in broadly conservative ways . . . then start really to produce fruit . . .? The Clause [28] would be one example.

Wilshire: . . . There may be 'thus far and no further' as an issue . . . I certainly had a sense myself then and have a sense now that people with 'fashionable ideas' (i.e. ones I don't agree with) have quietly been changing things, and slightly started to become more successful, so that the amount of change made started to stack up a bit, so even the most dim of people like myself suddenly became aware of it . . . A lot of social change which had suddenly stacked up into a, 'Hang on a minute! Do we the adults, middle-aged particularly, like what we are suddenly seeing here?' . . . I think also by the '80s we had those who had made a lot of change gradually becoming bolder in their assertion of *their* values to the point of causing public offence and *that* started to stack up a little bit, as well.

He added that post-1979 Conservative governments gave 'some comfort to those who felt crotchety' and talked about his consciousness of 'a dreadful sense of aimlessness'. 'We are', he concluded, 'a slightly more Godless society at the moment now than we have been for some period in our history.'

> RJ: . . . you really see this as reactive . . . to . . . radicalisms or too rapid change?
>
> Wilshire: Yes . . . Revolutions get counter-revolutions.

In education, the sexual 'counter-revolution' was clearly connected with other issues, with the attack on the relative autonomy of teaching as a profession, with the delegation of powers to individual schools and the weakening of local authorities. Section 28 and the sex education measures ran along the grain of all three restructurings as well as being a key 'moral' demand. As David Wilshire put it:

> I wanted to stop local government wasting public money . . . Nowhere will you find me expressing an opinion about homosexuality or homosexuals. You *will* find me saying that I do not consider it proper to use taxpayers' money to encourage things which the majority of people don't wish to be encouraged, even if those people are prejudiced and wrong . . . bearing in mind I hadn't been here very long and that I had come here via the leadership of a local council and I had very clear views then, and still do now, on what is the proper role of local government. And campaigning positively for homosexuality is not a proper function in my judgement of local government. I do, however, defend your right to stand on the pavement out there and shout to the rooftops that homosexuality is a marvellous thing and why don't you try it . . . but you are not entitled to expect the taxpayer to fund you . . . We are back to the politician leading within what is the norm of society at the moment.

We will return to Wilshire's 'norm' later, but responding to the argument that the Clause stimulated lesbian and gay campaigning, he added that he 'was not at all keen on encouraging something I am not at all sure I can live with'. His own position was that of a conservative Christian on questions of marriage and sexuality.

If anything is characteristic of a 'New Politics', Section 28 is (Stacey 1991; Cooper 1994; Reinhold 1994; Smith 1994). Based in a traditionalist reaction to the 'too far too fast' (but actually very hesitant) policies of some local authorities in working against sexual discrimination, it brought together traditionalist and free-market strands, focusing them on issues of educational control. The Conservative government took over the issue and melded it with a project to regulate local government, a power base of opposition parties. Section 28 was a particularly paradoxical example of centrally imposed regulation to curtail 'illegitimate' interventions by the (local) state. It was opposed by an alliance in which radical movements of sex and gender were central, in this case the lesbian and gay movements and some forms of feminism. Finally, the Clause condensed sexual interest around the strong binary – heterosexual versus homosexual. As Anna Marie Smith puts it, the Clause involved a 'homosexualization of local government autonomy' (Smith 1994: 185).

A fuller account of the mid-1980s shift would require a closer look at the dynamics of power within the Conservative Party itself, especially John Major's balancing acts between his 'Thatcherite' and 'Conservative' wings and the search for issues to restore electoral fortunes. On the whole, however, the last ten years does not bear out Martin Durham's prediction that 'Major will not take the party in a moralist direction' (1991: 4). Willingly or not, Major has presided over a marked moralization of the political scene, in which traditionalist themes have acquired political prominence, often with an unexpected twist. Crucial too has been the growing sense of social decay and disorder produced by government policy but feeding moralistic discourse. The effectiveness of minority moral campaigning is not necessarily a sign of strength. It has been a sign of weakness in government and the ruling party, seeking to stick together a disintegrating social alliance and a very contradictory set of discourses. At another level, however, a certain hegemony has been sustained, since moralizing discourse shifted New Labour further to the right in its search for the political centre.

From the mêlée of sexual news, we have chosen four main episodes for closer analysis, concentrating on debates in Parliament. The debates around Clause 28 were formative for 'the New Politics' with some devious connections with education. More central to schooling were the sex education debates, our second case study. Our third case study, the debate about the age of consent for gay men, raised issues about youth and sexuality, innocence and corruption central to our topic. Finally, debates around the 1996 Divorce Act allow us to analyse the central place of the conjugal couple in contemporary discourses.

In addition to reading political sources, we wanted to interview a range of activists, especially those on the Right. We wanted to understand the personal commitments from which right-wing policies arose – so different from our own. Richard therefore wrote to six MPs requesting an interview on 'family policy'.[2] Only David Wilshire agreed.

Dominant strategies? moral traditionalism, neo-Conservatism and neo-Liberalism

The differences within dominant discourses can best be seen in the Commons debates on the age of consent of gay men in February 1994 and on the 1996 Divorce Act.

It was the Conservative MP Edwina Currie who moved the resolution for the age of consent to be lowered to 16, the current age of consent for hetero-sexuals. Currie is well known as ex-Minister for Public Health who was forced to resign when she spoke out about salmonella in eggs. Some arguments in her trenchant speech were certainly drawn from this 'expert' public health repertoire:

> As a former Health Minister, I have a particular concern. How can we advise young gay men about the danger of AIDS, how can we talk to them straight about safer sex, when what they are doing is supposed to be strictly against the law?
>
> (*Hansard*, 21 February 1994: col. 78)

Later she insisted that the way to combat HIV and AIDS and the high rate of suicide among young gay men was to 'have open, intelligent, well-trained, well-informed, talk, advice and support', not 'to turn our young people into criminals'.

Currie's position can be understood in terms of different Departmental affiliations, which privilege different discourses. Rachel Thomson, in a key analysis of the politics of sex education, distinguishes between 'moral authoritarianism' and 'public health pragmatism', a tension she relates to differences between the Department of Health (DoH) and the Department for Education and Employment (DfEE) (Thomson 1993, 1994). This fissure is an important and persistent one. In April 1994, for instance, Baroness Cumberledge, Junior Health Minister, supported a family planning nurse in North Birmingham who gave condoms to girls under 16. Health workers got support from some Conservative MPs, including Currie and Teresa Gorman, but were attacked by others, Dame Jill Knight and Harry Green-away, who are leading moral traditionalists (*The Guardian*, 26 April 1994).[3] 'Public health pragmatism' is a useful term to characterize aspects of liberal responses: especially the preoccupation with sexual pathologies and the preference for apparently technical solutions – above all the magical condom.

In Currie's speech, however, public health issues are framed by a particularly consistent version of a classic liberal argument, linked to her own Conservatism and to European comparisons:

> As a lifelong Tory, I can only say that I believe that the state should be kept out of the personal lives of the men and women of this country. Everyone is entitled to his or her privacy. What my neighbours get up to in private is their business and not mine, and it is not for the state to interfere. If we are to have a nation at ease with itself and a nation at the heart of Europe, the most unpleasant homophobic nature of current legislation must be changed – and the sooner, the better.
>
> (*Hansard*, 21 February 1994: col. 75)

In response to a particularly homophobic intervention from her fellow Tory Mr Marlow she commented:

> I do not consider the private sexual practices of other people, including the hon. Gentleman, to be any business of the law. The debate in recent weeks has taught me that one person's sexual perversion is another person's preferred sexual practice. We should all be careful about pronouncing on what goes on next door.
>
> (*Hansard*, 21 February 1994: col. 77)

For Currie, there are different individual preferences in sexual matters. These are private matters in which the state should not intervene; nor should it enforce the preferences of any particular group. The discrepancy between the age of consent for heterosexuals and for homosexual men is a problem because it stops decent health education, but is also prejudicial, discriminatory and oppressive.

Discourses deployed in Currie's speech are a good example of the neo-Liberal strategy in contemporary Conservatism. Her most vociferous opponents were members of her own party. Her relationship to her male-dominated and homophobic party gains poignancy from her authorship of *A Parliamentary Affair*, a popular novel about the links between parliamentary power-seeking and sexual 'affairs'. Against her view of sexuality as private, her opponents insisted on the national interest in private matters, coming close to denying a private sphere at all. As the Ulster Unionist Rev. Ian Paisley put it:

> It has been argued that private morality should not be a matter for the House. If we followed that principle, how many Acts of Parliament would have to be destroyed?
>
> (*Hansard*, 21 February 1994: col. 113)

Conservative differences were even more visible over divorce. One cluster of positions came from government speakers defending the original Bill and from professionals with experience of divorce law, counselling, or social or probation work (*Hansard*, Commons, Family Law Bill, Second Reading, 25 March 1996: cols 738–805; Committee Stage, 24 April 1996: cols 443–543). The main problem with earlier legislation and practice was the availability of relatively easy, quick divorce through the ascription of 'fault'. This procedure, which accounted for over 70 per cent of divorces in 1994, allowed little time for reflection and incited mutual recrimination. The resulting damage to children was a key reason for change. The Bill provided for 'an active period of reflection and consideration' for mediation and possibly reconciliation. Partners could settle their financial affairs and make more amicable arrangements for children. Divorce was a social evil, but couples can make more or less rational decisions to part. They should be helped by a new apparatus of mediation services, without too quick a recourse to law. Marriage is seen, usually implicitly, as a contract between equal adult persons, the main social consideration on break-up being the protection of children. An unusually explicit neo-Liberal version came from the official Liberal Democrat speaker:

> Just as the individuals freely choose to come together, so either one or both have the right to choose at any time to take steps to dissolve that partnership and to go their separate ways. Parliament's job should not be to stand in the way of that choice, but to ensure, so far as possible, that the responsibilities that the individuals accept when they enter into marriage are properly exercised, if necessary for the rest of their lives.
>
> (Chris Davies, *Hansard*, 25 March 1996: col. 767)

Against this liberal utilitarianism, moral traditionalists insisted that the state must defend marriage as a moral institution. Urged on by the Conservative press, especially by the *Daily Mail*, they first opposed the Bill and then sought to amend it. In particular the 'no fault' principle eroded the responsibility for partners to keep a marriage alive. Here the law is more than an enabler of civil transactions. It has 'a declaratory effect on behaviour' (Jeremy Bray, *Hansard*, 25 March 1996: col. 763). As speaker after speaker put it: it 'gives out a message from this House'. Often the preferred message was linked to a religious view of the state, as a kind of theocracy. This was associated with a neo-Conservative commitment to a single, Christian, 'national' way of life, a commitment which marginalizes members of other faiths, and also the non-believing majorities. It privileges, indeed idealizes and sanctifies Christian marriage. Certain moral values are essential in the nation's character and history; they must be inculcated generally through the law. Edward Leigh's version was particularly apocalyptic:

> The Bill would have a great impact on millions of lives and it is also of enormous quasi-constitutional importance. Many of our institutions are based on the concept of the Judaeo-Christian state . . . The gospel view of marriage is clear: marriage is for life. The Bill would advance further down the dangerous road of ending the concept of a Christian state laying down the framework of social life.
>
> (*Hansard*, 25 March 1996: cols 783–4)

Parliament should make divorce as difficult as possible. It should stress 'the rough tough stuff of reconciliation' rather than 'mediation and the divvying up of spoils' (John Patten, *Hansard*, 25 March 1996: col. 763). It should lengthen as far as possible the waiting time and restore 'fault'. Liberals decried this as an impossible 'moral audit'; traditionalists called it the 'recognition of culpability'.

This insistence on a directive public interest in private morality starts by refusing a more pluralistic conception of the nation. It treats all citizens in a culturally diverse society as though they were Christians, if only by default. However, in the divorce debates, this position was moderated once defeat threatened. Traditionalist activists, forced to recognize some limits to the nationalization of Christian versions of marriage, started to claim special exemptions for Believers. They argued for the right to opt into a 'more binding promise' under the new law, a curious variant on the right to withdraw children from (Christian) worship in schools or from sex education programmes.[4] In the debate as a whole, however, little recognition was given to other forms of sexuality. Even heterosexual cohabitation was pushed to the margin, some rights to women in these circumstances being given, but the distinctions with marriage being preserved. The rising rate of divorce was cited by speaker after speaker, alongside the insistence on 'stable' heterosexual marriage as the strongly preferred sexual form.

> Let no one doubt that marriage is intended for life. The current level of divorce at about 160,000 each year in England and Wales is a matter for regret and its relatively high rate in comparison with that of other European nations is a matter of concern. The purpose of the Bill is to strengthen the institution of marriage by encouraging the process of reflection and consideration . . .
> (Roger Freeman, for Government, *Hansard*, 25 March 1996:
> col. 738)

> Families are the natural, fundamental units of our society, and safe, secure marriages are the most certain buttress of those families.
> (Paul Boateng, for Labour, *Hansard*, 25 March 1996: col. 753)

Marriage, the ideal, occupies the centre stage even though the topic is divorce, the failure of the ideal to hold. Several speakers insisted that the Bill was on the 'wrong' topic – the government, influenced by the hyper-liberal Law Commission had come up with a Divorce Bill (actually called the Family Law Bill) when what was needed was a Marriage Bill, a Bill to strengthen marriage. The family and marriage were thus inextricably linked or conflated. Marriage was declared ideal just where its troubles were being addressed. Yet because it is idealized, it is hard to talk concretely about its difficulties and limits, the reasons in fact for many of those divorces. Only occasionally does the actual diversity of arrangements for sexuality, intimacy and living together come to view: in traditionalist discourse as disapproval, or in liberal discourse as 'fact'. As Jeremy Bray put it:

> The increases in marriage breakdown and divorce have occurred over the same period, and among the same age groups, as changes in the pattern of sexual behaviour. In the sterilized, fault-free world in which the Bill seeks to operate, it is almost necessary to remind the house that marriage and sexual behaviour are related . . .
> (*Hansard*, 25 March 1996: col. 764)

He argued that the erosion of marriage was part of a process of (deplorable) sexual change which included increased rates of premarital sexual activity, of cohabitation and decreased rates of marriage among young adults. Generally, marriage is presented as the guarantor of childhood and the reproduction of population and nation. Often, however, it is presented as the only fully legitimate way of being sexual at all.

The Normal, the Natural and the Perverse

Just how narrow the idea of the sexual can be is clearest in debates on homosexuality. In the age of consent debate, for example, Conservative men, in particular, identified sexuality with procreation and therefore with fucking. They seemed to have the utmost difficulty in conceiving of sex in non-genital terms. It followed that the peculiar abnormality of homosexuality was the act of 'buggery' – as Sir Nicholas Fairbairn put it, 'Putting your penis in another man's arsehole is perverse'(*Hansard*, Commons, 21 February 1994: col. 98). Fairbairn's statement was unusually explicit; highly-charged references to 'sodomy' or 'buggery' do, however, galvanize the debates. We also find decorous distinctions: 'homosexuality in theory' versus 'homosexuality in practice' for example. The practices are 'unmentionable' but 'well-known'; abstinence is often the only way to win approval.

Notions of normality and perversity in traditionalist discourse almost always have a procreative/non-procreative criterion lurking somewhere.

> *Wilshire:* At a personal level . . . it [homosexuality] is a natural part of the human condition but it is not normal. That is the distinction I have always sought to draw. It is natural, it is there . . . it is a natural part of the human condition . . . so it is natural . . . it is, however, not normal in the sense that I use the definition normal to be a biological definition. Until such time as the human species can reproduce homosexually, then in my book, it's not normal.
>
> *RJ:* Or reproduce , I suppose, without sexuality at all.
>
> *Wilshire:* That's not normal either . . .
>
> *RJ:* Umm.
>
> *Wilshire:* . . . would be my . . .
>
> *RJ:* Would 'not normal' be, again, back to your religious absolutes then?
>
> *Wilshire:* No, that's back to my biological absolutes. We are a heterosexual species that lives in societies. I don't need to rehearse it to you. You are well aware of the biologist's view of *homo sapiens*.
>
> *RJ:* Yes . . . Yes . . .

Wilshire: And I think we get ourselves into a lot of trouble when we
seek to tell ourselves that we are somehow no longer part of
the animal kingdom and masters of everything we survey,
free to change our characters, free to change our roots, I'm
afraid we ain't.

RJ: But biology and religion do sort of go together rather here
don't they?

Wilshire: Probably yes . . . I'd actually say that we neglect what we are
and who we are at our peril . . .

RJ: Yes . . . and are you worried that what you would have seen
as the promotion of homosexuality might also weaken
family attachments, or family life or heterosexual relations?

Wilshire: Yes, it undermines what I consider to be a fundamental
norm of the human condition.

RJ: Even though it's a norm it can still be undermined. Some
would say that's a contradiction I suppose.

Wilshire: *[Sighs deeply]* Erm, yes, because it . . . I'm not an expert on
the subject . . .

Richard's first thought in this puzzling conversation was that by 'normal'
Wilshire was referring to an earlier discussion about religious and moral
absolutes, or about societal norms held, 'rightly or wrongly', by his own 'Alf
Garnett-like' (his phrase) constituents. It turned out, however, that 'normal'
(unlike 'natural' – which is more like 'empirically observable'?) was rooted
in 'biology', but evidently as a highly normative science. The argument only
holds if it is assumed that procreation is the only justifiable reason for sexual
activity or relationships. The exchange shows how strongly neo-Conservative and religious discourse centres on sexuality as 'sex' and on 'sex' as the
procreative act.

The procreative couple is privileged against (any kind of) homosexuality
in this scheme. In more soppy, patronizing versions, compassion is extended
to the 'handicapped' or 'disabled' lesbian or gay man who is excluded from
'family life and normal parenthood' – an outcome devoutly to be secured,
where possible, by discriminatory regulations.[5] But it is important to stress
the full range of exclusions and otherings on which this construction rests.
It is not just sexual identities that are excluded but whole aspects of the
sexual domain: sexuality as fun or pleasure, or sexuality as personal identity
or even, surprisingly perhaps, sexuality as intimacy. Such definitions do not
address, except as a looming 'nothing', the particular sexual position of
teenagers or young adults or, for that matter, post-procreative heterosexually inclined individuals and relationships. In the meantime the procreative
assumption certainly underpins 'compulsory heterosexuality' and also dic-
tates what the main forms and bodily zones of erotic significance and pleasure shall be.

It is crucial to Conservative positions that despite being unnatural or abnormal, homosexuality can be 'promoted' and learnt. This was the leading theme of Clause 28 and the age of consent debate. Section 28, as it passed into law, prohibited local authorities from 'intentionally promote[ing] homosexuality' by publishing material or promoting teaching in schools 'of the acceptability of homosexuality as a pretended family relationship'. As Anna Marie Smith put it (1994: 238):

> For the supporters of Section 28, homosexuality operated like a ['dangerous'] supplement: they rightly claimed that lesbian and gay identities – like all identities – profoundly depend upon political intervention, and that if homosexuality were politicized, it could indeed have a tremendous subversive effect on the 'normal'.

Yet there is something paradoxical about the possibility of 'promotion'. Political opposition to the work of feminist and lesbian and gay local government committees compels the notion that it must have evil effects, must 'promote'. Yet the underlying conviction remains that homosexuality is unnatural, abnormal or in some way 'impossible'. Is this the tension that underlies Wilshire's not untypical categorical acrobatics around the natural and the normal? Or has he been forced to take on board some of the arguments about the 'naturalness' of homosexuality from the other side, so strengthening his conception of the norm with biological reinforcements?

As Jonathan Dollimore has shown, a key 'solution' has been the idea of 'the perverse'(1991). A defining feature of the perverse is its closeness to the normal. The pervert is 'us', so to speak – but for grace of God. It is the normal gone wrong, twisted, changed or *influenced* in some way. This 'solution' to the homosexual conundrum, however, serves to make matters worse because it brings the danger even nearer. If the Other is a perverted version of the normal, 'we' and 'they' are still harder to disentangle and greater watchfulness is needed.

This 'proximity' of the perverse is clear in conservative discourse. It is illustrated in the figure of the 'good homosexual' of course – who is 'just like us' (but not quite). But accounts of 'bad' homosexuals may also be accompanied by propositions so hotly pursued and so earnestly exaggerated that they suggest the speaker is far from disengaged. While accepting the elements of 'rational' realpolitik in these constructions (Smith 1994: 189), the standard claim that anti-discriminatory policies are actually a *promotion* of homosexuality is an emotionally invested exaggeration of this kind, only qualified in the final Section 28 by 'intentional'. Similarly, it is sometimes argued that the local state has granted special rights or privileges to sexual others as though sexual identities stood on even ground in the first place. When Lord Halsbury introduced his precursor to Section 28 he presented anti-discriminatory policies as a fearsome and ungrateful threat to heterosexuals in general: 'they will push us off the pavement if we give them a chance' (*Hansard*, 18 December 1986: col. 310). This recognizes the inter-relations of different sexual identities but articulates it only as fear, hatred, and a certain self-justifying pleasure in these feelings. It is inconceivable that the heterosexually inclined might enjoy, celebrate or choose to live with homosexual desire, or ally with lesbian or gay politics, or emulate gay styles. Some forms of lesbian, gay and especially 'queer' activism do challenge the privileges and borders of heterosexuality, but why is this a problem, exactly? Again, Wilshire's phrase is interesting: homosexuality is 'something I am not at all sure *I can live with*' (emphasis added).

The aversion to perversion is expressed most often through fears for others, particularly for the young. In the Wilshire interview and in several parliamentary speeches, references are made to boarding ('public') school homosexuality – by Lord Longford and, very defensively, by Halsbury himself in the debate on his 1986 Bill for instance. This currency suggests that the experience of boarding school homo-eroticism, romantic or sadistic, often hard to negotiate as 'gay', is critical in explaining the strength of homophobia among elite men. In these 'personal' stories, told quite abstractly, 'perversity' is seen as abnormal development:

> I was, however, at a boys' boarding school, which is probably as good a place as any to get anecdotal evidence of what happens to teenage boys in their development as animals [*sic!*] and I observed, then, and nobody seems to want to contradict me, that there is a stage that boys go – I pass on girls . . . They go through a phase where homosexuality is there, quite near the surface as an experiment with their developing maturity and it occurs to me . . . that if you, ah, sort of stunt the emotional sexual development of somebody you might sort of fossilize them in an adolescent position where they would develop through it. And by taking, ah, by appealing to youngsters, by telling them that that is a normal, natural or marvellous state of adult maturity, I'm desperately worried about it.
>
> (Wilshire interview)

Here perversity is identified (in a sense as 'natural'), yet dismissed (as temporary, as a 'phase') and pushed away (as abnormal, stunting), yet it also remains to be desperately worried about. Perversion as maldevelopment provides the space for 'promotion', especially the corruption of the young. Youthfulness becomes the focus for the wider adult anxieties, which are personal and individual as well as social, to condense around. Some of the emotionally wildest, most invested representations of the sexual occur in debates about 'youth'. In the age of consent debate, resistance to lowering the age to 16 centred on 'those whose sexual orientation is not properly determined', 'the mass of undetermined, seeking, evolving, immature youngsters', adolescent males especially. They might be cheated from normality by the seduction of older men or confused by the 'vortex' of homosexual clubs, or be 'redirected' in the context of 'a highly organised self-conscious community'(*Hansard*, Commons, 21 February 1994: cols 102–3). It is in this discursive context that lesbians and gay men who work or wish to work with children encounter the heterosexist assumption that they are more likely to be abusers of children than heterosexuals (Chapter 6).

Sex education is another topic where adult heterosexual anxieties run rife. In moving a moral traditionalist amendment to the Education Bill of 1986, Viscount Buckmaster attacked contemporary sex education practice and blamed it for most sexual evils:

> [A] great deal of the sex education today, particularly in our maintained schools, is amoral, if not downright immoral, dealing as it does, with human reproduction in the most provocative and explicit way, with no element of moral guidance.
>
> Indeed, the theme running through most of this literature [*sic*] is that sexual activity among teenagers of whatever age is quite normal and natural, and also quite harmless, provided one takes appropriate precautions to avoid pregnancy or a sexually transmitted disease.
> (*Hansard*, Lords, 15 April 1986: col. 647)

There could be little doubt that the type of sex education advocated by the Family Planning Association, the Brook Clinics and the National Marriage Guidance Council had led to increased sexual activity among teenagers, had encouraged 'furtive fumblings in cars', had rendered homosexuality acceptable, undermined stable marriage and increased the divorce rate.

> And is it not also possible to link some of the appalling sexual crimes that are apparent nowadays, the increase in rapes, the attacks on children? Is there not perhaps some connection between these and this appalling sex education?
> (*Hansard*, Lords, 15 April 1986: col. 649)

Again, what is especially interesting here is the projection of sexual evils onto children as the victims several times over of sex education, the inability to think of sexuality except as fucking or 'fumbling', and the tendency to hysterical exaggerations about causation. These discursive and psychic moves fuel the very odd assumption that 'sexual activity [of all or any kind?] among teenagers' is abnormal or unnatural.

'Sit down and shut up': children, parents and pedagogy

Discursive constructions around childhood and child–adult relations will be explored in more detail in Chapter 4 since they tend to be held in common across different discursive sites and are vividly present in media forms and debates. But it is important to stress that liberal inhibitions can more easily be set aside in the case of children. This applies both to state (or school) regulation and to parental rights or 'choice'. The rights of children to receive an adequate sex education, to make choices about their own sexuality, or to have any kind of sexual autonomy are not topics within neo-Conservative discourse and only rarely within neo-Liberalism. Rather the emphasis is upon enhancing the power of parents against the state or school or teacher. The child is subsumed into parental and other interests. Much the same can be said of preferred pedagogies including the whole idea of 'healthy' moral, familial influences upon the child. Where school pedagogies are specified, they are highly didactic and authoritarian, with the teacher all activity and the child infallibly pacified. Asked if he was in favour of educational policies since the 1988 Act, Wilshire replied that he was 'in favour of a lot more things we haven't pursued':

RJ: Such as?
Wilshire: Being taught to recite their tables. Being taught to spell properly. And punctuate. And to sit down and shut up. And do what they're told. And I'm old and reactionary. I used to be a teacher. I am all in favour of whole class education: 'You sit there and listen, Sunshine, while I describe this to you.' It didn't seem to do me any harm.

It is clear that the idea of a private space is always qualified when it comes to childhood, as though the child has no privacy even in sexual matters. The sexuality of children can be regulated, interfered with, all under the rubric of education or protection. It is this, together with gay/straight inequalities that is at stake, of course, in the age of consent debate. Those, like Wilshire, who favoured 18 did so on the basis that this age marked the onset of adulthood according to the existing state of law. Asked why he voted this way, he replied:

For the very simple reason that if it's legal, and if you are defined as an adult at 18 then I do not think that I as a politician, though I disapprove, I think it follows, though I wish these things didn't happen, I don't think the law has any place in what consenting adults do providing they don't outrage other people . . .

It undoubtedly does have a place, however, in the sexuality of those aged 16 to 18 if they are gay, or under whether gay or not. When asked if he would wish to see further changes in the age of consent, Wilshire replied:

No. If pushed I might have some views about the age of heterosexual consent rather than about the other. If I am told I am being illogical . . .
RJ: In what direction?

Wilshire: Upwards . . . If one is required to be dispassionate and logi-
cal, I have to give you that reply, which gets hoots of
derision, which only makes the point that I don't think the
law has all that much of a place . . . Unless it outrages public
decency . . . by cavorting, but then, of course, I would wish
to ban heterosexual performances of sex on the lawn out
there, let alone homosexual activity.

The logic of much conservative discourse is the desexualization of children and young people. The child, even the young person, is produced in this
discourse as not legitimately sexual. This is part of the same logic that exalts
heterosexual and preferably Christian marriage as the 'mature' form of the
sexual. After all, if marriage is the only legitimate form of the sexual we have
nothing to do but wait. Exclusion from the sexual defines the politics of
sexuality for children and those concerned, like teachers, with child–adult
relations in this sphere. The logic of this discursive strategy is that sexuality
can only be lived by the young, secretly, as a naughtiness, under erasure. We
will explore the impacts on children's lives more closely in later chapters, but
may note that given the usual youthful resistances, these prohibitions invite
sexiness as a 'naughty' act, but discourage thought and discussion.

Neo-Liberal limits

We can lay out the typical dichotomies of dominant sexual discourses in the
following ways:

Themes	*Neo-Conservatism*	*Neo-Liberalism*
Sexuality?	Procreation/perversion	Different natures/choices
Sexualities?	'The family'	Individual diversity
Homosexualities?	Perverse	Individual/private
Gender relations?	Gender natural	Gender blind
State role?	Protects 'the family'	No role in private sex
Moral position?	Traditional values	Choice
Parent/child	Protection/innocence	Parental rights
	Parental responsibility	

On occasion neo-Liberal discourse can oppose and even qualify the authoritarianism of neo-Conservatism. Currie's advocacy of equality of the age of
consent of 16 was the clearest (albeit unsuccessful) example we could find.
In Wilshire's case, the neo-Liberal/neo-Conservative opposition is internal to
his Thatcherite politics. He stressed the liberal limits to state intervention
and had a strong sense of the public/private split. He insisted on the limited
role of the politician: a representative of the social norm, not a 'staring-eyed
revolutionary'. He narrated himself in the interview as a responsible man

torn between difficult choices: his desire to do good according to his moral and religious values; his understanding of the proper relationship between 'politics' and 'management', a relationship he studied at Brunel University. Politics was about handling the tensions between intervention and freedom, striking a personal balance and respecting those of political colleagues. Unlike moral traditionalist colleagues, however, he was careful to distinguish between moral 'gurus' as sources of 'absolute' values and the limited role of politicians. He only wished the Christian churches would do their job:

> If the churches consider that homosexuality is a sin they should preach it from the pulpits. They should not expect us to legislate what they cannot preach effectively from the pulpits.

Similarly he regarded the attempt to align the Conservative Party with a call for 'Back to Basics' as politically 'crass', much though he yearned for a return to Christian fundamentals himself.

This *combination* of neo-Liberal and neo-Conservative strategies, sometimes contradictory, sometimes complementary, marks Wilshire as a more typical Thatcherite than Currie or his own traditionalist allies. As a separate basis for policies, neo-Liberalism has familiar weaknesses. It involves an under-social version of the individual – a radical individualism. It is neglectful of relations of power and difference, except as state coercion. The play of power in everyday life is minimized or discounted. The 'social' in this old Socialist sense – the forms of cooperation which link human beings but also divide all and oppress many – is denied. It is hard within this framework to make an issue of the subordination of the interests of children to parental power, since 'rationality' is seen as a feature of adulthood alone. It is hard to question the subordination of women or of lesbians and gay men except as a critique of bad law. It is hard to engage with the complexities of sexual difference, gender power and child–adult relations in their interrelations. Sexuality is seen as an individual matter which should be protected by relations of privacy. This neglect of power relations can also be seen in the limits of the contractual approach to divorce which ignores the centrality of gender and other struggles in the making and break-up of marriages, and the need to support the economically weaker party, often a woman. This neglect makes liberal versions of marriage and divorce vulnerable to critiques from the Right, which at least grasp the possibility of conflict and discrepant desires, if only as moral misdoing.

One further accompaniment of individualism and its weak sense of the social is a failure to see the importance of sectional political organization. This failure was, perhaps, the limit of Currie's considerable radicalism on the age of consent. In her advocacy of the abolition of legal discrimination she took care not to identify her cause as that of homosexual men, especially not of an organized gay movement. For her the campaign was 'not an issue for gay men alone, and no longer a minority issue, but one of human rights, which touches us all' (*Hansard*, 21 February 1994: col. 75). There is a version of this argument which expresses lesbian and gay confidence. Homosexuality is not a minority issue since homosexual assertion changes the terms on which heterosexuality is lived. But we do not think that this was Currie's version. Rather, though she took many arguments from gay campaigning, she also distanced herself from the demonstrators outside the House of Commons and, according to some reports, blamed them for the parliamentary defeat.

Against the individualism of neo-Liberalism, neo-Conservative strategies offer an over-social or socially coercive and conformist view of social order. There is indeed a social interest in 'private' matters which should, where social cohesion and moral absolutes demand, be enforced in law or moral conformity. In the sexual domain there is one right way, or at least one most legitimate or mature way of being sexual. Often these moral absolutes are traced to God's 'law' and fundamentalist religious belief. In a more 'scientific' discourse, sexual morality is seen as rule-bound and given, especially biologically, linked to procreation and not a matter of discovery or education. True, sexualities may be 'promoted', but promotion is a route to the perverse. In any case our 'promotion' is only natural!

The liberal/conservative combination sets up many of the typical antinomies of dominant sexual discourse. These can be traced in the whole sexual culture, but also in legislation and practices in schools. Neo-Liberal themes are worked into New Right policies along with traditionalist elements. Sex education provides a rich example of the double-binding and self-defeating contradictions that result. We can now reread the detailed regulations as laid out in the Acts of 1986 and 1993 and DfEE Circular 5/94 in the light of our analysis.

The inclusion of 'biological' aspects of sex in the National (science) Curriculum corresponds to the reductive view of sexuality and the tie to procreation. Non-procreative sexualities of all kinds cannot really be discussed within this framework. There is a case, indeed, which we explore in Chapter 8, for disarticulating sex education from 'biology', certainly not starting there. The equation of sex with biology also limits sexuality education, as a possible theme across the National Curriculum. Moral traditionalism, however, and public health considerations, require that sex education, within a 'moral' framework, privileging marriage and the family, be taught in all secondary schools. This puts pressure on teachers to act as moral directors of the young, running against the tendency to pupil-centredness in liberal sex education. Moral direction is also likely to be ineffective because of the distance between the sexual cultures of teachers and pupils and the dynamics of control and resistance in the school (see Chapter 5). But neo-Liberal emphases also underpin the right of withdrawal from the school's sex education lessons. Note, however, that the right of withdrawal is an (ungendered) parental right, not a right for girls or boys. This neglects (or sanctifies) conventional gender power relations and it also constructs an authoritarian view of child–adult relations, which denies choice and autonomy to the child. Having removed a child from sex education lessons, parents are under no obligation to give reasons or to make some alternative provision. Presumably it is supposed that such parents will give moral instruction of the kind approved of by the government. This enhancement of parent power, in general, makes it harder for teachers or other professionals to intervene in oppressive family relations, including the sexual abuse of children. Similarly the DfEE Circular limits the young person's autonomy and rights in relation to confidentiality in a pastoral school context. Major obligations are imposed on schools with the minimum of legislative enablement or protection and a maximum exposure to irresponsible parental contestation and to adverse publicity.

More generally the dominant discourses give out *contradictory* messages from this House to the schools and elsewhere. Is the giving of a full sex education a matter of public interest? Or is it a matter of individual conscience and private or familial practice? Sex educators risk being labelled as corrupters of innocents when they speak of homosexuality or any form of non-procreative sexuality. When they use children's own sexual languages, they risk being accused of obscenity. They trespass on the very disputable rights of parenthood. If they act, as government wishes, as givers of the moral rule, they run up against ethico-cultural diversity in the communities they serve. If they raise moral issues in a genuinely educative way, they run up against adult hang-ups and discursive dissonances but also the dogmatic convictions of religious minorities and significant sections of the ruling groups and their local supporters. It is not at all surprising that sex education is now often seen in schools as an impossible practice.

In sum sex education is now constrained and disorganized not only by a moral traditionalism, which has always attacked it fiercely, but also by the sexual dissonances which run right through the cultures of politics and affect the wider cultural formation.

Social liberal discourses on sexuality

In the age of consent debate, several speakers argued for equalizing at age 16 but according to social rather than individual interests.[6] We term this strategy 'social liberalism'. On the other side, social liberalism shares with neo-Conservatism a sanctioning of state intervention in sexual matters. However, intervention is justified on different grounds, the sexual domain is theorized differently, and state action takes different preferred forms.

In the age of consent debate, social liberal discourses embraced a sexual ontology of different sexual natures. Most speakers operated a distinction between a biological or given sexuality and its social concomitants or consequences. While the first is fixed, the second may be changed. This view of sexuality was the commonest defence against discrimination and against the argument of Conservative speakers that young men, of indeterminate sexuality, could be corrupted by older men or by an assertive gay culture.

> I do not believe that sexuality is determined by persuasion. The overwhelming evidence – scientific or indeed merely experience of life – suggests that being homosexual is not something that people catch, are taught, or persuaded into, but something they are.
>
> (Tony Blair, *Hansard*, 21 February 1994: col. 98)

Chris Smith made a similar point, clearly based in a history of gay defences:

> We are who we are. No amount of attempts by anyone to convert us into something else would pose a threat or danger.
>
> (ibid.: col. 111)

This was also a main line of attack on Clause 28.

> We are what we are. It is impossible to force or encourage someone into a different sexuality from that which pertains to them. What is needed is not to be involved in changing, persuading, forcing, encouraging people into different sexualities. What is important is to enable people to understand the sexuality that they have, and that cannot be changed.
>
> (Chris Smith, Commons Committee Stage on Local Government Bill, 15 December 1987: col. 1007)

The stress on different sexual natures, which are all 'normal' and 'natural', creates a space for arguing for the injustice of discrimination and for claiming equality of recognition for lesbians and gay men. In this version of the sexual nation, homosexualities have visibility and some measure of recognition. Social liberals, however, draw different conclusions. Some continue to work with a familiar sexual hierarchy. While voting for 16 in the age of consent debate, Neil Kinnock continued to privilege heterosexual relationships and to patronize young gay men and lesbians:

> Let us tell young people that a heterosexual life, in the sense that it is what most of us live and want to live, is the norm; that it is and will remain the basic human relationship upon which the family is founded. But let us also tell young homosexuals that we still have regard for them and want them to live in a society that accepts their nature and will give them the same chance as others for personal happiness.
>
> (*Hansard*, 21 February 1994: cols 85–6)

Kinnock's version of social liberalism operates with the same condensed version of 'the family' as does traditionalist Conservativism, only it appears to be rooted in a preferred social norm rather than in nature. This combination of a 'social' familialism and 'toleration' of homosexualities is perhaps the typical social liberal strategy. It is a position which has become increasingly explicit in the official voices of Blair's New Labour Party, often indistinguishable from traditionalist accents:

> Therefore, the law can never be value-free. We have somehow to build into what we are doing in this place in the next few weeks some messages about values. If we do not do so, the continuing escalation of the breakdown of the family and the undervaluing of marriage, which we all regret on both sides of the Committee, will continue. This is a difficult task, but it is one that we have to embrace.
>
> (Paul Boateng, Family Law Bill Commons, 3rd Reading,
> *Hansard*, 24 April 1996: col. 483)

It is not suprising that traditionalist Conservatives claimed that 'it is common ground among hon. Members that the family is the foundation of our society and that the basis of the family is marriage' (Simons, ibid.: col. 493).

So *both* heterosexual and homosexual identities have a natural basis and are unchangeable, but it is still possible to privilege heterosexuality, socially and politically in the most heterosexist of ways. The whole construction rests upon the active splitting off of sexual categories. Kinnock splits off gay identity from 'the family', holds 'the family' in the centre and gay identity on the margin; he preaches a toleration for the Other so long as it does not disturb the central categories. What cannot be grasped from this liberal position is the 'truth' of conservative homophobias: that the recognition of legitimate sexual difference always has implications for the dominant positions. Nor is it possible, it seems, to conceptualize gay or queer families and, especially, families or households which embrace both gay and straight relationships. A similar splitting operates, especially within social liberal discourses, in the debates upon divorce. On the one hand, an ideal of marriage and the family is eulogized; on the other hand evils are recognized with which adequate legislation must deal: gender inequalities within marriage and on break-up, 'loveless marriages', sexual violence towards women, and the effects of poverty and male unemployment. Many of these evils are plainly internal to marriage as an institution, or mark the effects of a changing social context upon it. Yet very few speakers really put these two sides of the discourse into an imaginative or practical relationship, allowing evidence of oppressive social relations to question the exclusive marriage ideal. Consequently marriage itself is not scrutinized, nor are the usual equations – marriage = family = parenthood – deconstructed. This is so rare, in parliamentary debates, that even modest versions are startling:

> We make a fundamental mistake if we assume that marriage is the same as a family . . . If people do not want to marry, the state should

not moralize, find fault or blame. Many people – of whom I am one –
live outside marriage. I can tell hon. Members that my children are perfectly happy . . . The problem is that marriage has come to be seen as
a passport to happiness . . .

(Mr Soley,[7] *Hansard*, 24 April 1996: cols 495–7)

The belief in different sexual natures can, however, underpin more consistently liberal positions. In his speeches on the age of consent and on Clause
28, Chris Smith, the only out Labour MP, uses the argument about the
natural basis of sexual difference more pluralistically. There are many sexualities, they are equally natural and legitimate; they should be equally recognized; the great evil is the imposition of one version on another (e.g.
Hansard, 21 February 1994: col. 112).

Within social liberal discourse, the state has a role in negotiating the
relationships between relatively discrete sexual identities or 'communities'.
There is no ground for discriminating between heterosexual and gay male
sex on the age of consent. The state ought to act against illegitimate sexual
discrimination in the way it does against sexism or racism. Similarly, in the
complex manoeuvres of the divorce debate, social liberal discourse pointed
not only towards mediatory and reconciliatory services, adequately
resourced through the state, but also insisted on the splitting of pensions
between partners, legal redress against sexual violence and civil and social
rights for the more 'vulnerable' partner, usually the woman.

All this is allied to definite conceptions of 'society', of social groups and
of social progress. For Blair, 'any strong society' needs 'good and decent
principles'; it should learn from and evaluate 'its progress' and 'build its own
future' (ibid.: col. 100). The appeal of communitarian political philosophy
to Blair and other New Labourites illustrates the retention of 'the social' in
their politics but also its conservative inflection. Similarly different sexual
identities are viewed not merely as individual choices, but as social groupings or interests. To these social interests or 'minorities', collective rights
may be attached. It makes sense within this framework to talk of gay and
lesbian 'communities' or even 'the lesbian and gay community' – as a social
group that is 'vulnerable' or faces social discrimination and in whose interests a claim for 'equality' can be made. Social liberalism is different from
Currie's liberalism or Wilshire's Thatcherism in that it relies less on a
public/private division (and therefore some notion of the closet) or on
child/adult boundaries (and therefore an idea of childhood asexuality) to
regulate the nature and limits of state action. Anti-discriminatory policies
presuppose a visible community; they are meant to enable the process of
coming out. For Blair, for instance, it is wrong for gay men to have to 'hide
their sexuality in fear' (ibid.: col. 100). Within this framework, then, it is
easier to speak openly about sexual issues and 'speaking out' can be an
important dimension of strategy.

Childhood and child–adult relations are also central to the social liberal strategy. In the divorce debates, the strongest defences of the interests of children were expressed within this framework. Speaker after speaker insisted that the main societal interest in divorce was the well-being of 'the children' – so much so that the possibility of childless marriage and divorce was often overlooked. Attitudes to children differed, however, between those more conservative speakers who constructed them as the 'innocent victims' of divorce and those who stressed that the voices of children should be heard throughout the processes of mediation, possible reconciliation and break-up. Conservative traditionalism certainly addresses the evils of divorce for children but tends to speak for them, sometimes generalizing from personal experience to attack divorce in general (e.g. Jill Knight, *Hansard*, 24 April 1996: col. 523). Liberal speakers, often drawing on professional experiences of familial diversity, went beyond these broad moralistic strokes. They pointed to the difficulty of long procedural delays for children's security, the importance of minimizing legally-incited fault-finding between parents, and the importance of legal representation of the children's interests. In general, within the social liberal framework there is less of a tendency to infantilize children and present them as sexually innocent. Rather, children are treated as part of the social future, even where this future is assumed in quite conservative terms: they are future husbands, wives, mothers, fathers, sexual partners and citizens.

Accordingly, the preferred form of state action is educational. Education for marriage, for parenting or for relationships, elaborated health education programmes, and a liberal sex education in schools and outside have been characteristic social liberal demands. Aside from the traditionalist amendments, the main liberal amendment on the 1986 Education Bill in the House of Lords was for an extended programme of Health Education in which sex education should play a part (*Hansard*, Lords, Baroness Masham's amendment, 17 April 1986: cols 771–2). It is within this framework that 'public health pragmatism' finds its more general philosophical justifications. There is an historical affinity too with professional expertise and social research, though also a recent history of backtracking on these alliances by New Labour. It is this discursive space that has been occupied by progressive sex educators of all kinds whether working in schools, or the Health Education Authority, or in the voluntary agencies.

The limits of social liberalism

Emphasis on the social interest in public health promises less inquisitorial policies around schooling and sexuality. Within limits, social liberal discourse is pro-state, pro-sex and pro-education, especially the latter. Yet it is important to note the limits.

In part its vulnerability can be understood historically. The shorter-term history is that of the rise of New Right hegemony (Hall *et al.* 1978; CCCS 1981; Hall and Jacques 1983). Just as Thatcherism can be understood as a critique of social democratic traditions, so New Labour, potentially the main legatee of a social liberal tradition, is post-Thatcherite. It lacks, however, the peculiar strengths of Thatcherism as a long-term hegemonic project: there is no thoroughgoing critique of its predecessor, no counter-hegemonic impulse. Rather New Labour has attempted to outmanoeuvre Conservatism by purging itself of past liabilities. Without fundamental transformations however, social reforming liberalism remains vulnerable to the New Right's critiques of the state, the expert and the professional, even, or especially, where it wriggles to escape the old label 'Socialist'. In practice, therefore, the larger supports in public discourse for positive policies around sexuality and schooling remain unreliable. Because New Right fundamentals are unchallenged, New Labour's positions are pulled towards individualism, individual freedom, choice and market forces. In its increasingly moralizing tone and uncritical familialism, New Labour has also come to resemble neo-Conservatism in its most traditionalist voice. In education policy, the sacro-sanctity of parental choice has, in recent years, often overridden the insistence on social justice and the recognition that immediate parental self-interest (including that of party leaders) and progressive social outcomes may often be in contradiction.

Blairite limitations correspond to a much longer Labour history of electoral pragmatism and ideological caution (Milliband 1964; CCCS 1981). Crucial here has been the long-term abandonment of a popular educational–ideological role of a transformative kind. In the absence of a campaigning counter-hegemonic project within Labour, the traps set by Thatcherite hegemony remain in place. The pursuit of a passive kind of 'popularity', that trembles to give offence, can hardly be supportive of practices which traditionalist campaigning has made controversial. New Labour reads voter attitudes conservatively and takes over many Thatcherite themes, including anti-professionalism. Professionals who work in highly contradictory areas may not gain more support from the Labour Government than from the previous Conservative government, though they could scarcely have less.

It is important, however, also to specify this Conservatism in tighter discursive terms. In any case, social liberalism as a discursive strategy is not simply identifiable with Labour as a political formation. *Discursive* formations do not always tally with *political* divisions.

We wish to stress two ways in which discursive strategies of the centre-left do not escape the traps set by New Right hegemony. The first is the preservation of a view of sexuality or sexualities as natural. Within this framework, to recognize diversity is simply to proliferate 'natures'. As Tony Blair put it in the age of consent debate: 'It is not against the nature of gay people to be gay; it is in fact their nature.' Although this argument seems to have defensive value against the accusation of 'promotion' levelled at a few Labour local authorities, and makes sense of aspects of everyday experience and of gay organization, it is in many ways self-defeating, conceding much ground to anti-educational and illiberal positions. It undermines the claim that education, and cultural processes more generally, are important in determining our conceptions of the sexual: that sexuality, for instance, is more than a matter of natural urges, controlled or uncontrolled. It perpetuates thoroughly reductive ideas of the sexual itself, returning them to the dominant model of penetration and procreation, cutting out the growing centre points of sexuality in contemporary culture – as sources of pleasure and identity. Indeed, the equations between the natural and the procreative are so powerful that to use the argument from nature at all countermands the support for diversity. Nor in the era of genetics and neurology is the appeal to the natural any better safeguard to oppressive manipulation than the argument from culture. As Eve Sedgwick (1994: 163–4) puts it:

If anything, the gestalt of assumptions that undergirds nature/nurture debates may be in process of direct reversal. Increasingly it is the conjecture that a particular trait is genetically or biologically based, *not* that it is 'only cultural', that seems to trigger an estrus of manipulative fantasy in the technological institutions of the culture.

The second and allied problem is the tendency to split off 'other' sexual categories and practices, in the name of 'toleration', but as though they hardly existed in the same social space as heterosexuality, marriage and 'the family'. Sexual differences so separated in pluralistic discourse flow together again with great emotional energy in popular Conservative fantasies. A rationalist social-reforming politics, which focuses on the untruths of opponents' arguments, is not equipped even to grasp the nature of this Conservative advantage. For these reasons it is hard, in the current conjuncture, not to see social liberal discourse as always contained, disorganized or subordinated by the dominant strategies, always working within the limits set by the Thatcherite contradictions, rarely succeeding in exploiting or transcending them.

This is one of the reasons why later in this book we attempt to identify certain emerging discourses from which to form more adequate oppositions.

Notes

1 For the research in the press and other sources on which this account is based see the beginning of Chapter 4 below.
2 Harry Greenaway, Edwina Currie, Jill Knight, David Wilshire, Ann Winterton, Peter Bruinvels.

3 There is a similar argument in the work of Peter Redman, a researcher on sexuality and masculinity who has also worked for a local Health Education Authority. Redman distinguishes 'the new moral traditionalism' and a liberal and progressive practice of sex education which developed in the 1980s, moved away from the narrowly biological model implied in the National Curriculum, and employed student-centred approaches (Redman 1994).

4 See amendments to the Divorce Bill to create a 'hard' form of marriage/divorce (*Hansard*, Commons, Third Reading, New Clause 9, Statement of Conscientious Objection, 17 June 1996: cols 561–81).

5 For example in relation to the use by lesbians of artificial insemination, to lesbians and gay men in fostering cases, and in decisions about rights of custody and access to children on divorce. For an example of the 'compassionate' version see Alison, *Hansard*, 21 February 1994: col. 103. Wilshire's activism around issues of 'virgin births' and fostering should be noted.

6 These speakers were mainly members of the Labour Party and included Neil Kinnock, Tony Blair, Chris Smith and Simon Hughes (Liberal Democrat).

7 However, for other instances of more radical arguments in the Family Law Debate see the speeches of Jean Corston, Hilary Armstrong, Paddy Tipping, and Elfyn Llwydd, professionals with experience of a range of family situations.

CHAPTER 4

Scandals for schools, schools as scandals: the press and sexual regulation

The state is only one of the institutions which regulates school-based identities and constructs the wider sexual culture. The power of mainstream media is important too. In this chapter we focus on the national daily and weekly press. We are interested in the press for four main reasons.

First, the press is the medium most closely linked to formal politics, though news and documentary forms on television are candidates too. Unlike television, however, newspapers are often closely linked to political parties, even to tendencies within them. Sometimes proprietors impose a political line; sometimes editors develop personal relations with leading politicians. Piers Morgan, editor of the best-selling Sunday tabloid, the *News of the World,* had to clear his editorial line (including the dropping of nude photos) with his proprietor Rupert Murdoch. Murdoch has also intervened publicly to discipline 'his young man' who had 'gone over the top' (*The Guardian,* 12 May 1995). Sir Arthur English of the *Daily Mail* was a close ally of Mrs Thatcher and the Thatcherite connection continues under the editorship of Paul Dacre (*The Guardian,* Media Section, 12 February 1997). Until very recently the built-in Conservative advantage across the national press was politically very significant.

Second, the cultural form of the press sexual scandal is a key moral regulator, more popular than political debates. Historically, scandals around sexuality and power have been a staple of popular journalism. From the street literature of the eighteenth and early nineteenth centuries, to the popular Sundays of the mid-nineteenth century, to the popular daily and especially Sunday newspapers of the twentieth century, sexual news has been a source of entertainment. Many of the sex scandals of the 1990s were sparked by the investigations of journalists of the *News of the World*, which claims a circulation of over 4.5 million (4.7 m in 1995). It specializes in sex scandals among the rich or famous, including film, soap and pop stars, ministers and MPs, the late Princess Diana and her family, and the bishops and clergy. (Interviews with Piers Morgan, *The Guardian*, Media Section, 17 October 1994; 17 April 1995.) The world's news is definitely sexual. But all the tabloid newspapers in Britain are strongly sexualized. The imperatives of sexual news may be as compelling as political allegiances. Despite the Conservative hue of the national press, most recent press scandals have concerned Conservative ministers and MPs.

Third, scandals add further dimensions to our analysis of political discourses. In particular this press genre brings to view the deeply anti-educative nature of public sexual culture in Britain. This is not just another instance of the dominance of moral traditionalism in recent debates. It has to do with aspects of the liberal inheritance too.

Finally we use press analysis as a way into two particular themes that directly link scandals and schools: the sexual regulation of professionals, especially in this case teachers, and the construction of child–adult relations in the sexual domain. Sex education scandals provide a convenient focus here.

The material for this chapter was collected in two ways. We followed up particular stories in a range of media, adopting a 'case study' approach. Throughout this chapter, we draw on Debbie's previous research on the Jane Brown case, see Epstein (1996a, 1997c). The sex education scandals of spring 1994 and the political sex scandals of early 1994 to 1996 are examples here too. We also covered specific media less selectively for particular time spans, keeping an eye on sexual, and especially lesbian and gay matters. In addition we collected material on a regular basis from *The Guardian* (as a chosen newspaper of record) and from the *Times Educational Supplement* as the standard source for education. For the national press our intensive period studies were October 1993–May 1994 and February–March 1995.[1] We also compiled an index of all the references to sexual matters in the Clover Index from 1985 to 1993 in order to place our mainly 1990s materials in a long time span.[2]

'Giving out a message from this House' – another way

At the Conservative Party Conference in October 1993, John Major attempted to heal divisions in his own party by making a speech, strongly angled to the Thatcherite and moral traditionalist wings, calling for a return to 'our roots' – 'to more Conservatism of the traditional kind that made us join this party'. In the phrase that was to return in eerie parody over and again in the following months:

It is time to get back to basics: to self-discipline and respect for the law,
to consideration for others, to accepting responsibility for yourself and
your family, and not shuffling it off on the state.

(*The Times*, 9 October 1993)

Restating his themes three months and half-a-dozen scandals later, Major
insisted that Back to Basics 'carries a moral dimension, but it is not a matter
of personal sexual morality'. He attempted to direct attention further from
home: 'eliminating the mugger, slovenly educational standards, poor service
from public bodies, things like benefit fraud, bad housing and so on' (*The
Guardian*, 15 February 1994).

It is true that there was little in his original speech about sexuality, a
promise to deal with 'the loathsome trade in pornography' apart. What
proved critical, however, was the adoption of a moral traditionalist tone,
including the usual references to 'the family' and 'responsibility', and the
labelling of the Conservative Party as the party of morality. The party was
now vulnerable to every personal moral disclosure, around financial and
political corruption, but also, given the press's own agenda, around sexuality. For editors and journalists, the high-profile espousal of morality
offered additional justification for the papers' risky stories, and a further
defence against threats to introduce privacy legislation against press intru-
sion. It was indubitably 'in the public interest' not to hush up misdemeanours within the Back to Basics party, however private. Morgan for
the *News of the World* foregrounded 'hypocrisy' as a reason to publish:

I think it's wrong for people in positions of power to commit adultery
if, by so doing, they leave themselves or their jobs exposed. And it's
wrong if they are preaching one thing and doing another.

(*The Guardian*, Media Sections, 17 October 1994)

The reason for publishing a story about the new Bishop of Durham's cot-
taging offence of 26 years ago, for example, was that he was 'guilty of rank
hypocrisy' for speaking out against gays in the Church. The Conservative
leadership's rhetorical strategies and the sexual codes and publication needs
of the press led to instant sexualization. The Back to Basics sex scandal genre
had arrived.

In the next nine months there were eight sexual scandals concerning
members of the government or its MPs, ten if we include the stories concerning David Mellor and Stephen Norris (both ministers) that began before
Major's speech, eleven if the much earlier saga of Cecil Parkinson, Sara
Keays and their child is included.[3] In addition Sir Peter Harding, the Chief
of Defence Staff, was forced to resign over a well-publicized affair. The next
two years saw several new cases of this kind including two ministers, two
MPs, the Deputy Director of the Bank of England and the Director of Public

Prosecutions, top banking and legal posts respectively. Tangled stories with legal ramifications often continued beyond the first news.

What was so scandalous about this sexual news? And what does sexual scandal tell us about the sexual culture into which young people are educated?

Of the 16 or so cases we have listed, all featuring a man as the central character, only one case was straightforwardly the outing of an unmarried gay man. Michael Brown MP was forced to resign from the Whip's Office after a story in the *News of the World* about three men in a bed. He publicly acknowledged his homosexuality and joined Chris Smith as only the second openly gay man in the House of Commons. In the second case in which gay identity was an issue, the *Sunday Times* accused David Ashby MP, a married man, of sleeping with a male friend on a rugby tour, so being a closet gay or bisexual. Ashby's denial and subsequent libel case against the newspaper produced, of course, further news, often farcical as much as scandalous (e.g. *The Guardian*, 30 November 1995). In the third 'gay MP' scandal, the *News of the World* bought a story from Paul Stone, a previous male lover of Gerry Hayes MP, who had approached the publicist Max Clifford with the story including Hayes's letters. Again Hayes was a married man and is suing for libel.

Even a hint of gay sex in high places still creates immediate notoriety. Even in scandalous stories the heterosexual presumption (that everyone is heterosexual) operates, so that a gay connection adds news value, especially where outing is involved. Newsworthiness was accentuated by Back to Basics and the conflicts between Conservative traditionalism and liberal opinion over the age of consent and lesbian and gay rights in the churches and the forces. Conservative gay connections were taken as evidence of hypocrisy or of the failure of Conservatives to live up to their own creed. The improbability of his defences apart, the evidence for Ashby's gayness as presented in the press was tenuous, while Brown seems straightforwardly the victim of press homophobia. This included the spectre of young gay men making a kind of club of the House of Commons. The Hayes storyline – 'Tory MP Two-Timed Wife with Under-age Gay Lover' – had many of the same features as the heterosexual scandals – only on this occasion the lover was an under-aged (18) young man (*News of the World*, 5 January 1997).

Other stories were scandalous because, like the gay stories, the sex was seen as abnormal, unusual, or, in the tabloid term, 'kinky'. That 'kinkiness', even if apparently heterosexual, was itself a cause for scandal is clear in the case of Richard Spring. Spring, a parliamentary private secretary, was forced to resign on the basis of another *News of the World* story, a five-pager, front-page headlined, 'Tory MP, the Tycoon and the Sunday School Teacher'. The three-in-a-bed happening was tape-recorded (or remembered with unusual detail) complete with the MP's remarks about fancying the Prime Minister's wife Norma and Princess Anne. The 'kinkiness' of the episode was accentuated by emphasizing that Odette Nightingale, the woman concerned, was a devout Christian and Sunday School teacher. (*The Guardian*, Media Section, 17 April 1995). Undoubtedly the most painful of these stories to read, however, concerned the death of Stephen Milligan MP, another parliamentary private secretary who was found in circumstances that suggested he died while seeking to increase the pleasure of masturbation by partial asphyxiation and cross dressing. His death unleashed a flood of moralizing and speculation.

Most of the remaining causes célèbres, 11 in all, concerned married men who had heterosexual relationships outside their marriages. One married man, and one further MP who was unmarried at the time, had had 'love children' outside marriage, an offence in traditionalist eyes in any case, but exacerbated in relation to Conservative policies. Here were Conservative men actually creating the single mothers whom Conservatives blamed for social ills! In other cases too, the charge of adultery – of being, in the tabloid terms, 'a love rat' or 'a love cheat' – was worsened by particular circumstances: by vocal support for 'Back to Basics' or for traditional 'Christian' morality (Hartley Booth MP, a Methodist lay preacher; Rodney Richards, a 'Back to Basics' supporter); by security implications (Sir Peter Harding, the Chief of Defence Staff); by conducting the affair in part at the official place of work (Richards in the House of Commons; Pennant-Rea at what the *Sunday Mirror* called 'Bonk of England'); for allegedly using an official position for sexual exploitation or advantage (Robert Hughes who had an affair with a constituency worker who came to him for help from an abusive relationship); or for having multiple or serial extra-marital relationships (Alan Clark, Stephen Norris).

If we look closely at a few of these cases we may see how they work as scandalous narratives and how they reveal and hide problems with the central sexual identities. Three stories of married men, all fairly late in the sequence, bring to view different themes: the sacking of Welsh Minister Rodney Richards, the confession and resignation of Robert Hughes, Minister for Public Service, and the resignation of Rupert Pennant-Rea, Deputy Governor of the Bank of England. Although this was not a Conservative resignation, the circumstances produced some unusually thoughtful responses which extended the argumentative range of the press.

Scandals and dominant discourses

Press scandals deploy similar discourses to those we have already analysed. The tabloids wielded a version of moral traditionalist discourse, often with a strong class inflection. As the conservative Catholic writer Mary Kenny put it in the *Daily Telegraph*:

In this there is an element, too, of class resentment – the desire, which George Orwell identified as the real moving force behind the disgrace of Oscar Wilde: to bring down a swell.

> ('What's the Matter with Us?', 22 March 1995)

Most of the Conservative tabloids (and some of the broadsheets) supported the Back to Basics campaign; some, especially the *Daily Mail* and the *News of the World,* were leading agents of it. In their way of telling the scandals, the erring man was centre stage. Rodney Richards, for example, was a 'love rat' cheating on his wife and children. His actions were dishonourable and hypocritical, the more so since he had 'preached Back to Basics' in his strongly religious Welsh constituency. As a local Tory activist put it:

> We are having a campaign to restore family values and it is unfortunate because Mr Richards has been spearheading that campaign.
>
> (Quoted in the *Daily Mirror*, 3 June 1996)

For the *Daily Mail*, the *Sun* and *The Times,* it was important that such men, who let down their government and constituents, should quickly resign from the government or be sacked: ' "One bonk and you're out" is one of Mr Major's few successful policies . . . He should stick with it' (quoted in the *Daily Mail*, 16 March 1995). Each new scandal led to a recapitulation of the 'roll of dishonour' with assessments of how adequately the Prime Minister had responded. His speedy sacking of Richards was praised by the *Daily Mail*, the *Sun* and the *News of the World*: Major should not repeat his mistakes with Mellor or Yeo, 'dithering' and further harming the party and government. There were few reservations about the role of the press here; indeed the tone of much writing is not only unapologetic but campaigning: 'It has always been the role of the *News of the World* to probe into the dark corners of high places' (6 June 1996). While activating very similar discourses, the *Mirror,* which supports Labour, was in a better position than the Conservative populars to draw out the contradictions of the Conservative Party's stance:

> The Conservatives set themselves on a pedestal to lecture the rest of us on right and wrong. They appointed themselves the high priests of modern morality – not just sexual, but in relationships, finance and even how we live our lives.
>
> But they are not the party of morality, family values and sound money, but of adultery, hypocrisy and fat cats.
>
> . . . The Tories have created a climate of immorality where greed is good – whether it is sexual or financial.
>
> Yet they still preach to everyone else. To single mothers, the low paid, the unemployed, the sick, the elderly, our European partners.
>
> (*Daily Mirror*, Leader, 3 June 1996)

While disapproving of 'love rats', the popular press has always sought to entertain their particular readerships through them. The *News of the World* featured the Richards case for the second Sunday running (9 June 1996) in a four-page frolic through the affair, aided by details supplied by Julia Felthouse, his lover: from page 1, 'We Had Sex in the Commons', to page 2, 'Randy Rod Fondled Me Hours after He Resigned', to a full page of photos and the story of the night that Richards wrote a speech in between 'the most amazing sexual marathon of her [Julia's] life'. In many ways narratives like these are the other excluded side of moral traditionalist discourse. As we have seen the idea of sexuality as pleasure is largely absent from the Conservative framework. It reappears, however, in the form of naughtiness, risk, transgression, 'kinkiness'. In the 'sex marathon' story in the *News of the World*, 'the subheads ran: 'Message', 'Chatted', 'Intimate' (code for sexual in tabloid language), 'Dirty', 'Risky':

> He has more staying power than any other man I know and knew how to please a woman. I have never known anything like it.
> He was so exciting – never able to resist the buzz of taking risks like our sessions in his office.
> It was the same thrill when he took me to his constituency home, forbidden territory I would have thought.
> (*News of the World*, 9 June 1996)

Though the 'Randy Rod' construction exemplifies this particularly well, similar themes – secrecy, risk, the fear of discovery but also its erotic possibilities – run through many of the other stories told by both press and participants. Even 'respectable' tabloids like the *Daily Mail* or *Express* use scandal stories to entertain and evoke particular forms of sexual fear and pleasure. Apart from its traditionalist campaigning, the *Daily Mail* seeks out the points of view of women participants in scandals, often focusing on the pain and courage of betrayed wives:

> Yet as she clutched his hand and nervously proclaimed her love for him at the obligatory press conference, she looked anything but a tower of strength – however hard she tried. Her dark eyes, ringed by shadows, betrayed only fear and shock.
> (*Daily Mail*, 7 March 1995)

Mary Ellon Synon, Pennant-Rea's lover, wrote an article in the *Daily Mail* giving her point of view ('My Love, His Lies and the Affair that Has Left Both of Us Losers', 23 March 1996). The paper also ran its own debates on how contemporary women were responding to their husbands' affairs. The 'womanist' perspective of the *Daily Mail* contrasts with the routinely pornographic presentations of lovers and wives in the news pages of the *Sun*: Julia Felthouse was presented there as 'curvy PR executive', 'leggy divorcee' who also managed to two-time the 'Tory Bonker with a Russian Banker' (*Sun*, 3 June 1996).

In liberal discourse, which tended to be dominant in broadsheet news-papers, especially in *The Guardian,* affairs are not morally approved of, but nor are they seen as inevitably a cause for resignation, dismissal or moraliz-ing newspaper coverage. As a typically lofty *Guardian* leader put it:

> Mr Spring seems a smutty-minded boy. That's not a nice thing to be. But being a smutty-minded boy is not a crime even so . . . MPs are not good or bad; they are only human beings. Some are sympathetic, some not. Some have lovers, some not. But they are politicians not priests. They should be allowed to make fools of themselves in private.
>
> (*The Guardian,* 10 April 1995)

Several commentators argued against resignations on the grounds that sexual relationships were a private matter and did not affect competence in a job. As Pennant-Rea's wife's sister put it, 'He's not a politician and he's not the keeper of the country's morals, he's an economist and a very good one' (quoted in the *Daily Mirror,* 20 March 1995). The most extended defence of not resigning came from an MP on the libertarian side of the Conservative Party, Teresa Gorman. Commenting on the unpromising Richards case, she stressed the differences between past and present and between Britain and other countries. Like many other liberal commentators, she stressed the differences with France, especially in relation to President Mitterrand's long-term lover and their child. (For a more extended comparison with 'Euro-pean' ways see *The Guardian,* 23 March 1995.) She was critical both of press and public for believing 'that we will create a healthier society if every dark secret of every person's life is laid bare'. Believing that male politicians were not, nor should be, 'plaster saints', she was in favour of a privacy law to contain press intrusions and even a certain level of secrecy within mar-riages themselves:

> Alternatively our representatives will be drawn from a decreasing pool of people whose narrowness of mind will belie the natural instincts that go with human nature.
>
> (Teresa Gorman, *Daily Express,* 3 June 1996)

Gender, nature and sexual discourses

The naturalization of sexuality – more strictly sex – is once more plain in both liberal and conservative discourse. The dominant version of the sexual in the scandal literature is what Wendy Hollway has called 'the male sexual drive discourse', a belief in a virtually unstoppable masculine desire to fuck (Hollway 1987: 231). This drive, it seems, is heightened by the peculiar pur-suits of power. As Geoffrey Wheatcroft in the *Daily Mail* put it:

What's for sure is that the 'aphrodisiac of power' works both ways: there is a connection between sex drive and the power urge and thirst for fame which drive people into politics.

Politics is adrenaline-charged, which is almost to say testosterone-charged. It has to do with seeing something you want and going and getting it.

('A Sorry Catalogue of Inept Adultery', 7 March 1995)

So sex and power operate here at the level not of moral but of chemical basics. The slides between power and sexuality, which are surely intended by the writer, are deeply troubling especially if as a reader you take the position of the 'something' that is wanted and will be 'got'. Within this framework there is a strong pressure towards the (almost always masculine) conviction of the untrammelled right to sexual satisfaction and the strong expectation that men, especially powerful men, will err. This is both to do with nature and to do with the strains of office.

> Politicians live very unnatural lives. Separated from their families for most of the week it is inconceivable [*sic*!] that men living on politically charged adrenaline should confine their sexual urges to Friday to Sunday when they return to the constituency.
>
> (Gorman, *Daily Express*, 3 June 1996)

Puzzling with her usual incisiveness over why it was men not women who got 'caught like this', Edwina Currie also stressed the pleasures of danger, risk and walking 'on the wild side', but also the fact that this behaviour was tolerated and even envied for men, but would be disproportionately punished for women (*Mail on Sunday*, 12 March 1995). Anyway women were far too busy doing sensible, practical things!

The naturalization of sex as the male sex drive coexists with the other dominant version of the sexual – Hollway's 'have/hold discourse' (Hollway 1987: 232–3), or the conventional story of love and marriage. If liberal opinion reaches for exoneration in terms of unchangeable masculine proclivities, conservative traditionalism usually presents a version of marriage as a moral 'gold standard'. Marriage – and good women – should control 'the drives'. From this point of view, the trouble with (some) men is that '[they] have no control over their loins' (Max Clifford on David Mellor, quoted in *The Guardian*, 8 November 1994). As one Conservative backbencher put it: 'You have to set an example. There are standards to be set and if a Minister misbehaves in this way, that's it' (David Evans MP, quoted in the *Daily Mail*, 3 June 1996).

Men and women in these stories are invariably positioned in the contradictions between 'male sexuality' and love-and-marriage, handling this tension more or less creatively. The men concerned marry and have extra-marital affairs, often secretly until they are forced to disclose publicly.

They then must choose between their wives if their wives will have them, or separation, divorce and serial monogamy. Women, on the other hand, are polarized between 'faithful wives' and mistresses who are almost always strongly sexualized and are presented as 'gold-diggers' or whores, or, alternatively, as victims. Often decisive in these representations, paradoxically, is the mistress's relationship to the press: kissing and telling and getting paid for it is taken as the decisive comment on their morals. Julia Felthouse clearly struggled to present herself as someone who loved her lover and believed he loved her. She also had an interesting professional identity as a public relations worker for animal charities. Once she had told all, however, stories began to appear about other relationships – the fact that she was dating another man during her affair with Richards for instance. Throughout she was labelled as a '28-year-old divorcee' and pictured in sexualized ways. By headlining a fairly straightforward story about her professional activities as 'Bubbly Beauty's Animal Passion – the Lover', the *Daily Mirror* (3 June 1996) managed even to frame her campaigning for the Canine Defence League in a sexualized way. This particular instance shows how difficult it is for any 'mistress', even if she is English, to escape the kinds of representations which had full scope in the exoticizing portrayals of Bienvenida Sokolow, formerly Buck, Sir Peter Harding's mistress, and David Mellor's lover, Antonia da Sancha (see the interview in *The Guardian*, 5 November 1996 and the paper's reflections on Spanish mistresses, 16 March 1994).

In other ways too this is a drama in which women must lose out. Wife and mistress or both are betrayed in turn, the wife by the relationship itself and its secrecy; the mistress, usually, when publicly renounced. It is not a conceivable outcome of these scandals that both relationships will be sustained or honoured; indeed affairs are entered into, it seems, precisely because of the danger to man, wife and lover(s). Upon discovery, dishonour for the man and betrayal for one woman (actually for both in turn) is inevitable. Women must react to circumstances they have not chosen, but rarely, except perhaps in the act of going to the press, are they presented as really active. Will she (the wife) 'stand by her man' or will she, as Marjorie Proops unavailingly urged Tory wives to do – 'fling their husbands out'? (*Daily Mirror*, 7 March 1995). The *Daily Mail* and other traditionalist papers highlighted the courage and the 'dignity' of wives. At best some of the reasons for this passivity are grasped. Feature writers stressed how, given the usual power discrepancies, the need to protect children and to secure a material future, not to mention the political context, flinging a husband out is not at all easy (e.g. 'I Wish I Had Your Dignity, Helen', Lady Sarah Graham Moon, *Sun*, 23 March 1995). Will the 'Other Woman' be left, and if so, will she be vengeful or accepting? Underlying the dramas are implications about the quality of relationships, especially perhaps the marriages. Is the affair a matter of love, lust, or material ambition? Who really loves whom? Will love or lust win out? Or, most cruelly of all, was this marriage flawed? What was it like sexually?

Dominant narratives; possible openings

Most press coverage on the scandals – and this includes broadsheet commentary – is unthoughtful and highly formulaic. It is a fair assumption, from personal and other experience, that the situations faced and the strategies pursued are always more complex, nuanced and often more difficult to evaluate than the public versions declare.

One partial exception to this conservatism in mainstream media was some of the coverage of the Pennant-Rea case. In some ways there was nothing very unusual about this case though it revolved around the fortunes of a particularly well-connected intellectual family.[4] Pennant-Rea himself had been married three times; on two previous occasions he had left his wife for his new lover. His relations with Mary Ellon Synon, an Irish–American financial journalist of 'free market' persuasion, had been going on for three years (they had known each other much longer), with familiar risk-taking episodes, including making love at the Bank of England and using the private dressing room of his boss, Eddie George. When forced to choose, he chose his wife who had known about the affair for at least a year and was extremely composed and impressive in public. It was Mary Ellon's strategy, however, that led to the interesting commentaries. Angry at his betrayal, insisting she loved him, she campaigned vigorously across a wide range of media in Britain and in Ireland. Her campaign, which more than matched those of other scandalous campaigners, David Mellor or the publicist Max Clifford for instance, had three main features. First, she did not accept money from the media. Second, although she insisted on the history of love between them, she minimized the sexual dimensions. Third, she made it hard for the media to present her either as a 'gold-digger' or as a victim. For Angela Lambert and Vicki Ward writing in the *Independent* (23 March 1995) this made her 'A Thoroughly Modern Mistress', the equal of her lover, determined to punish him for his betrayal, or perhaps persuade him to return. For Mary Kenny, the case not only showed some familiar lessons – including 'man being prey to original sin' – but prompted some reflections on 'British society' and its changing sexual culture. Dismissing the usual comparison with French insouciance, she focused on 'Americanization':

American culture is both more outspoken and more puritanical. American women always demanded more than European women, and were less ready to play at polite social games which required the tacit acceptance of a certain degree of hypocrisy.

(*Daily Telegraph*, 22 March 1995)

'The Americanized formula' takes love as the most serious thing, is obsessively open at all costs and involves the acceptance of divorce. If anyone in a marriage 'cheats', the divorce lawyers 'must be brought in instantly'. There is less protection of top people by polite hypocrisies. Openness is illustrated by 'confessional television genre' (the Oprah Winfrey Show for example) and the abandonment of privacy and shame. Of all this, together with the actions of Mary Ellon Synon, Kenny clearly disapproves. She is especially worried by the collapse of distinctions between private morality and public competence. Her analysis is suggestive, however, not so much for the theme of Americanization – which, as we have seen, is a common British construction around the sexual – but for the interesting theory that puritanical morality and 'openness' coexist in the contemporary period, or, to translate into our own terms, that moral traditionalism feeds off scandalous revelations, including the disgust at pleasurable wickednesses.

Perhaps the most interesting of these mainstream responses was the article by Rhoda Koenig, 'Why Women Will No Longer Put Up with Unfaithful Men' in the *Daily Mail* (23 March 1995). Citing Mary Ellon and Princess Diana, she argued that what had changed was the willingness of women, whether as wives or mistresses, to be loyal and hypocritical. Women were no longer prepared to put up with betrayal in silence. This change was related to a shift in the gendered relations of power and dependence. Unlike most of the women in the political scandals, younger women know that they can support themselves if need be. Moreover the expectation of sexual pleasure in marriage has changed the stakes of infidelity:

> If a wife is expected to be a satisfying sexual partner, it's natural for her to think that her husband ought to be satisfied with her alone; any betrayal of her is much more hurtful than it was when society assumed that 'good' women didn't enjoy sex.
>
> (Rhoda Koenig, *Daily Mail*, 23 March 1995)

Like Kenny, Koenig sees modern women taking love more seriously (though still, it seems, on masculine terms), being less pragmatic or practical about relationships, and demanding more. This goes for wives but it may also go for mistresses:

> Whether it's wiser for women to tolerate infidelity or reject it remains an open question. One thing, however, is true: married men out for what they see as harmless fun ought to think as well as look before they leap.

Like most commentators, Koenig and Kenny fail to stress the very specific class locations of their stories. Their implied histories are also very generalizing. We would argue, for example, that it is important to be precise about the historical point where women's expectation for sexual satisfaction within heterosexual relationships became a real possibility and ask, 'For which women, precisely?' Nor do any mainstream commentators acknowledge the importance of feminism in shifting the balance of women's expectations. Yet they do argue that women's expectations have risen, and that this change in gender relations is a fundamental motor of social and sexual change. This does move the analysis towards more critical, in this case feminist, perspectives.

Limiting the damage: some strategies

A key question that flows from a feminist perception of the scandals is how the contradictions of marriage and hegemonic heterosexuality are handled and contained, and how the borders of heterosexuality are patrolled (Steinberg *et al.* 1997). After all, the most obvious (to us!) reading of the scandals is that they signal difficulties in the institutions of heterosexual marriage, even for elite groups of males themselves. Moreover, they strike at a vulnerable point in the linkage of nation and family, at men who make a profession of constructing such links. It seems reasonable to suppose that they might also exemplify them in their lives. These political scandals have much of the symbolic status of scandals in the royal family: whatever liberal opinion may say, the personal is political in these cases. How then do scandal narratives and their commentaries defend marriage itself, as an institution, from the disruptions which the scandals themselves present? Why did not an apparently unending series of high-level scandals produce a fully-blown moral panic on marriage?

One defence is to personalize all issues intensely – this man, this woman, this scenario. This form of biographically led narrative makes it harder to develop a theory of events that goes beyond the descriptive–evaluative categories in use: it is just a question of how far the characters play their usual parts. Individuals in the story, especially the men, are often represented as exceptional. This has a particularly odd effect when the representation is also a familiar stereotype. Examples are the representation of public men as power-crazed and 'over-sexed', supercharged versions of the usual testosterone model. Humour often plays around with this monstrous normalcy:

> Unfortunately like a lot of men these days, he seems to have his eyes below his belt.
> (Relative in the Hughes case, quoted in the *Sun,* 10 March 1996)

> We're all after the tablets, if he's doing it five times a night.
> (Local constituency publican in the Rogers case, quoted in the
> *Daily Mirror,* 3 June 1996)

On the one hand the men are just, well, men, in the familiar naturalization; on the other hand the individual specimens are just a little bit crazy. As Suzanne Moore put it in relation to the Hugh Grant case:

This [they just can't help themselves] is what it always comes down to – what women are saying to each other. Men can't help it, even men who have to fend off Madonna in the middle of the night. Sometimes they want meaningless sex, devoid of emotions, sometimes they want to take risks. Sometimes they do stupid pathetic things, sometimes they get a little crazy . . . and so what?

(*The Guardian*, Tabloid, 29 June 1995)

Stress on the 'kinkiness' of the sex, or the Toryness of the offenders, or the temptations of male MPs, have similar effects. It naturalizes male sexual incontinence and closes off discussion of wider meanings. Debate is contained within sexological/scatological, high-'political', party-political or, at best, class-political parameters.

Discussion is also foreclosed by disorganizing thinking about possible alternative ways of living. In general, there is very little engagement in the mainstream media, especially the press, with the actual variety of households and relationships. Gay visibilities rarely extend to discussion of forms of family or household. At the same time, as we have seen, even Conservative media spend a lot of time 'exposing' gay identities and especially lesbian and gay politics. The insistence on the negativity of gay alternatives at a time of heterosexual scandal is an obvious defensive resource. It may also be that stories about sexual relations between adults and children, often coded as homosexual (despite the evidence of heterosexual predominance) and certainly coded as 'kinky' or monstrous, have a similar effect, even though they are often directly related to heterosexual troubles – for example, child sexual abuse in families.

The dialectical relations of gay and straight sexual stories are very clear in the national press in both of our most intensive case study periods from October 1993 to the late spring of 1994 and February–March 1995. The extraordinary saturation of the media with different issues of public sexuality from October 1993 to the late spring of 1994 is very striking. In retrospect it is possible to identify two overlapping strands of sexual news. The first of these followed John Major's speech. It featured Conservative sexual scandals – in this period nine in quick succession from January to May. The New Year, however, saw the emergence of another strand of sexual news that centred on lesbian and gay stories. In this respect the Jane Brown case was important and helped to mark the shift of emphasis. This shift was sustained by the media attention given to the parliamentary votes on the age of consent for gay men in February.

The Jane Brown case also marked another shift: from high politics to schooling; from Conservative politicians to ridiculous professionals; from Back to Basics to Political Correctness and a revisiting of 'the loony left'. On this rebound the press, aided by John Patten, picked up a series of education-based sex stories: the sex education 'outrages' of March, sex education book stories of March and April, the debate about new DfEE Sex Education Guidelines in April–May, and, in the late spring days, a series of stories about sexual relationships between women teachers and their male pupils. We are not necessarily arguing press intentionality here, though the 'knowingness' of some campaigns, the anti-gay campaigning of the *Daily Mail* for instance, is clear enough (Epstein 1997c: 194–5). Each of these stories can be read, however, as a kind of answer to the sexual scandals, or to a critical reading of them, pointing up gay or lesbian identities not as alternatives – this precisely is denied from the time of Clause 28 onwards – but as threats – the real sources of all the sexual disorder. As we shall see the sex education stories also do this: family values are at risk from the sexual precocity of children and the irresponsibility of their teachers. All this is happening, we must remember, while readers can also see that the self-acclaimed protectors of 'real families' are tearing them apart, threatening the stability of their households, betraying their wives and children and creating single mothers.

In our second case study period, the coexistence of (hetero) sexual scandal and lesbian and gay themes is even more striking. This period (February–March 1995) sees the cases of Robert Hughes and Rupert Pennant-Rea with the Richard Spring case following in April. There was also much discussion about *The Politician's Wife*, a television drama with 'stark parallels' according to the *Mail on Sunday* with several scandals (12 March 1995). There was also coverage of several other heterosexual scandals including an unsuccessful case of rape brought by a woman police constable against a male colleague and a story about an alleged relationship between the Dean of Lincoln Cathedral and his female verger.

Lesbian and gay stories during this period were exceptionally prominent. They included the comic Freddie Starr's gay relationship with his gardener; a minor 'loony left' story about grants to a young women's lesbian and bisexual women's group in Bristol; features about a gay actor Rupert Everett; an extended debate about the gay assistant bishop of Ripon, the Right Rev. Derek Rawcliffe; coverage of a lesbian family (two women and a foster daughter) pursuing claims against the RAF for unfair dismissal; discussion about the film *Priest,* the plot of which concerns a young gay Catholic clergyman; the coming out of the British actor Nigel Hawthorne; and extensive coverage of the outing campaigns of the gay political organization OutRage! and its leading figure Peter Tatchell, especially the naming of ten bishops of the Church of England as gay. The flood of gay news prompted the *Daily Mail* columnist Richard Littlejohn (plagiarizing from Ken Plummer) to demand a moratorium on all sexual news whatever: 'These Days the Love that Dare not Speak its Name has become the Love that Can't Keep its Mouth Shut' (10 March 1995).

In part Littlejohn was right to ascribe lesbian gay visibility to deliberate campaigning especially around the forces and the Church, but it is also clear that the journalists showed great interest in gay stories in this period. We have already discussed the main drive of much of this coverage in comparing the treatment of Peter Tatchell and Nigel Hawthorne: the heightened distinctions between good and bad homosexuals, especially on grounds of 'quietness' or activism. In this period, once more, activist gay politics of most kinds come under severe attack, except when one group (e.g. Stonewall) can be used to criticize another (e.g. OutRage!). OutRage!'s policy of 'outing', first clergy and then politicians, gave plentiful ammunition to Conservative media. It could benefit three-fold in these circumstances. It could carry stories about clerics who had been outed, for example the Bishop of London's admission of his 'sexual ambiguity'. It could attack gay militancy in the shape of OutRage! and throw suspicion on anyone who came out voluntarily. Finally, it could seek to distinguish itself morally from OutRage!'s use of outing as a politics. Coverage of politically active or culturally assertive lesbians and gay men was strongly homophobic. Coming out, for example, was seen as imposing your sexuality on the public, something unusually said of heterosexual identity! Thus the Rt Rev. Derek Rawcliffe who made a point of being out, was described by the *Mail on Sunday* (12 March 1995) as 'a slimy unctuous old creep'. Tatchell's or OutRage!'s tactics were variously described as 'fascistic', 'shrill', 'aggressive', 'terror tactics of the Tatchell gang' and the product of a 'twisted road of religion, rancour and repression' (*Daily Mail*, 16 March 1995).

We understand and share OutRage!'s anger about hypocrisy but we believe that outing is a tactic which is deeply problematic. It makes a weapon of a very double-edged kind from a common but informal and often very subtle queer strategy of naming names in gossip – often a kind of subcultural play. It is problematic, however, to use a weapon whose effect depends on the very homophobic conditions which lesbian and gay politics seeks to combat. It is also problematic to present the press with homophobic storylines of so many shapes and sizes. The form of outing adopted by OutRage!, where leading figures are first contacted by letter to encourage public confession under an implied threat of exposure, also rests upon assumptions about sexual identity which are increasingly questioned in radical theory, specifically the idea that sexual identity is definitive, one way or the other. Of course it is true that coming out almost always transforms the fields of force around gay identity and that the overall effect of the campaign is to raise the visibility of issues. The great difficulty, however, with OutRage!'s outing strategy is that it does what the tabloid press does, only inverts its evaluations.

The unveiling of sexual identities and practices is intrinsic to the scandal genre whether the subjects are heterosexual or homosexual. This strategy depends on 'the closet' and other forms of the liberal public/private division. Yet outing as a gay tactic is attacked as though it is something entirely different, as though the press practice of sexual revelation never existed. In practice many of the same criticisms that are made of OutRage! could be made of those who are victimizing someone like Jane Brown or the sex education teachers. Here is the *Daily Mail* in full flood against OutRage!:

> The evil depths of a campaign of intimidation by militant homosexuals against the heart of the Church of England were exposed yesterday. The pressure group OutRage! stood accused of blackmail in trying to menace one of Britain's most senior bishops into admitting he was homosexual. It effectively told the Bishop of London, the Rt Rev. Dr David Hope, that it had enough dirt on him to 'out' him unless he came out voluntarily.
>
> ('Blackmailing of the Bishop', 14 March 1995)

It is an interesting exercise to substitute the word 'journalists' for 'militant homosexuals' and 'the pressure group OutRage!' in this quotation. The argument is recognizable even if we limit the case to the Church of England, which has been subject to a flood of very intrusive sexual news, gay and straight. But the experience of 'blackmail' which the *Daily Mail* conveys through the person of the Bishop of London in this quotation is in fact a common one for the subjects of sexual news more generally. Chris Holmes, for example, was the second man in the Richard Spring case. Shortly before the scandal broke, he was approached by a *News of the World* journalist:

> 'We have everything, Mr Holmes, there is no use denying it.'
>
> We went inside and talked. I was given a choice. They said it was going to look bad for me but that the paper didn't go to print until that afternoon. There was time to change the article if I co-operated . . . I said I would not co-operate and that they would have to do their worst. And they did.
>
> (*The Guardian*, Media Section, 17 April 1995)

Press power and outing: Jane Brown revisited

The full implications of the power of the press in outing lesbians or gay men are best exemplified, however, in the treatment of Jane Brown. Activists in the successful campaign to defend Jane as headmistress of Kingsmead Primary School have stressed the hostility of Gus John, the Director of Education, and of a group on the Hackney Borough Education Committee, including the then Chair, Pat Corrigan (Radford 1995–6). According to Bea Campbell, for instance, it was the Council leader, John McCafferty who took the decision to name Jane Brown to the press (quoted in Radford 1995–6). When the press story broke, the Council also issued a statement disowning Jane and forced her into a humiliating public apology in front of the TV cameras. Nor did the then Secretary of State for Education John Patten hold back on condemning her. Even the Prime Minister commented on the case in a coded reference to 'political correctness'.

We can, however, look at the case in a way that brings out the role of the press in this form of 'queer bashing'. The power of both local and national state was limited in this case, partly by successive changes in the law which had delegated powers of appointment and curriculum to the schools themselves. Unless Kingsmead could be presented as a 'failed' school, which was very far from being the case, it was hard for local and national authorities to intervene. Because of the solidity of local support for a successful and popular head, the opposition was forced to rely upon public attacks and the formidable power of Conservative media. As Debbie has shown, the original incident, in which Jane refused subsidized tickets for the ballet Romeo and Juliet allegedly on the grounds of the ballet's exclusive heterosexuality (in fact on a range of issues), only became a cause célèbre after being reported in the *Evening Standard* three months after the LEA had been informed of the incident by the charity concerned (Epstein 1997c: 186–7). Publicity alerted central government to what was now 'a case', and sensitized Labour politicians in Hackney to the threat of a replay of the attacks on ILEA and London authorities over 'positive images' and 'political correctness' in the mid-1980s. Though the precise facts remain obscure, it seems as though the publicity hardened official attitudes from 'rather unfortunate' to 'gross misconduct' between September 1993 and January–February 1994. Press coverage also helped to escalate the case, foregrounding the issue of Jane's sexuality by representing her as a threatening 'butch dyke' and by spying upon her and her partner. As Debbie puts it: 'Thus we see a progression of attacks on Jane Brown for being "politically correct" (bad) to being a lesbian (worse) to being a PC lesbian (worst)' (Epstein 1997c: 185). One newspaper (the *Daily Mail*) elaborated a whole mythology around Jane to mesh with its ongoing campaigns against lowering the age of consent for gay men and against lesbian and gay activism more generally. Similarly the sanctions that were visited on Jane, her partner, friends and family were characteristically those which the press can wield. While she was strongly supported by parents and local activists, exonerated by a local committee of inquiry and praised by an Office for Standards in Education (Ofsted) inspecting team, she was forced to make a humiliating public apology before national TV cameras, was attacked repeatedly in the press over a prolonged period, her privacy was invaded, she received hate mail, death threats, was physically assaulted and forced into hiding, her partner outed, her partner's children and ex-partner harassed and her work and career deeply affected.

Such action against an individual has a much wider impact on those who identify with the experiences the person represents. At stake in the Jane Brown case was the attempt to define lesbian teachers, especially if they dared to criticize the exclusiveness of dominant sexualities, as inappropriate people to head a school and perhaps to teach there at all. More generally still, lesbianism itself as a way of life or a social identity was being stigmatized and 'expelled' from the nation. These messages were not lost on those who identified with Jane as a lesbian and as a teacher. As Jill Radford has put it, the spectacle of her public humiliation sent shock waves 'beyond the school encircling the lesbian communities in Hackney and beyond'.

> They impacted in particular and immediate ways on lesbian mothers and their children; and on lesbian teachers and educators whose limited and tenuous security as residents and professionals living and working in the borough was threatened by the council's betrayal.
>
> (Radford 1995–6)

Although in some ways the Jane Brown case was a success story for local oppositions, it illustrates very well the use of outing by the press as a coercive strategy, and the ramifying effects this has on family, friends, job security and prospects, and in policing a whole community.

Press scandal as an anti-educational form

If we look at the sexual scandals in the national press as a form of recognition it has to be seen as deeply conservative. The scandal form reproduces conventional power discrepancies between men and women, often in a heightened form. In its portrayals of 'the other woman,' and sometimes of wives, it is frequently misogynistic. As the Jane Brown case shows, misogyny and heterosexism are often conjoined so far as the representation of lesbian professionals or activists is concerned. Morally, or in explanatory terms, men hardly fare better. No real insight is offered, aside from the usual biological closures, for the sexual insistence of some men, no challenge to the widespread cultural assumption that men have a right to 'satisfaction' or to the assumption that this means fucking. In this kind of media representation, different ways of being a man are not on offer.

The lessons which this form teaches, then, are mainly negative, cynical, disorganizing. It does not pay to be lesbian or gay, especially to be lesbian or gay and proud of it, and even more so to come out and say so. It does not really pay to be married, even if you are a man. Wives should not trust husbands; husbands cannot really be expected to be faithful to wives. Sexual pleasure is something won (mainly by men) by taking risks and endangering those you live with and maybe still love. It is certainly something to live up to, in 'marathons' or risky multiple partnerships. Sexual pleasure only counts as anything like legitimate if limited to fucking and 'foreplay'. It is legitimate – but rarely celebrated or discussed – within marriage or marriage-like relations, but there is often an implication that married sex is rather dull. In heterosexual relations men should 'control themselves', though women have a certain power in controlling men too. Sexual life is to be bounded by privacy and secrecy; yet discovery can be an additional source of risk. It does not pay to be open with lovers or with a wider world about your sexual practices, feelings and identities. On the other hand, your friends, 'mates', family, neighbours and 'the public' in general are insatiably curious about this private domain, and would like to have your secrets. Confession (this kind of openness) is not incompatible with stern moral judgements; it is the condition that allows them free rein.

Perhaps the most important cultural structure that holds this nastiness in place is that around secrecy and openness. Historians of sexuality, especially Eve K. Sedgwick, have recently argued that around the beginning of this century a particular repertoire of categories arose, organized centrally around the hetero-/homo- divide and the figure of 'the closet' (Sedgwick 1990, 1994). The closet, according to Sedgwick, is a key structure for thinking about the relationships of heterosexuality and homosexuality, a relationship with 'lasting potentialities for powerful manipulation'. But the closet is also an epistemology (or version of knowledge relations) which organizes modern conceptions of sexuality more generally. As a version of knowledge relations, of speaking and silence, of learning and ignorance, it is also, we would add, especially relevant to education. According to Sedgwick our understanding of the sexual is organized around recurrent oppositions of which the most interesting, in the context of our argument here, are as follows:

homosexual/heterosexual
feminine/masculine
private/public
secrecy/disclosure
ignorance/knowledge
innocence/initiation.

It may well be that historians of sexuality are often describing forms which, typically, are not just 'Western' but more specifically Anglo-American, even, since England (and especially the Oscar Wilde case) figures largely in the arguments as a key historical case study. Certainly the whole cultural configuration of homosexual/heterosexual relations appears different in other European contexts, let alone other parts of the world. It would be interesting to pursue this possible 'Englishness' of the closeting of sexuality more systematically. Very suggestive as starting points are the relative underdevelopment of sex education in Britain and the USA and the high rates of teenage pregnancy in both countries.

To return, in the British context, to our early twentieth-century dichotomies, then, we should perhaps add another couplet that makes the educational connection clearer:

closeting/education

In the paradigm instance – that of homo-/hetero- relations – it is easy to see how closeting and education are to some extent opposites, opposites especially for the heterosexual world. The closet is based in part on ignorance, and especially on the presumption, active in a million ways, that sexual desire is or ought to be heterosexual. Yet as queer theorists have argued, the closet is a kind of *open* secret; for lesbians and gay men it is often a necessary strategy with, however, serious costs, an enforced discretion, which also sometimes produces a shared world, a kind of 'community'. For heterosexuals the closet implies a kind of knowledge that is never fully conscious or critical, a suspicion, a half-spoken assumption, a nudge, a wink, a leer. One instance of this, well attested in lesbian and gay biography, is the sheer difficulty, sometimes, of coming out in a heterosexual context where a statement of identity is only half heard and often quickly repressed (Epstein 1994a: 220–2).

Education might be thought of as the opposite process to closeting and has a close relation to coming out, where coming out is possible. For as all accounts of this process show, coming out, as well as being a moment of great danger, may also cause major shifts in the relations of knowledge and power. To say this is not to put the onus for sexual education on lesbian and gay men alone, and emphatically not on lesbian and gay teachers. (School, as we have argued in Chapter 6, is one of the most difficult places to come out in.) Rather it is to argue that 'coming out' about sexuality, not just by individuals but *in the culture generally*, may be a condition for a more transformative educational process. Again, we are not arguing for an unconditional and undifferentiated openness about personal sexuality here. Central to this view of an alternative must be understandings of the relations of power that determine inner and outer identities, speaking and silence, openness or discretion, the private and the public. These relations operate between lesbian and gay 'communities' and a predominantly straight public culture of course, but also between the sexual cultures of schools (their overt and hidden curricula) and the sexual cultures of schoolchildren and between the 'adult' public world of sex and childhood experiences more generally. One of the tragedies of the current situation – the general state of discourse in this area – is that the rather fragile successes of the New Right have made strategies of coming out – at an individual, professional and general cultural level – more difficult to achieve, and often more risky. Indeed in several areas we are seeing a marked tendency to a kind of imposed disclosure or refusal of professional and personal confidentiality which may mark the collapse of older formations, but which reinforces rather than changes the existing forms of power.

Our argument points rather to a more general 'coming out' about sexuality in educational institutions and in the culture at large, a process already occurring most unevenly and with high costs for some. Those who speak out about sexual matters, in many different contexts, including those of academic research, are still liable to ridicule or stigmatization.[5]

Schools for scandal: educational–sexual news

Like other professionals, teachers are subject to routine forms of press surveillance. The tabloid press in particular is always on the lookout for stories
of professional misconduct – by doctors, dentists, lawyers, clergymen and
teachers especially. In the case of education, there are well-established lines of
criticism, the product in large part of two decades of New Right campaigning against Local Education Authorities, progressive teachers, equal opportunities policies and teacher unions and professionalism. The systematic
anti-professionalism of Conservative governments, backed by criticism in the
media, has meant that many if not most teachers are deeply alienated from
government educational policies which they have none the less to implement.

There are also some well-established teacher and sexuality storylines in
the tabloid press, particularly stories about sexual relationships between
women teachers and boy pupils (e.g. 'My Sex Lessons with French Mistress',
Daily Mirror, 7 February 1995). We don't have much doubt that such
episodes are indeed problematic, while insisting on the importance of a kind
of seduction in successful teaching/learning situations (see Chapter 6). What
happens in press and policy often, however, is that the danger of cross-generational sexual relations, where discrepancies of power are gross and easily
exploited, spills over into all discussions of schooling and sexuality, including discussions of sex education. This fuels the elements of moral panic on
the part of the press or school authorities, a panic likely to be particularly
intense if the teacher is lesbian or gay.

The case of Vincent Pedley illustrates some of these dynamics. Pedley was
a biology teacher responsible for teaching sex education in a Jewish state
secondary school in Manchester. According to the governors of the school,
he was supposed to teach only 'the mechanical aspects of reproduction'; sex
education in a broader sense was supposed to be covered by religious
teachers. He was accused of gross misconduct following complaints from
parents of 15- to16-year-olds. His main misdemeanour was to breach the
boundaries of 'the mechanical' by responding to children's questions more
generally, including questions about oral sex and masturbation; his main
defence was that he was trying to deal with sex education 'openly and hon-
estly' and that it was necessary to use 'a slang phrase for oral sex' so that the
children would understand what he was talking about.

> You cannot teach sex education without talking about sex. Even if a
> child is highly religious, they need to know about modern issues like
> how HIV can be passed on.
> (Pedley, quoted in the *Daily Telegraph*, 17 February 1995, and see
> also 14 February 1995 and the *Daily Mail*, 17 February 1995)

The charge of breaching guidelines, however, was extended to unprofessional sexual conduct including telling pupils that teaching sex education

was 'a turn on', commenting on a girl pupil's cleavage and allowing pupils to call him 'a dickhead'. He was dismissed in December 1992 and his case for wrongful dismissal came to an Industrial Tribunal in February 1995. He was awarded compensation for unfair dismissal and the charges against him were dismissed as 'fabrication'. Despite being out of work since 1993, he could not be reinstated because of the poor relations with his employers. There was obviously a political difference within the school over sex education which underlay the case, but it is interesting to note that the 'fabricated' part of the evidence against him concerned his own sexuality and his alleged sexualization of relationships with pupils. His own conclusions about the case were significantly cautious:

> Teachers must beware. I advise them to get a cast iron statement from the governors laying out what they are required to do. I have no regrets about how I conducted my classes. I am certain the children were behind me. They enjoyed my class more than most.
> (Quoted in the *Daily Telegraph,* 17 February 1995)

On the whole the press coverage of Pedley's case even in Conservative papers was quite sympathetic, but most sex education stories conform rather to the scandal genre. These stories are revealing, however, not only for the ways they discipline professionals, but for the way they portray the relationship of children to the sexual domain.

On 23 March 1994, the *Sun* carried a story about sex education lessons in Highfield Primary School in Leeds at which the school nurse had explained what a 'blow job' and a 'Mars Bar party' were in response to pupils' questions. According to the *Sun* she also encouraged the class 'to make up dramas about jealousy and love – in which one boy shouted "You've been s******g my wife"'. The following day the Education Secretary John Patten, who was addressing a meeting on sex education organized by the *Catholic Herald*, was widely reported as condemning the nurse. All of the tabloids condemned her, and were joined by several Conservative MPs, the leader of Leeds City Council, and David Blunkett and Ann Taylor for the Labour Party. On same day the press reported the Health Minister Brian Mawhinney telling the HEA to withdraw *Your Pocket Guide to Sex*, written for 16- to 25-year-olds by Nick Fisher, the agony columnist of the girls' magazine *Just Seventeen. Your Pocket Guide* and other sex and HIV-related education publications were withdrawn from the HEA's recommended list in April despite plaudits from health educators. In the days that followed, the popular press sought similar stories and found a few, focusing on primary schools. The *Daily Express* (24 March 1994) asked parents to call its newsdesk, if 'you have had a frightening experience over the sex education of your children'. In early April there was a flurry of stories about sexual relationships between women teachers and secondary school boys, including one about a sex education teacher who 'Ruined Our Boy's Life'.

The key arguments hinged on the age and 'innocence' of the children concerned. There was a marked tendency for the age of the Highfield class to drift downwards in different reports: 11-year-olds (*The Guardian*), 10- to 11-year-olds (*Times, Telegraph, The Guardian*), 10-year-olds (*Star*, Janet Daley in *The Times*), 9- to 11-year-olds (*Mail*), 9- to 10-year-olds (*Independent*), 9-year-olds (*Sun*), 'very young children' (Patten). More strikingly, the *Mirror* described *Your Pocket Guide to Sex,* clearly aimed at late teenagers and young adults, as a 'Porn Book for Five-Year-Olds'.

The key assumption here was that children of primary school age were too young, too 'innocent' or too 'immature' to be told about oral sex or to imagine their parents having affairs. As Patten put it: 'I am incensed to think that very young children could be exposed through role play and teaching to things which they should not even be beginning to think about understanding, never mind understanding' (e.g. *Daily Mail,* 24 March 1994). According to the *Mail*'s leader-writer on the same day: 'Childhood is over soon enough. How crass to foreshorten it with sad, self-indulgent diatribes on sex.'

The argument about innocence is deeply problematic. First, it seriously mis-recognizes the position of children. They are assumed to lack sexual curiosity, knowledge or beliefs: they ought to be wholly unconscious of 'such things' – 'should not even be beginning to think about understanding, never mind understanding' them. Either that, or in an alternative and more thoughtful version, children are victims of the 'free market' in sexual representation, with sex education as a counter to media corruptions (e.g. *Daily Telegraph,* 24 March 1994). Absent or mis-recognized in both these versions of innocence/protection are the sexual cultures of schoolchildren themselves. It must be thought that children are immune from the daily saturation of the sexual in news and entertainment forms, not least – or most of all – from the same tabloids which ridicule sex education as premature. It must also be assumed that children don't draw conclusions from the visible, invisible and imagined sexual behaviour of the adults and children around them. In the concerned anti-media view, common among teachers themselves, children are none the less seen as passive recipients of sexual representations.

There is much research now that shows that sexuality figures strongly in the cultures of schoolchildren, with changing agendas and forms certainly, right through the school years, including the infant and junior school (Walkerdine 1981; Trenchard and Warren 1984; Lees 1986, 1987; Wolpe 1988; Holly 1989; Holland *et al.* 1990a, 1990b; Mac an Ghaill 1994a, 1994b). These sexual cultures are powerfully formed by the relative powerlessness of children and their attempted exclusion from 'family secrets'. Though the cultures of school students have their own sexual silences and emphases – they are often systematically hostile to gay and lesbian identities for instance – they also carry practical knowledges, express desires, and take distinctive points of view. As we shall show in Chapters 5, 6 and 7, children, even young children, are capable of a complex grasp of sexual issues. Some of this is visible, even, in the press accounts of 'scandals'. In the Highfield School case, for instance, it was children who introduced the offending topics, a fact sometimes handled by splitting off these children as precocious (corrupt?), to preserve the innocence of the rest (e.g. Janet Daley, *The Times*, 24 March 1994). Since children of all ages develop understandings of sexual life, 'innocence' is something which adults wish upon children, not a natural feature of childhood itself.

As the image of the precocious child suggests, it is not only a mis-recog-nizing projection that is involved here; the theory of childhood innocence also endangers children. As Jenny Kitzinger has argued in relation to child sexual abuse, belief in innocence inhibits communication between abused children and adults who might help, while ignorance itself is dangerous for the child (Kitzinger 1988, 1990). Moreover, in sexual representation inno-cence is commonly seductive, and the child who provokes sexual interest or succumbs to adult advances may be viewed as corrupted and dangerous, and no longer worthy of protection. In short, the innocence/protection couplet functions in favour of adult control and against a notion of children's rights (see also Davies 1993).

The exploitative relations are clearer if we return to the tabloid press: on the one hand, its themes of innocence blighted or parents affronted by 'dirty language' or sexual explicitness and on the other its daily exploitation of sexual scandal. The language of scandal and of pornographic representation even spills over into the accounts of sex education lessons: 'kinky sex lessons' (*Sun, Daily Star, Daily Mirror*), 'Marianne mouthful' (*Sun*, 24 March 1995). The same papers that condemn attempts to discuss sexuality seriously with children give a daily education in a narrowed, voyeuristic, male-dominated (hetero) sexuality, available to children of all ages in words and images on the kitchen table.

So educational programmes must therefore make their way not only against the closeting of the sexual in the culture but also against the belief that sexuality is an 'adult' matter, not to be discussed in front of, or with, the children and only then by a figure of authority, moral or professional. It is interesting that 'adult' has this specifically sexual connotation. The 'ethno-graphic' truth – the recognition of children's sexual cultures – makes an indispensable contribution here. It deconstructs the idea of childhood inno-cence as a kind of desirable ignorance and therefore puts a question mark against the forms of 'protection' that this justifies. From this point of view, 'innocence' is a state which some *adults* mistakenly *wish* upon children and which confirms their power. The failure to recognize the prior involvement of children in sexuality may do great harm, especially, though not exclu-sively, when their experience of sexuality has been, or threatens to be, abu-sive.

The role of the press in relation to sexuality and schooling is deeply dis-organizing. On the one hand, through the scandal genre, it produces and reproduces existing contradictions around gender power, sexual pleasure and lesbian and gay identity. It plays around with the contradictions of exclusive heterosexuality implying that no one, especially the rich and powerful, is 'better than they should be'. At the same time it blocks or dis-organizes critical and constructive thinking and practice and hides or stig-matizes existing alternatives. In the same pages it idealizes marriage in general, helping to create heightened and romantic expectations – then cyn-ically shows the results. The policing and punishing of sexuality education, including any open response to children's questions, is part of the same anti-educational pattern. It inhibits educational solutions on the lines of practices in many of the countries of continental Europe. In the broader sexual culture, the consequences are curious and destructive: daily discursive ex-plosions around sex as naughty but nice; the stymieing of discussion about sexuality in a broader sense, including more sustainable and egalitarian sources of intimacy and/or pleasure. We have to look elsewhere in the media, sometimes in surprising places, for more emergent and hopeful sexual dis-courses, especially perhaps to television soaps, to advertising and to girls' magazines (see Chapter 8).

Notes

1 We are particularly grateful to Judith Green for researching the period February–March 1995.
2 We are grateful to Louise Curry for working on the Clover Index.
3 The chronology and outline description of the different cases are based on reports in *The Guardian* unless otherwise stated. See also the *Independent on Sunday* special supplement: 'Sleaze: A Guide to the Scandals of the Major Years', 23 July 1995.
4 His wife Helen is daughter of Douglas Jay, former British Ambassador to Washington; she and her twin sister were 'feted as "the Beautiful Twins"' during their time at the University of Sussex (*Daily Telegraph*, 22 March 1995).
5 Witness the coverage of the British Sociological Association's Annual Conference which took 'Sexualities in Social Context' as its topic in 1994, e.g. *Daily Mail*, 1 April 1994; *Independent*, 1 April 1994.

PART TWO

Sexualities in schools

So far, in this book, we have concentrated on questions of nation, sexuality and schooling and on political and media discourses. In this part of the book we shall be turning to the specifics of schooling and, indeed, of particular schools and particular students and teachers. Here, we want to explore what schools are like for lesbian and gay teachers and students and through that, to think about what schools should be like for them. It is our contention that doing so will allow us to think about how their experiences relate to wider structures of inequality and, in particular, the ways that compulsory hetero-sexuality is an organizing matrix for these. We do not mean to imply that sexuality must always be privileged in the way that we have done in this book. There are other key differences through which structures of inequality are organized. Sexualities are shaped by, among others, class, dis/ability, ethnicity, gender, and religion, but sexualities also shape them. The ways that these processes take place in school are our primary concern in Part Two of the book.

Histories of the present

The burden of representation

Our investigation of these processes was qualitative, consisting of a combi-nation of school-based ethnography and in-depth interviews. When we started to do this work, we needed to access not only school students (which we did through participant observation in three secondary schools and, later, a primary school), but specifically young people who identified as lesbian, gay or bisexual. Because of the difficulty which young people face in coming/being out within the structures of schooling discussed in Chapter 5, because of the high age of consent for gay men,[1] and because of the potential for public scandal in the popular media, it was clearly not going to be possible deliberately to seek out lesbian/gay identified students within the schools where we were doing our observation. For this reason, we contacted most of our interviewees through letters in the gay press, through our friends and through a process of snowballing which helped us find further respondents. Our letters said that we wanted to interview 'lesbians and gays who are currently involved in the school system, or were involved in it during the late 1980s, as teachers, school students or parents of school pupils'. Most of the interviews were with individuals, but some were with couples and others took the form of focus group discussions. In addition, we spoke to members of KOLA, the black[2] lesbian and gay group in Birmingham at the time, who also taped two discussions for us in our absence and within their regular meetings.[3]

In this way, we managed to get information from some 50 people who identified as lesbian or gay. It is important to realize that this does not constitute a 'representative sample' of people participating in the school system who desire members of the same sex, or even of those who identify as lesbian or gay. The people who responded to the letters were, by definition, those who had access to the journals to which we wrote (or their friends). This meant that, for the most part, they were people who went to lesbian and/or gay venues where they could pick up the free papers. This excludes significant numbers of those, young and old, who are not active on 'the scene'. Furthermore, very young women and men still at school are less likely to be on 'the scene' since it is constituted largely of pubs and clubs; the age at which young people can legally purchase drink acts in concert with the age of consent legislation to mean that those under the age of 16 (the age at which compulsory schooling ends in the UK) are relatively unlikely to frequent such places.[4] The effect was that our appeal for interviewees was answered mainly by teachers in their twenties and thirties (but with some much older) and university students, most of them out on the scene and several involved in lesbian/gay activism of some kind. Equally, those who attended the meetings of KOLA were, by definition, out. Accessing research subjects is a well-known difficulty in the conduct of research on sensitive areas and the practice of 'snowballing' which we adopted, though common in this and other 'sensitive areas',[5] has been criticized for leading to samples where similarity is emphasized and difference is lost (see, for example, Lee 1993), as people ask their friends to take part and there is a tendency to make friends with those perceived to be similar to oneself (Hey 1997).

We have no problem with a lack of representativeness, since what we are interested in is, precisely, the situatedness of the production of identity and the discourses within which people speak themselves and are spoken about. Indeed, we are sampling these discourses through the stories that people told us and through our observations, rather than trying to get a representative sample of people. Much of the evidence we have from lesbian and gay identified students is in the form of stories from the past recounted to us in the process of an interview or group discussion. In this context, we would wish to insist that the personal histories we heard and use in this chapter are histories of the present. They construct a relationship between past and present. Present reality does colour memories from the past, even reconstitutes it in the process of retelling it 'as it is now'. Furthermore, if, as Stuart Hall (1996b) – among many other contemporary writers about identity – claims, identity is always a process of becoming and never achieved, then it must be recognized that the telling which obtains in an interview situation is itself a way of constituting identity in the here and now, using narrations from the past and present entwined in complex ways. Moreover, for many of our informants the period they were telling us about was one in which they moved from presuming their own heterosexuality to identifying as lesbian or gay, often through a period of great uncertainty. None of this, however, invalidates stories of memories as a legitimate way of understanding people's lived experiences in the past and present. What is required of the researcher, as of all other forms of material, is a critical interrogation or method of reading.

Racializing the coming out story

When, for example, the KOLA group began their first taped discussion for us, part of what they were doing was to use their recollections to establish who they were at the time of the discussion through narratives of their childhood experiences. Thus Robert, who organized the group at the time, opens the discussion with the following statement:

> I think, to start myself, as I was saying earlier when it was not being taped, the watershed for me came around about the age of 11 when this guy came over from Jamaica.

In this opening statement, it is clear that the discussion prior to the group switching the tape recorder on was about a remembered shifting identity in childhood with, as a subtext, the ubiquitous question, 'When did you realise you were gay/lesbian/bisexual/queer?' The question assumes a fixed, essential identity, one with which the person is born, rather than one which is achieved dialogically, through complex processes of self-construction in conditions not of one's own choosing; and the coming out story, the story of a 'watershed' after which things were never the same again, is a response to this question both when asked directly and often in its absence. Such stories play an important part in the lives of lesbians and gay men, forming, as Ken

Plummer (1995: 82) points out, a dominant narrative of lesbian and gay experience. It is a story which lesbians and gays tell to themselves, their straight friends, their families, other lesbian and gay friends, privately and in print. It is one which builds a sense of collective identity. Plummer characterizes the coming out story in the following way:

1 It starts in childhood and follows in a linear progression . . . Chance and contingency is (*sic*) usually overrun by cause and continuity.
2 Childhood is usually seen as an unhappy time, often the source of being gay or lesbian. There is often a strong sense of difference: 'I never felt as if I fit in. I don't know why for sure. I felt different. I thought it was because I was more sensitive.' A deterministic tale suggests that something happens at birth or childhood which sets up this 'difference'.
3 A crucial moment appears – often in early adolescence – where problems appear that lead to a concern – or a discovery – over being 'gay'. Problems abound and are usually documented: secrecy, guilt or shame, fear of discovery, suicidal feelings.
4 Problems are resolved in some fashion, usually through meeting other lesbians or gays in a community.
5 A sense of identity or self is achieved as gay or lesbian along with a sense of community.

(Plummer, 1995: 83)

As Plummer himself points out, this is too simple an account, but it is striking how many of our informants' stories followed a narrative structure very similar to the one he suggests. Indeed, Robert's very next statement leads into an interchange between himself and Clint which focuses on a sense of difference and exclusion (Plummer's Stage 2):

Robert: But I think before that what I did have was very much a sense of being different to other boys and not feeling a kind of emotional involvement in the things that they seemed to be involved in, and not wanting to do particularly the kind of activities that they wanted to do and other kinds of behaviours and subtle messages that adults around gave out about what it meant to be a boy and what you should be doing. I felt quite early that it wasn't appropriate to me.

Clint: Can I ask a question over it? This thing of you not being, or feeling different to the boys in schools. [What] I wanted to find out was [whether] they deliberately isolated you or you deliberately isolated yourself because, at the end of the day, perhaps you weren't sure or could not put your finger on the fact that you were sexually different to those boys?

Robert: Your question is very much a kind of either/or, sets a very either/or scenario. 'Did you deliberately exclude yourself or were you deliberately excluded?' I don't think it was that simple. I think it was more dynamic than that. There was certainly recognition that I didn't feel the same . . . So, here I was, knowing myself to be a boy and not wanting to be any different to that, but feeling *really different* to other boys and finding other boys as a group quite fascinating and being somewhat out of all that.

A discourse of early difference is strongly in play here, combined with a discourse about early attraction to people of the same sex. This continues for several more pages of the transcript with other men and women joining in with their own stories of childhood difference. There is also a thread about the way people were positioned by others (did you isolate yourself, or did they isolate you?), which leads into a series of stories of discovery of the self as gay/lesbian combined with stories of attempts to escape one's true destiny/self (Stage 3). Goodwin, for example, tells about how:

I actually felt really ashamed of myself and I was thoroughly ashamed and thought *[5 second pause]*. And, I mean, soon after I realised what was happening and stuff like that. And it took me ten years 'til I actually come to terms, almost eleven years to actually come to terms with what I actually felt. And from eleven I knew I was gay and I, I mean, during that time I was so desperate to become heterosexual. I mean, in the end, I mean, like, I went into [a nightclub] to become heterosexual and, y'know, all sorts of really dubious things like that. I dunno, I mean we really are, in my mind, um, we've had all this propaganda about our sexualities and what we should be like and what we shouldn't be like and I was running away from my sexuality because I was afraid of what people might think of me for not being what they wanted me to be and I was afraid of never getting married.

Goodwin's 'desperation to become heterosexual' is also a well-worn aspect of the dominant lesbian/gay coming out story and the 'really dubious' action of going to a nightclub signifies something much more than the simple (and rather ordinary) action involved. The nightclub stands for all that Goodwin is rejecting in heterosexuality and, we would guess, more particularly heterosex. Our point, here, is that in the course of this discussion the group are constructing themselves within a set of well-known lesbian and gay narratives through which they are able to establish a common identification with each other as queer. In this context, reference to ethnicity or 'race' did not occur until page 16 of a 27-page transcript, when one of the women mentions kissing a white woman. This is clearly not because the members of the group do not define themselves in racialized terms – after all, the group is self-defined as being a 'black' group – or that 'race' was not part of the agenda which we had asked them to discuss in their taped conversations – the request had been that they discuss the ways that 'race'/ethnicity, gender, sexuality and class had intersected in their experiences of schooling. Rather, we would suggest, (at least) two other things are going on.

First, it may be that the establishment of common identification on grounds of 'race' has already been achieved within the group while commonalities on grounds of sexuality are still in the process of exploration and simultaneous construction. This may be partly because a person's ethnicity and 'race' are not usually open to question in the same way that their sexuality might be. People are not usually asked whether they are sure that they are, for example, Jewish or Irish if they say they are, even though, in the current context of the anglophone world these ethnicities are generally not immediately visible.[6] 'Blackness' in the terms established by the group could, in this context, be assumed. Here the physical absence of any white people is a key factor. Much has been written about the power relations involved when white researchers seek information from black informants (see, for example, Mac an Ghaill 1989; Edwards, 1990). After discussion with KOLA (when Debbie attended part of one of their meetings to explain our research project and ask for their assistance), they offered to tape some discussions for us in their regular meetings and without the presence of a researcher. The participants were obviously aware that the intended audience of the researchers consisted of two white people, and that the majority of readers of the published, edited version of one of their discussions (KOLA 1994) and of any writing we did drawing on their conversations would be likely to be white. Nevertheless, the context of the black group provided a situation in which blackness could become a taken-for-granted, 'normal' identity (in the same way as whiteness is taken for granted as 'normal' by nearly all white people nearly all of the time).[7] Indeed, the purpose of the group was to provide just such a context in order to make a relatively safe space in which black people (people of colour) could deal with issues which arose from their sexual identities, with the coming out story as one of the key narratives told and retold amongst the group.

Second, notwithstanding the emergence of many coming out stories by lesbians and gays of various ethnicities and nationalities, the narrative *framework* of the story does not include, perhaps actively excludes, narratives of 'race' precisely through the relatively simple structure outlined by Plummer. If the story is told in these terms, then the complexity of the mutual shaping of racialized and sexualized identities can be submerged in the driving force of the heroic genre of the coming out story where monsters are overcome to reach a point of sexual self-confidence as a lesbian or gay man. This is epitomized by Dave in two focus group discussions held with a group of white students, both of which ended with a declamatory statement from him about the power of coming out:

I've gone through all of those horrible things. [What] just overwhelms and overtakes any of these horrible experiences I can have or ever had about being a gay man is that I know that what I'm doing is such a positive choice for me to make. It's not a choice [that] I'm gay but it's a choice about the way I deal with it. It's just what I've learnt about myself and about everything from coming out is just amazing and that's the thing I always get whenever I think about it is that what a much happier person I am now that I've come out. And no matter what might happen to me from this point on, whether I get the shit kicked out of me or whatever, I'll always know that what I've done has been the right thing.[8]

The ways in which the narrative of coming out, as told here, constitutes a history of the present is particularly clear in this quotation from Dave. His life, including his earlier account of feeling suicidal (see Plummer's Point 3 above), is glossed in a linear progression towards (almost a Whig history of) coming out. The certainty of rightness expressed here is, we would suggest, part of a psychic and unconscious process of strengthening the identity boundaries which Dave has constructed, boundaries which are fluid, indeed fragile, not specifically in Dave's case but in identity construction generally.

Co-constructions of meaning

We would argue, then, that the processes of interviewing and of being interviewed are not simply about the giving and receiving of information but at least as much about speaking identities into being, solidifying them and constantly reconstituting them through the stories we tell ourselves and each other (see and cf. Kehily 1995). The interview, or group discussion, is a discursive space within which meaning is co-constructed by researcher and researched – though the researcher tends to set the agenda and has the ultimate power of interpretation in public versions like this one. This is a general point, but, as suggested above, it may be particularly significant in the context of identities which are not only stigmatized, but about which there is coercive legal power deployed to (try to) prevent the identification in question, though, as Foucault (1978) points out, the attempted coercion may actually incite and produce the identity in question. In the British case this takes place through Section 28 of the Local Government Act 1988,[9] the unequal age of consent and the establishment of sexual 'offences' for gay men for which there are no heterosexual equivalents[10] (see also Chapter 3). Thus, while one might work with, for example, ethnic minority or disabled young people in schools, it would be virtually impossible overtly to seek out young gays (or lesbians) *in the school context*, though in a prolonged project about other issues one might get to know them[11] and, of course, there are many other contexts (like lesbian and gay youth clubs) in which one is much more likely to meet them.

Sexualities in schools

This section of the book consists of four chapters, followed by the conclusion to the book as a whole. Chapter 5 focuses on the school as an institution. Here we examine the ways that the organization and dynamics of schooling contribute to the production of sexualities (or sexual identities) amongst both students and teachers. We draw particular attention to the way that the inequalities structured into schooling result in one of the primary dynamics being that of control and resistance. In this context, we trace the ways that both sides of this dynamic involve recourse to sexuality, in ways which can be both regulative and disruptive.

Chapter 6 turns the spotlight on to lesbian and gay teachers. In this chapter we argue that the apparently ever-increasing surveillance of teachers and schools is partly to do with anxieties produced by the seductiveness of the best teaching. In turn, the chapter points to the ways that the best teaching is constricted by the punitive surveillance of schools, teachers and sexualities. Any exploration of the stories of lesbian and gay teachers will involve narratives of constraint and punishment, but our central story in this chapter is much more positive. It concerns the reactions of a class of primary schoolchildren when their teacher came out to them, the steps they took to protect him and their sophisticated analyses of the ways they (and he) had to negotiate homophobia as a fact of everyday life.

Chapter 7 explores the gendered and racialized ways in which lesbian and gay students experience schooling. It uses this exploration to develop an understanding of the sexual dynamics of schooling, the particular problems of school-based masculinities and possibilities for anti-sexist practice. Chapter 8 builds on that exploration to take a close look at sex education in schools. In this chapter we reflect on a variety of different approaches taken by sex education teachers and the constraints that they have to work with. The chapter finishes with a consideration of the resources, drawn mainly from popular culture, that students bring to school with them and some ways in which this might be brought into the classroom in an effort to improve the experience of sex education for school students.

Notes

1 18 years old now, but 21 at the time when we were collecting data.
2 The group used the term 'black' in its widely used British sense, to signify anyone

discriminated against on the racist grounds of phenotypical or cultural characteristics. In the US, they would have called themselves 'people of color'.

3 See KOLA (1994) for an edited version of one of these discussions.

4 On the other hand, the 'scene' is predominantly young, including, for the most part, those aged between about 17 or 18 and their early to middle thirties.

5 See, for example, Khayyat (1992); Appleby (1995, 1996); Melia (1995).

6 Historically, this would not always be true. Jews were, for example, perceived as very visible in the 1930s and 1940s, not only in Nazi Germany but across Europe. Equally, Irish people have been made visible in certain historical contexts, especially in the UK.

7 For important discussions about whiteness see Ware (1992); Frankenberg (1993); Roediger (1994); Dyer (1996).

8 For an edited version of this discussion see Alistair (1994).

9 For discussions of some of the Foucauldian effects of the introduction of Section 28 see Stacey (1991) and Epstein and Johnson (1994).

10 It is frequently claimed that male homosexuality was 'legalized' in the UK in 1967. This is not strictly true. Male homosexual acts were 'decriminalized' in particular, tightly defined circumstances – that is, between gay men over the age of 21 (now 18) in private, with privacy being legally defined as in a private dwelling with no one else present in the house or with the door locked. Thus gay sex in a locked hotel room is not defined as 'private'.

11 See, for example, Máirtín Mac an Ghaill's important work on masculinities, during which he worked closely with a group of black and South Asian gay young men (Mac an Ghaill 1994a, 1994b).

CHAPTER 5

Producing one's self: sexuality and identity dynamics in the school

So far in this book we have been concerned about the way sexuality has figured in general debates, including those about schooling. In exploring these
debates, we have identified certain discourses which testify to adult confusions about sexuality and also impact upon practices in schools. In this
chapter we turn to a closer examination of processes of schooling and the
ways in which discourses about sexuality and about childhood are imbricated
in the production of sexual and other identities and in discourses of schooling itself. By providing a general map of sexuality and identity in schools, this
chapter presages a more detailed examination of the experiences of particular actors in schools in Chapters 6 and 7, and of sex education in Chapter 8.

We want to use this space to explore three sets of arguments about sexuality, identity and schooling. In schools, as several commentators have
pointed out, sexuality is both everywhere and nowhere.[1] Indeed, schools, we
will argue, are important sites for the production and regulation of sexual
identities both within the school and beyond. This gives rise to paradoxical
situations. On one hand, schools go to great lengths to forbid expressions of
sexuality by both children and teachers. This can be seen in a range of rules,
particularly those about self-presentation. On the other hand, and perhaps
in consequence, expressions of sexuality provide a major currency and
resource in the everyday exchanges of school life. Second, the forms in which
sexuality is present in schools and the terms on which sexual identities are
produced are heavily determined by power relations between teachers and
taught, the dynamics of control and resistance.[2] Third, schools are not the
only sites for the production of sexual or other social relations; neither is
everything which happens within schools the result of schooling alone.

Those differences which make a real difference, such as class, dis/ability, ethnicity, gender and 'race' are actively present in the school, produced not only there but in other social sites as well. One consequence of this is that it is impossible to discuss sexuality, even where it is most in focus, outside the matrix of these other social relations or to detach schools from other social structures. Sometimes these connections are the product of deliberate state policies and conscious administrative and legislative controls. At other times, such connections are best thought of as continuities with surrounding social and cultural formations, while at others they may be made through disruptive importations by either children or adults.

Equally, in pursuing strategies of resistance or control, both teachers and pupils draw on cultural repertoires which they live elsewhere but which acquire new meanings in the context of the school. Important in our analysis are commercial popular culture, discourses of adulthood (and, therefore, of childhood), of national identity and of assumed heterosexuality. As we have seen in Part One of the book, these repertoires or discursive clusters change their meanings as they are transported from site to site. The centralization of schooling in the years following the Education Reform Act 1988 has meant that schools are much more tightly articulated to other sites, in particular the economy and 'the nation'. This articulation has been achieved largely through the introduction of the National Curriculum, but the apparatuses of centralized surveillance which have taken the place, to a large extent, of Local Education Authorities have also been important. Teachers experience Ofsted inspections as highly stressful. Indeed, Debbie has noted that Ofsted inspectors are so conscious of their unpopularity and of the stress that their presence induces that when they attend courses they usually refrain from informing the rest of the class of their work! The dynamics of teacher–pupil control and resistance take place within a context of the control of teachers (and teacher training) through formalized surveillance of the strongest kind by Ofsted, which, of course, includes inspection of sex education specifically and, more generally, the kinds of behaviours and school-based cultures which we will show, in this part of the book, are connected to the production of sexualities in schools. Furthermore, the more informal surveillance of schools by the media and by politicians, often themselves informed by media scandals, also impacts upon schooling practices. As we shall see, the shaping of the sexual landscapes of schools is recognizable in its similarities to the ordering of sexuality through the discursive frameworks explored in Part One.

Sexualities assembled

Assembly is, in the English context, a particularly good place to start a school ethnography concerned with culture and power, identity and sexuality within school contexts.[3] When Debbie did ethnographic work at Heathlands School, a large girls' comprehensive in quite a poor area of a large (post-) industrial English city, her first day began with an assembly. In Debbie's observation of this particular assembly, we see encapsulated many of the characteristic cultural dynamics of the school. Like other particular sites, schools set distinctive agendas for the cultural work of agents and the production of social identities, including the identities of teachers and head teachers, students, governors and parents and other carers of children. What we see in any assembly are the two social categories most involved in, and present throughout, schooling – that is, those of students (pupils) and teachers – though sometimes other actors (for example, school governors and even researchers on schooling) might also be present and, indeed, take an active part in the proceedings:[4]

> I am sitting at the back of the school hall as the girls come into the statutorily required 'act of worship'. The fact that most of these young women are Muslim does not alter the fact that, by law, the act of worship must be 'predominantly Christian'.

Here, Debbie has already picked out certain central features of schooling related to the theory with which we are working. In her description we can see, for instance, the imposition of a hegemonic version of white Englishness in the form of a 'collective act of predominantly Christian worship' as prescribed by the Education Act 1993. It is open to schools which have majority populations from another religion to opt out of the Christian aspect of this worship, but in order to do so they must make a case and few schools other than those specifically set up within another religion (e.g. Jewish schools) have taken advantage of this option. Parents also have the right to withdraw their children from assembly (and religious education), but again few do so. Insofar as the school enforces Christian forms and beliefs, then, it will be distanced from the everyday cultures of most of the students in a multi-ethnic, multi-religious, but mainly secular, society. General features of the hegemonic culture are inscribed in the rituals of the school through state policy and the surveillance imposed on schools.

Within this context, the girls individualize their uniforms as far as is possible within the school regulations. This is done partly with an eye to fashion, but also through the use of signifiers of adherence to Islam, and often through a combination of these concerns:

> The girls are in school uniform – the regulation appears to be green skirts and/or trousers with a white blouse. I think about how familiar this sight is to me as a frequent observer in British schools with large numbers of Muslim students. Ten years ago (approximately) a Muslim parent won a case under the Race Relations Act about the compulsory wearing of skirts as school uniform. Now the Muslim girls often wear

a pair of trousers – in a variety of Western or Punjabi styles – under their skirts. This is an act which may signify communal solidarity or pressure but something else is going on here. There is a subversion of Western style, but also of school uniform rules.

Other girls (white, African–Caribbean and South Asian) have personalized their uniforms in a variety of ways. One, I notice, has her skirt so tight that she can barely walk and certainly has trouble when she has to sit, cross-legged, on the floor for assembly. Another presents a startling image. She is wearing the head-covering scarf usually associated with strictly orthodox Islam but carrying a bag with a raunchily androgynous image of the current pop super-star group Take That. Several have skirts with lengths at mid-calf, the current fashion. There seem to be no (few) pleats, but several splits either at the side or the back of the skirt. Blouses, too, are individualized. Some girls have them daringly unbuttoned so that their cleavages show. Sleeves are of many different styles. Clearly, there is a conscious attempt going on to individualize the uniform. This attempt is most clearly seen in the huge variety of bags which the girls carry. Clearly unregulated by uniform, these vary in size, shape and colour. Bright, shocking pinks vie with purples and greens. Some carry images of the latest pop stars. None seems to be very practical for the carrying of heavy books! . . .

The teachers come in with their forms and take their seats down the sides of the hall (unlike the girls, they do not have to sit, cross-legged, on the floor!). They face each other, across the hall, surveying the students with a disciplinary gaze. They, too, wear a kind of uniform. The few men wear grey flannel trousers and plain coloured shirts with a tie and a jacket (but not a suit). The women wear a variety of colours but similar styles. They are dressed to look 'respectable'. They wear 'sensible shoes' but nothing too unfeminine. There are neither stilettos nor Docs nor boots here. Rather there are small heels or flat 'court' shoes. There are no bang-up-to-the-minute fashions, straight or gay/lesbian, to be seen amongst the teachers. Rather they are safely dressed, not too smart but not too 'dowdy' either. Unlike their pupils, their individuality is played down rather than up. The PE teachers (all women) wear track suits and trainers. There are two South Asian women, both wearing Punjabi-style dress – shalwar-kameez in plain colours, none of the elaborate embroidery or mirror-work which one often sees in the city centre here. Only one white woman teacher is wearing trousers (apart from the track suits of course). I wonder about her. What kind of statement is she making? Is this acceptable in the school? Is it just chance that she is the only teacher wearing trousers on this, my first day here? . . .

There are two important related features of Heathlands School: that it was a girls' school; and that racialized and ethnicized differences were strongly accentuated. In the UK there is a strong demand for girls-only schools in the major urban areas. In part, this demand comes from the particular desires of many parents of South Asian origin for their daughters to be educated in single-sex settings. This is a desire shared by many middle-class, and often feminist-influenced parents, who see single-sex girls' schools as more friendly for their daughters and also as more likely to produce academic success, especially in non-traditional areas. The result of this is that very frequently mixed schools in these areas are, effectively, boys' schools. Their culture is dominated by forms of masculinity, but also numerically the proportion of boys to girls can be as high as 80:20. The effect of this is an increasing demand for girls-only schools. At this point, what we wish to note is that some, but not all, of the observations made at this school are specific to its single-sex character. Equally, examples drawn from mixed, boy-dominated schools will be in part specific and in part general.

It is well established in feminist research that girls and women both represent and are held responsible for sexuality in the larger society.[5] It is, therefore, not surprising that it is very easy to see the signifiers of sexuality when observing girls, whether they are interacting with boys directly or not. Indeed, many of the interactions with an explicit sexual content which we have observed in both primary and secondary schools are interactions between girls exclusively. Very often, in such interactions, boys, heterosexual romance and, amongst younger girls at least, marriage appear to be the primary objects of desire. In Edenfield[6] Primary School playground, for example, the skipping rhymes chanted by the girls included, among a multiplicity of verses about marriage, honeymoons and babies the verse:

Down by the riverside
We saw you kiss.
Elias, Elias, do you love me?
Yes, no, maybe so (*repeated until the skipper is out*).

The final two verses of this rhyme concern the production of babies:

How many babies will you have?
5, 10, 15 . . . (*repeated until the skipper is out*).
What colour babies will they be?
Pink, white, brown (*repeated until the skipper is out*).

The role of actual boys in the game itself is strictly marginal. Boys, in general, do not skip in the playground and certainly do not chant rhymes as the girls do, engaging, rather, in a competitive counting of the number of skips. Elias, himself, was called over by one of the participating girls to observe the game and the fact that it was being recorded by Debbie. He quickly dissociated himself from any interest in either the game or the girl who was chanting his name. This distancing made no difference at all to the playing of the game. It certainly did not cause any distress. If anything, it added to the fun.

Within the context of the all-girls secondary school, of course, girls' friendships, even when they revolved around heterosexual concerns, were also constructed in the absence of actual boys.[7] Another feature of these friendships, noted by both Debbie and Gurjit Minhas, was that they seemed to be constructed along racialized/religious/ethnicized lines. The vast majority of pupils in the school (about 90 per cent) were of South Asian descent and nearly all of those were Muslim. When classes settled down, and especially when they were working in small groups, it was almost invariable that Muslim girls sat exclusively with other Muslim girls, that Sikh, Hindu and, perhaps, secular girls of South Asian descent tended to sit together, and that the white and African–Caribbean girls sat with each other. Recognition of these dimensions, as of the all-girl nature of the school, is essential for reading the significance of the place of sexuality, both in relations between students and in their relations with school authority.

We have argued elsewhere (see Epstein and Johnson 1994) that schools are sites which are structured in age relations. Pupil and teacher cultures are centrally formed in these relations of power and are strongly influenced by the fact that there are few teachers and many students – and in classrooms usually one teacher and 30 or more students. It is partly for this reason that, in teacher cultures, issues of surveillance and control are often overriding. Pupil cultures, on the other hand, often hinge upon the blocking and under-mining of teachers' disciplinary powers and of those identities which the school recognizes and rewards. Although there are many other agendas for cultural production in the school, relations of control and resistance are inscribed in all other social relations of schooling and consequently in the construction of school-based identities. Neither teacher control nor pupil resistance are monolithic. They may be reversed on occasion, but, even more, they develop in contradictory and multiple relations with other forms of power. Both pupils and teachers constantly reposition themselves in relation to sexual discourses and develop complex psychic and social invest-ments in them. It is, then, important to view teacher and pupil cultures and identities together since each is produced in relation to the other.

The relations of power between teachers and pupils can be seen very clearly in our example. Here we have not only the infantilizing of young people-as-pupils by having them seated, cross-legged on the floor, but the visible hierarchy of adults-as-teachers sitting round the hall on chairs with the head raised on the stage. Central to this description is the attempt by school authorities to impose control through the prescription of uniform – a form of control virtually unknown in the state sector in countries outside the United Kingdom and some of its ex-colonies. Students, on the other hand, frequently subvert school dress to make it less uniform, a strategy which is perhaps more resonant for girls than for boys – though the rela-tively easily achieved variation around length and style of hair is often a major resource for boys. Both the infantilizing of students by having them sit on the floor and the imposition of uniform are fractured by the vision of fluorescent bags strewn around the hall and the girls struggling to sit cross-legged in pencil skirts under the surveillance of the teachers. Popular cultural references abound in the styles that pupils have adopted to punctuate the boredom and to disorder the uniformity imposed by school rules and dress codes. More is going on than resistance here. There is also much hard work around identities in all this play – including an overtly competitive seeking after 'street cred' amongst a significant minority of the students. Already we see, in this example, a characteristic tension between what is required from the 'good pupil' and their investments in commercial popular culture.

As we can see from the example, sexuality is not a discrete domain. It shapes and is shaped by all the surrounding social relations. Indeed, it is difficult to know where sexuality begins or ends. As we have seen, it enters into the power relations of schooling but it is also present in patterns of personal friendship and relationships; fantasies and expectations about future destinies; talk about popular cultural icons; teachers gossiping to teachers about teachers and about students; students' gossip about teachers and about their contemporaries; and in playground play, bullying and talk.

For girls especially, sexuality is clearly present in forms of dress whether within or outside the school. In the school it is, at once, visible and invisible, played up by some students, particularly through their overtly sexy versions of school uniform, and by many more through the adoption of clothing which is as fashionable as possible. One of the most interesting things about Heathlands School and others like it is the subtle way in which the young women who are the pupils here may simultaneously play up and play down a certain awareness of sexuality – their own and that of their popular cultural icons. In our example, a striking illustration of this was the girl in the headscarf carrying an overtly sexy image of Take That on her bag. Here we see a statement which is both about religious/ethnic identity and about a knowledge of and affiliation to the world of popular music, magazines and stars. Debbie wrote of this image as 'startling' in her research diary. This may be a specifically white response, albeit from someone who has spent most of her life immersed in anti-racist struggle of one kind or another in South Africa and in the UK. On the one hand, there is an unconscious assumption, and one which Debbie would contest if it were stated overtly, that, while white girls may occupy conflicting positions, Asian or black girls will not. Her reaction is indicative of the strength of, and the difficulty of stepping outside, non-Muslim common-sense notions about total separations between traditional Muslim cultures and Western youth culture. Both aspects of this girl's self-presentation, which she combines in her own way, can be read as oppositional to the official culture of the school where neither Muslim traditionalism nor popular youth culture are welcomed.

There is, then, a sparkling array of subtle differences achieved by the girls in defiance of school rules about dress, differences which bespeak a rich play on sexuality and the conspicuous visibility of fashionable styles. In stark contrast, there is a sameness about the informal uniform of the teachers. Here sexuality is played down rather than up, an issue we shall be returning to in the next chapter. These are images that are definitely not to be looked at in the terms which fashionableness demands. On the other hand, notwithstanding popular common-sense images of the 'scruffy (male) teacher' (with patches on his jacket sleeve) these teachers are determinedly 'neutral', while the head's dress, as Debbie noted in her diary entry, bespeaks authority:

> When the head comes in (after everyone has settled down and the hall is quiet), she is wearing a suit (skirt and jacket). Her hair is short and carefully set. She looks smart and very school-mistressy. She also looks authoritative. Is this just the semiotics of her clothes, or does it also have something to do with her body language, her air of knowing that she belongs here and that she is in charge?

There is nothing, in this context, that gets in the way of teachers being looked up to (rather than at), no diversionary sexual gaze, or so it is hoped. It is an unwritten rule that teachers should not appear to be sexualized people, a rule which these teachers observe in their neat but undistinctive dress. There is a similar functional deployment of dress between the teachers themselves: the head teacher's relatively formal, while feminized, dress signifies her authority and position; similarly, the tracksuits of the PE teachers not only signify the relative physicality of their work and the possibilities for bodily movement and freedom but, in themselves, make a statement about the particular identities of PE teachers. In the repertoire of teacherly types this offers a potential point of sexualization which may enter into the widespread assumptions made by pupils that all women PE teachers are, by definition, lesbian (see, for example, Rogers 1994). Women teachers, other than PE teachers, who wear trousers *may* be making a statement about the politics of gender and sexuality. At Heathlands, it later turned out that the teacher wearing trousers on this day rarely wore skirts and was one of the explicitly feminist women on the teaching staff. In later days at the school, it was usual that three or four of the women teaching staff would be wearing trousers although the majority regularly wore skirts. Notwithstanding the wearing of trousers (hardly a radical statement these days even in schools), we have never seen a woman teacher wearing men's clothing (for example, radical drag like men's suits, or even shirts buttoning the 'wrong' way) in school. Conventionally gendered dress is, then, an aspect of the 'neutrality' of teacher dress codes.

Making up identities

In this section we wish to maintain our concern with dynamics of control and resistance in relation to sexuality but focus more sharply on the question of identity formations. From this point of view, the school is a major site for the production of many different identities. In order to understand the specifics of identity work in school, we need first to develop a more general account of how social identities are produced, some of which have been explored in previous chapters. Our starting point is the self-production of individual and collective identities, processes which are often co-terminous. These are active processes on the part of the individuals involved. Struggling to acquire the means to represent themselves to self and others is part of growing up. However, this active work always occurs under socially given conditions which include structures of power and social relations, institutional constraints and possibilities but also available cultural repertoires. Furthermore, as we suggested in the introduction to Part Two, both individual and collective identities are constructed through processes of self-narration and self-imaging, particularly the telling and retelling to self and others of versions of the past, present and future.[8]

Self-narration of this kind cannot be understood simply in terms of conscious choices. Rather it involves involuntary processes of forgetting and remembering and, indeed, of re/membering differently. Nor does 'choice' explain, in these productions of self, the elements of phantasy, the rush of desire and/or disgust, of who we desire and who we wish to be – in psychoanalytic terms, the cathexis of object choice and identification. By stressing story and image in the construction of the self, we do not wish to separate representation and language from social practice. Rather, we are suggesting that identity is always 'performed' in the sense that we produce ourselves through what we do/tell ourselves/think. Inner performances and narratives may well rehearse a public identity or may never be performed publicly at all – indeed, may never be allowed. In other words, identity solidifies through action in the world in collaboration or tension with others and established social rituals.[9] In order to acquire a sense of reality about who we are, our versions, however represented, must be recognized by others as well as by ourselves. Such recognitions can take many forms: from personal intimate relations with family, friends and lovers to seeing oneself as represented in dominant versions of, for example, masculinity/femininity in such public forms as popular film, television and political discourse. Misrecognitions and stigmatizations, too, can take place within intimate relations and, as we have shown in Part One, in relation to public forms. It is these which commonly feature in the kinds of debates about homosexuality which take place in Parliament and in the scandals and moral panics of the popular media, especially the press.

Identity and make-up

One of the particular sources of struggles over sexual identities in Heathlands School was the wearing of make-up. Like dress, make-up is read both by students and teachers as overtly sexual. It is also connected with issues of ethnic and religious identity. One frequent subject for discussion within the school was the degree to which 'tradition' held sway for particular girls in, for example, dress, hairstyle, make-up and imagined futures. These discussions were sometimes instigated by the girls themselves and within pupil friendship groups, but frequently too by teachers amongst themselves and by teachers in classroom interactions with pupils. In this context, the wearing of make-up was both a way of constructing a sexualized and ethnicized identity and a frequent source of conflict between teachers and some students. While teachers presented a more or less united front in relation to school rules, student opinion was often more divided on these matters. Student judgements of their peers could be extremely trenchant. Gurjit took part in an exchange on themes of appearance and tradition among four Muslim girls, during which she was told:

> Shamira is not traditional. She is a big tart and wears lipstick that doesn't suit her and she walks around sticking her tits out.

This is an interesting example of the way in which feminine heterosexuality may be split between the figure of purity, defined in culturally variable ways, and the overtly sexual – in Western iconography, the whore. Not only have the girls set up an opposition around female sexuality, but also one which revolves around being a traditional Muslim or being a Westernized tart. What we see, here, is the deployment of the madonna/whore dichotomy which pervades public representations of women in a way which is both about ethnic identity and which is quite specific to schools, with their (often unsuccessful) regulation of students' self-presentation. Somebody like Shamira might find herself in multiply complex jeopardy over peer and teacher disapproval of her make-up and body language. Debbie recorded in her research diary how, in a lesson taken by the deputy head, Asma was told off for wearing bright red lipstick (Year 10 pupils turn 15 during the school year):

> Dep. H.: *[angrily]* You've been told time and time again that lipstick isn't allowed in Year 10. It's a privilege.
> Asma: *[sulkily, with a bored expression]* Yes miss.
> Dep. H.: Why do you wear it then?
> Asma: Just do.
> Dep. H.: Well, just don't!
> She then sent Asma out of the classroom to 'clean up'. Asma returned over ten minutes later, having missed almost a third of a 35-minute lesson. At the end of the lesson I watched her taking out her lipstick again and sitting at the back of the classroom putting it on before walking out defiantly! . . .
> Later I asked [the deputy head] about the make-up ruling. She

replied that it was about appropriate behaviour for the children's *[sic]* age. 'We don't think they should grow up too quickly.' [She also said] that it was useful to have some privileges for the girls at the top of the school. It makes them 'more responsible'.

This theme of being precocious was echoed in another lesson, when the same teacher told a girl who was wearing make-up 'to stop trying to act grown-up'.

Both Gurjit and Debbie noted that a substantial number of students in Year 10 (the year before it is permitted) did, in fact, wear some form of make-up. This ranged from the stridently overt, with bright red lipstick like Asma's (a particular bugbear of the teachers it seemed), to the subtleties of eyeliner. As Gurjit reports:

Nasreen, who was sitting opposite me, was wearing eyeliner. I asked her jokingly if she was wearing make-up but she totally denied it.

It was generally the more radical forms of subversion which were picked up by the teachers. Clearly, it would have taken more time than was available to police all the young women who were wearing some form of make-up!

Of course, regulating or foregrounding sexuality is not the only form of control and resistance open to teachers and students. Among those groups who are most consistently anti-school, but also amongst students in general, the school is often experienced as an alien and alienating place. Others have documented, in some detail, different ways in which both boys and girls resist schooling (see, for example, Willis 1977; Griffin 1985; Mac an Ghaill 1988; Wolpe 1988; Corrigan 1989). Most of these accounts emphasize the ways in which joking and 'having a laff' punctuate the boredom and formality of the school day and are used to puncture the authority of teachers. Within the repertoires of resistance open to students, playing up sexuality forms a significant part. Often it is only a minority of pupils who act out this sexualization of pupil culture fully but they, and the incidents in which they figure, tend to acquire a mythical significance within the school, both within pupil and teacher cultures. Shamira, for example, is labelled a 'tart' for wearing bright red lipstick although it is clear from the behaviour of the other girls that they, too, wish to defy school rules about make-up, albeit more discreetly.

It is around individuals such as Shamira that pupils and teachers alike construct more or less elaborate legends. The forms they take can resemble closely the structure of scandal in the press, and, like those stories, have consequences for their protagonists, both in terms of the ways in which they are positioned by others and the positions they take up themselves. Tracy, for example, was a young woman who was overt in her sexuality and constantly used it to bait the teachers, both in situations where sex was not the topic under discussion and, famously, in the middle of a sex education lesson about contraception observed by Debbie:

> LC asks the girls, who have recently talked about contraception in their science class, to volunteer to explain how the different contraceptives are used. As soon as they get to the condom, Nasreen called out, 'Tracy'. LC immediately said, 'You volunteered someone else. You do it', much to the embarrassment of Nasreen.
>
> 'Shall we start with the male?' says LC. (Translation: we will start with the male.)
>
> Immediately, Tracy whipped a condom out of her pocket saying, 'You stick in on the man's penis. It has to be hard.'
>
> LC was apparently unfazed by this interjection (which ruined her plan to have someone else talk about condoms), but in a discussion with me after the lesson said that Tracy was 'a sad case' who had been expelled from several schools for her bad behaviour and had been sexually active for several years at 15.

Somehow, in this account of Tracy, her sexuality and her general disruptiveness had become conflated. Rumour and reputation about her sexual exploits had spread among both teachers and students. On one occasion, a teacher who did not even teach Tracy commented to Debbie that 'she'll be pregnant before she leaves here'. Tracy, then, represented the 'whore' side of the madonna/whore dichotomy. She was sexually aware, possibly 'immoral' in sexual terms, 'a problem' for the school and, as such, came in for considerable disapproval. She was seen, iconically, as the single young mother of the future (which, of course, she may well have become). There were ways in which her activities and apparent sexual exploits were seen as threatening the stability and disciplinary regimes of the school. More widely, she embodied the scandalous figure of public discourses, the sexually active, even agressive, woman who threatens the institutions of heterosexuality and marriage, which we see in such films as *Fatal Attraction* and in press coverage of much sexual scandal. In fact, as Debbie got to know Tracy better, she formed the strong impression that much of her apparent sexual expertise was a form of bravado and that she was a good deal less experienced than she made out or than her reputation suggested. Indeed, the reputation of being a 'slag' was both courted in such incidents as that described above and endured as a form of misery – enough to keep her at home for several days as she told Debbie.

So what is happening which is specific to the school context around such symbolic figures as Tracy? Tracy is sexualized as part of the process of de-sexualization of the school. In other words, mythical individuals, especially girls, can be made to carry the denied (even repressed) sexuality which is everywhere present/'absent' in the school. In contrast, in boy culture, but especially among the 'macho lads', sexual exploits, real and imaginery are a positive asset (Willis 1977; Wood 1984; Willis *et al.* 1990; Mac an Ghaill 1994b). In the treatment of Tracy, the sexualized and disruptive girl, we see a characteristically gendered projection of those sexual desires and phantasies which threaten to disrupt the school. A version (aversion) of Tracy figures in the inner moral and sexual landscape of both teachers and pupils. She may be expelled, both literally and figuratively, or the threat of her overt sexuality may be diffused and contained by labelling her 'a sad case'.[10]

Though the production of figures like Tracy is a general social phenomenon linked, for example, to moral panics, there are specifically school-based features to the production of stigmatized pupils (and, indeed, teachers). Schools are systematically organized not only around child/adult relations but also around the development of 'the child' into adulthood in finely divided stages. Hence the notion that make-up was allowable in Year 11 but not in Year 10. As we have seen in Chapter 4, a key figure here is the innocence of the pupil-as-child – a major mis-recognition of many young people's investments in the sexual. The *alter ego* of the innocent child is the precocious or corrupted child. This discursive pattern is evident in both pupil and teacher responses to Tracy and in Tracy's own understandings, only valued differently. For teachers, Tracy seems straightforwardly to belong to that problematic category of 'sad cases'. They see her as a victim, but in their behaviour towards her, treat her like a culprit. Yet the salience given to Tracy and others like her is, itself, evidence of an underlying fascination with such stigmatized figures. In constructing her as 'Other', they also construct her as an object of desire.

For pupils, especially, figures like Tracy and Shamira are both exciting and dangerous. As Valerie Walkerdine has argued, for young girls (especially working-class girls) sexuality and sexualized performance and their accompanying glamour offer fantasies of escape and positions from which these girls can imagine 'being somebody'.[11] While for the generality of women pupils, these figures are regarded ambivalently, for the young women themselves, the burden of representation which they bear can sometimes be overwhelming however much it may also be enjoyed and exploited. Tracy and her friend Sarah, for example, talk about the effect of rumour and gossip on her:

> *DE:* So what would you say generally about the girls like in your class. 'Cos you said people were looking at you like you were a slag. I wasn't quite sure what that meant.
>
> *Tracy:* Oh it's like there were some rumours going round our area about me and this kid. And like, he spread it, someone spread it all round the Mid School, all round this school. People just looking at me, I just couldn't hack it no more. And like I was . . .
>
> *DE:* You must have been pretty miserable.

Tracy: Oh no, not. I was really angry, I just wanted to take my anger out on anybody that come along really.

DE: Sorry, what did you just say Sarah?

Sarah: No I just said she was, she was upset and that.

Tracy: I didn't come to school for about three days 'cos I couldn't face anybody. Didn't I, didn't I come to school on the Monday and Tuesday 'cos I, I couldn't face anybody.

DE: It's amazing how quickly those rumours spread isn't it?

Tracy: Oh I know, amazing innit?

Making collective identities

Of course, identity is not just a matter of individuals making themselves in relation to others. Collective identities are also produced in relation to their Others. Individuals also produce themselves in relation to such collective oppositions. These processes are clear from many ethnographic accounts of schooling. Some ethnographers[12] focus specifically on the collective construction of school identities. Kehily and Nayak (1996) argue persuasively that a major process in the making of these collective identities is the telling and retelling of stories which acquire a collective significance and become part of the mythology of the group. They also trace the process by which the stories of individuals are adopted by the group and collectively performed. They have analysed in detail the 'mythical' narratives told to and by a group of dissident working-class students with whom they worked in a large urban comprehensive school. This includes, for example, what they call 'the Christmas kiss' story. In this story, some of the students related what was obviously a well-worn tale about how Samantha had pursued their sex education teacher, Mr Smedley, around the classroom with a sprig of mistletoe demanding a Christmas kiss trying to 'get some lipstick on the top of his head!' As Samantha said, 'No wonder he had a nervous breakdown.'

Kehily and Nayak say, of this story:

> The Christmas kiss story indicates sexuality is a site where boundaries may be created by the school and tested by the pupils. The contestation reveals sexuality as a *playground* within which humour is used and power struggled over. In the story the negotiation/challenge of boundaries between the 'public' and the 'private' can be located.
>
> (Kehily and Nayak 1996: 214)

In the telling and retelling of this story for its comic value, the entertainment value of the teacher is treasured. The students made the assumption that the teacher was 'queer' and this played a significant part both in the comic value of the story and in the fact that he was supposed to have had a nervous breakdown as a result of the Christmas kiss episode. Another important aspect of the story, which contributes to the comedy, is the reversal of the expected power relations in the classroom. Interestingly, as the story ends, the students remember another episode in which Mr Smedley himself chased a pupil around the classroom. In the Christmas kiss story Samantha, not Mr Smedley, is doing the chasing, is in control of the classroom and of the expression of sexuality within it.

From our point of view, this story is about the construction of a particular collective identity – one which is working-class, dissident in terms of attachment to the school, cross-gender and heterosexual. In some ways the collective identities being constructed here resonate with those in the classic Willis (1977) study in which the 'lads' are defined by Willis and define themselves in a binary opposition with the more academic 'ear'oles'. Like other more recent ethnographers, Kehily and Nayak have been concerned to explore the more complex ways in which collective and individual identities are defined with, and against, the 'Others' of a range of groups. Recent studies have stressed both the very differentiated patterns of identity production in the school and the ways in which particular identities, especially hegemonic forms of masculinity, remain in dominance. In Mac an Ghaill's account, for example, the 'macho lads' are counterposed to a number of other groups: the 'academic achievers'; groups of girls who have a characteristically critical take on masculine identities; a gay group with striking insights into the sexual dynamics of the school; a cross-gender group of 'new enterprisers' who are oriented towards career and vocational qualifications; and the conservative, middle-class grouping of 'real Englishmen' who use their cultural capital to distance themselves from both parental and school cultures (Mac an Ghaill 1994b). Furthermore, these groups are not seen in isolation but always in relation to each other and to teacher groupings. They are also fluid in composition. Similar patterns of complex and fluid difference for training schemes feature in the work of Hollands (1990) and for schools and colleges in the work of Griffin (1993).

Teaching identities

We have already noted that teachers also construct their identities through their parts in the processes of schooling. Mary Kehily points out that the formation of teacher identities is, in fact, part of the informal curriculum both in teacher training and in schools.[13] This identity work is, as with the identity work of pupils, about a range of issues, not least around authority and knowledge. It is also, importantly, around the desexualization of teachers *as* teachers; as we have seen, they bear the primary responsibility for the desexualization of schooling required (however problematically) by government and the dominant sexual culture. As Teresa, in one of our group discussions, comments:

I know someone who is involved with teacher training and she said that sexuality is an issue that's a 'no-no' and that they still don't talk about it. They talk about every other form of oppression, but it's most obvious that they avoid sexuality.

(Alistair *et al.* 1994: 29–30)

At the same time, teachers have, and indeed are expected to have, 'exemplary' sexual lives outside the school. 'Exemplary', in this context, entails being, ideally, heterosexual, married and, for women at least, with children who are already at school.[14] Within the school itself, teachers' sexual identity is connected to the role of 'moral guardian', setting an example for children and regulating youthful sexualities. And where this 'moral guardianship' is questioned or rejected by teachers, then their lives may become the subject of scandal, even moral panic. In fact, there are formal professional requirements for teachers to be involved in questions of childhood and sexuality: sex education must be provided in all secondary schools and teachers must, by law, report suspected sexual abuse of pupils. Additionally, teachers are expected to report (including to parents) any child who reveals in a pastoral situation that s/he might be thought to be 'at risk' sexually:

Where the circumstances are such as to lead the teacher to believe that the pupil has embarked upon, or is contemplating, a course of conduct which is likely to place him or her at moral or physical risk or in breach of the law, the teacher has a general responsibility to ensure that the pupil is aware of the implications and is urged to seek advice . . . In such circumstances, the teacher should inform the head teacher. The head teacher should arrange for the pupil to be counselled if appropriate and, where the pupil is under age[15], for the parents to be made aware, preferably by the pupil himself or herself (and in that case checking that it has been done).

(DfE 1994: para. 40)

On the other hand, as we have seen in Chapter 4, teachers and other adults who talk openly about sexuality, even in the context of sex education, or come out as lesbian or gay are liable to find themselves figuring in tabloid 'scandals' and ministerial speeches.

Sexuality is, then, both inescapable and very dangerous territory for teachers. The tightrope which they have to walk between their public roles and private lives is one with an inbuilt insecurity (and no safety net to be relied upon). Thus, the instability of identity which contemporary theories argue for is exemplified in teachers' lives, perhaps in an exacerbated form especially in relation to sexuality. It is not only that there is a contradiction across the public/private line and within each side of that division. The boundary itself is permeable and sometimes shifts without notice. Well-protected identities in school may be destabilized by revelations outside.

One gay teacher we interviewed mentioned several examples of this process including the new and homophobic parents who had just become neighbours of a gay couple he was friendly with (which we will discuss in more detail in Chapter 6), and having his photograph in the local newspaper in a gay play he was acting in with an amateur dramatic company. Even less direct connections could cause anxieties:

> So there are various overlaps. I have to be quite careful, no matter how far away I think I am from work, suddenly someone picks up. It's like, I had an ex-student when I was teaching at the college, who I've kept in touch with and we've now quite a nice little friendship . . . She pops round to see me . . . and she was sort of saying, 'Have you got a new girlfriend yet?' and . . . I was just on the verge of saying, 'Well, actually, I'm in a relationship with an ear, nose and throat specialist, y'know' and she suddenly said, 'You're teaching such and such a child in September' and I said, 'Yeah, how do you know?' and she said 'I'm a good friend of the auntie of this young [child]'. And so there are all these links, this sort of great web in the area, and not even in the immediate area; this aunt lives . . . miles away from where I work and it could easily filter back to school.

As this example shows, the level of danger in this instability of boundaries depends upon relations of power. Any revelation about same sex relationships outside school presents a potential threat to the job of the teacher concerned. This is not the case for heterosexual relationships where the levels of transgression, especially for men, would have to be extreme, probably even illegal, outside connections to the school. Within heterosexuality, women, as bearers of sexual meaning and responsibility, are always more at risk than men. As we argued earlier, there is a sense in which sexuality in general is closeted in the school; however, this common feature applies differently, according to gender and sexuality, with grossly unequal consequences.

There are consequences, too, for students along the major line of force in the school – the pupil–teacher relation. Since sexuality is so difficult to deal with as an issue of teacher identity, questions of sexuality and 'good' and 'bad' identities are often projected by teachers on to their pupils.

> *Neil:* The other situation that occurred in my third year [of teaching was that] a boy who came to us from a high school, who was 16, and I didn't teach him for the first year, but I just picked up staff comments about him, [was] very, very effeminate. In fact he looked quite a girl; he had grown his hair into, he had it styled in a girl's style, he wore make-up, very high pitched voice, very, very confused, sort of pupil. There were various sort of sniggers around the staff room at the time about this [boy], Stuart. People were sort of coming into the staff room and going, '*(snigger)* I've

just had Stuart and he chose to do his thing', which they have to do, a talk, 'on skin care, and make-up'. And they were horrified. The Head of English [said], 'He can't do that!' and his particular teacher at the time, Isabel, said,'Er, why not, what's wrong with it?' and I said, 'Oh good for you, thank goodness for that, you'. She actively encouraged him and in fact he got a grade A because he had such a good oral, and then as luck would have it, he was having problems getting his GCSE Maths and he resat that year, failed, and the following year he was put into my GCSE Maths set so I thought, 'Perhaps I can do something [to help]' . . . A lot of the staff hadn't been nasty, but being negative, or being very frightened of him. In fact they didn't really know *what* he was, he didn't really know what he was . . .

DE: It was really the kind of 'gender bending' that was worrying them?

Neil: Oh yes, very much so.

In Neil's account, the intense focus on this young man illustrates the displacement and projection of sexual interest on to pupils. Stuart is, it seems, fascinating because he disrupts key borders through his gender-bending performance. Stuart's own position in relation to his (seemingly deliberate) performance is unclear. What *is* clear is that the teachers mentioned by Neil, including Neil himself, take up different positions in relation to Stuart: treating his gender ambiguity as a source of (homophobic) humour; banning, or attempting to ban, his performances; or supporting him. Each of these positions implies an identification with or against Stuart which is part of their own self-production. This is particularly clear in the case of Neil himself, whose desire to help is produced from his own sense of marginality as a gay teacher.

This self-production is about sexuality, but it is not only about sexuality. The teachers here are positioning themselves in relation to their work and identities as teachers through their relation to Stuart's gender-bending and perceived sexuality. In this context, they take up, for example, more or less liberal, student-centred or authoritarian positions. Here again, we see that sexuality shapes and is shaped by the relations of power between teachers and students, a connection more obviously made in the control strategies of teachers in the classroom and playground and students' resistances to them. AnneMarie Wolpe (1988, especially pp. 122–43) explores the assumption, often made by men teachers, that they have less difficulty in controlling classes than women. Wolpe argues that sexuality can enter into the control strategies of both men and women teachers but that there is no evidence that women consistently find control more difficult than men or are less successful as teachers. A degree of laddishness is often used between boys/young men and teachers to establish their relationships as men, to get the boys on the teacher's side and, simultaneously, to control the girls/young women (and even women teachers) through processes of objectification. Indeed, it is often hard to distinguish between this taken-for-granted sexism and easily recognizable forms of (hetero)sexist harassment. These dynamics are often most obviously visible from student points of view. Here, for example, is a group of boys in a boys-only school, making their own assessments of masculine/feminine repertoires among teachers and how they respond to them:

T: Do you react differently to male and female teachers? If you do, why? Tell us.

D: [sotto voce] Battyman.

M: If you talk with a male teacher, you can talk about girls. We treat all teachers differently . . .

P: Some people take more notice of a male teacher than a female teacher, they think they're more masterful, they're going to get in more trouble if there's a male teacher.

S: 'Cos you think of him as a, a – he reminds you of your father and the command he holds around the home.

H: . . . [M]ale teachers are bigger than us – they look down on you so you have to look up to them . . . But a female teacher is always having to look up into your face so it's like you've got the power of her, 'cos you're just looking down on her . . .

S: Sir, . . . you have to be careful when . . . you approach a female teacher, not to appear with any sexual references or anything . . . I mean, you could . . . go up to like . . . a man teacher and tap him on the shoulder and say, 'Sir, you gonna give us homework or something'. But if you touch a woman, I mean she'll probably think you're trying to come on to her or something . . .

N: Some of the students do touch the teachers up and then say, 'Oh Miss, I was only trying to get your attention'. Some of the students are trying to touch them up and the teacher sometimes interprets that they want their attention. So you see it works both ways.

(Bansal 1995: 41–2)

What is striking in this extract, and, indeed, in the transcript as a whole, is the excessive/obsessive preoccupation with gender and size and the implicitly sexual nature of 'looking up' and 'looking down'. Indeed, it is significant that the discussion moves quickly from the relative sizes of male and female teachers and boy/young men students to explicit discussion of sexuality, sexual harassment and the complexity of these relations.

Teachers may also use their 'popularity' with both female and male students, more or less aware of its erotic content. We are defining the 'erotic' broadly, here, to include a much broader sense of excitement, passion and love than is usually intended. The figure of the intensely loved teacher is well-known in popular culture, perhaps iconically represented most strongly in *The Prime of Miss Jean Brodie* and *Dead Poets Society*. Both popular cultural stereotypical images of teachers – that is, the dreary, boring, pedantic and passionless *and* the vibrant, entrancing, passionate object of the 'crush' – are easily recognizable in many people's experience and in the published school ethnographies. In the first of these images, the teacher is strongly desexualized, while in the second, there is a strongly erotic content. Being desirable or loved is a reward for, and perhaps a condition of, being a successful teacher. Desire may, of course, be 'desire for' and/or 'desire to please' and/or 'desire to be'. In this way, the teacher becomes cathected by the pupil as part of the learning process. This may also fuel students' choices of subjects, topics and disciplinary identities as indicated in the story of Mr Lefevre quoted in the introduction to this book (Redman 1997). For the student, then, an engagement with the subject is intimately connected to a relation with a teacher who is him- or herself passionate in teaching and learning, a relation which we will argue in the next chapter can be understood as a kind of metaphorical seduction. Equally, the rewards of teaching are intimately connected with a particular kind of love for one's students and the love one receives back from them.

We will be arguing, in the next chapter, that good teaching is inherently seductive, in a metaphoric sense. In this way, it can be said to carry a kind of erotic charge. It is, therefore, important to develop ways of distinguishing between erotic dynamics which are productive in positive ways, help students to develop their abilities to learn, and encourage independent thinking, and those which exploit the inequalities involved, impair the student's own learning processes and appropriate the student's energies and knowledges. There has been significant debate about these issues on the 'safer' ground of higher education (see, for example, hooks 1994; Gallop 1995), enough to show how explosive a similar debate might be for schools. Nevertheless, there are important reasons for having such a debate even on the quicksands of the politics of schooling and sexuality whose dangers we have already signposted. The failure to have such a debate serves to (re)produce the closeting of sexuality in school contexts and, thereby, to increase the danger of exploitative erotic dynamics through a failure to recognize them. Indeed, as Wolpe (1988: 134–41) points out, the biggest problem in relation to sexuality and schooling is the way oppressive sexual behaviour, especially by boys and men, is overlooked, naturalized or condoned.

Conclusion

Throughout this chapter, we have stressed how the key structural features of schooling, that is, the power relations between teachers and students, shape the ways in which the sexual is played out in school contexts. In particular, schooling sexualities are lived out through the dynamics of control and resistance. In this context, we would neither affirm nor condemn in any singular way either side of this dynamic. Within the structural conditions of the school, the ability to control a class is a prerequisite for other uses of the teacher's power and example. Nor is student resistance necessarily productive of positive outcomes. Our argument is rather that, under existing conditions of policy and practice, the control/resistance dynamic almost invariably produces negative outcomes in the sexual domain. One of the most important contexts, here, is the social framing of sexuality, both within mainstream media representations and political discourse. The main impetus of both media and politics is towards the further closeting of sexuality within schooling contexts. In particular, it reinforces the split between the treatment of sexuality within student culture, with a focus on fun, excitement and identity as well as anxiety, and the dull regulation of the official sexual (desexualized) regime of truth produced in schools – the regulation of clothing and make-up; the denial of the libidinous in teaching and learning; the caution of the sex education lesson; the policing of masculinities via homophobic abuse; enforced invisibility of sexist harassment. The result of all this is that any challenge to the status quo of sexual politics, either in terms of gender relations or in terms of heterosexism, is made immeasurably more difficult. In particular, the policing of sexuality through regulative institutions makes it difficult for even the inspiring teacher to engage in passionate pedagogy, especially around the sexual.

As we have seen in this chapter, the sexual landscape of the school is familiar, tracing the contours of patriarchal relations between men and women, girls and boys. These relations, organized through a matrix of heterosexuality, draw on resources from outside the school. Dominant, hegemonic discourses, always classed and racialized, are deployed to identify 'who' different pupils and students are in the collective (school) imagination. There are ways in which all the participants in heterosexual in-school 'scandals' about girls like Tracy live out the narrative frameworks available in other places, particularly popular culture and formal politics. The stories that are current in the popular sphere offer subjectivities which can be inhabited, objectifications which can be projected on to others. However, the specific processes of regulation of and within schools can be expected to impact on formations of sexualities in specific ways – for example in the use of sexual bravado (even bravura) to disrupt teacher control. Boys have featured little in this chapter, which has focused specifically on girls. We shall be exploring sexualized masculinities in schools in much greater detail in Chapters 7 and 8. The exploration of the policing of heterosexuality in schools, which we have undertaken in this chapter, will be illuminated further in the next two chapters, where our interrogation of the sexual dynamics of schools will be conducted through a central concern with lesbian and gay teachers and students.

Notes

1 See, for example, Wolpe (1988); Kelly (1992); Epstein (1994, 1995); Redman (1994).
2 When we use the term 'resistance' here, we are not in any way suggesting that such resistance is either uncomplicated or inevitably progressive. Neither would we suggest that control is always unnecessary.
3 We specify 'English' because British education is diverse. Scotland and the north of Ireland have their own forms of school organization, governed by statutes other than those governing schooling in England and Wales. Welsh schooling always includes tuition in Welsh and there are many Welsh schools where the first language of tuition is Welsh. There are, of course, also differences between urban and rural schools and between schools with differing social class catchment areas.
4 Extracts are from Debbie's research diary. While she was in school, she made notes about observations and wrote down some short interchanges which were not taped, as interviews and some group discussions were. Later the same day, or as soon as possible thereafter, she composed a diary, written in prose, and including some of her reflections as well as the descriptions.
5 See, for example, Coward (1984); Vance (1984); Winship (1987).
6 This primary school was situated in a relative poor and very ethnically mixed area in London. At the time of writing, Debbie had spent one term doing fieldwork in this school, concentrating on a Year 5 class, but also spending much time in the playground. For a fuller discussion of her work there, see Epstein (1997b).
7 See Valerie Hey (1997) for an extensive discussion of the construction and structuring frameworks of girls' friendships in schools.
8 See also Kehily (1995) on questions of self-narration and gender.
9 For further discussion of identity and performativity see Butler (1990, 1993).
10 For extensive discussion of the cultural significance of marginalized, despised and fascinating figures see Stallybrass and White (1986).
11 See Walkerdine (1990, 1996, 1997). This particular formulation is drawn from a seminar she gave for the Centre for Research and Education on Gender at London University Institute of Education in 1995.
12 See, for example, Willis (1977); McRobbie (1978); Wood (1984); Mac an Ghaill (1988, 1994).
13 This is part of her work-in-progress argument for her forthcoming PhD thesis.
14 For an interesting discussion of the pressure on women teachers to marry (even during the period when that entailed leaving teaching) see Miller (1996).
15 For boys identifying as gay, thinking about or engaged in same sex sexual activity, 'under age' means under 18. At the time when the circular was published, however, it meant under 21 – i.e. any young man still at school!

CHAPTER 6

Teaching sexualities

I drew my teacher very traditionally with glasses, conservative clothing, in front of a chalkboard, a woman. I don't think I was thinking
about myself as a teacher but more what many of my elementary
school teachers looked like. What a stereotype! . . . *[I]t's funny how
many of the pictures drawn by my classmates resembled mine.*
(Renee, student teacher, quoted in Weber and Mitchell 1995: 29.
Emphasis added by Weber and Mitchell)

Surveillance, survival and teaching

In Chapter 5, we drew together public discourses around schooling and
sexuality with a discussion of the school as an institution in which sexualities are shaped and actively produced by participants in schooling. This
chapter will focus more narrowly on teachers both in relation to their own
sexualities in the school context and with regard to their interactions with
students and (potential) impacts on student sexualities. In Part One of the
book, we traced the ways the sexualities are shaped through discourses of,
for example, family, (male) desire, marriage, love and romance, deployed in
the 'public' spheres of the popular media, politics and the state. We pointed
out the ways that sexualities are policed, often through the deployment of
'scandal', with normative forms of heterosexuality rewarded and other
forms of sexuality, from single parenthood to same sex desire and identity,
punished more or less severely. We have also shown how discourses of
'childhood innocence' come into play, particularly in relation to schooling,
to produce moral panics around sexuality and schooling.

The surveillance of teachers (and schools) with regard to the 'academic achievement' of their pupils has reached unprecedented heights in the UK during the late 1980s and the 1990s and teachers in the Anglophone world generally have been at the sharp end of what Jane Kenway (1987) has called 'discourses of derision' (see also Ball 1990). These discourses, combined with those around sexuality and schooling, mean that the surveillance of teachers in relation to sexuality is particularly strong. This is a process which disciplines all teachers (or teaches them to discipline themselves by punishing some), but is gendered and racialized and bears particularly heavily on teachers identifying as lesbian and gay.

This was graphically illustrated in the case of Jane Brown, the head teacher of Kingsmead School in Hackney, whose refusal of subsidized tickets to take her pupils to see the ballet of Romeo and Juliet reached the headlines across the Anglophone world. We have discussed this case in somewhat more detail in Chapter 4.[1] Here we wish only to point out that the fact that she was 'outed' by the press in this way led to her experiencing what amounted to a siege: she had to go into hiding with her partner and her partner's children for a while; she was beaten up by young men as she left the school after a parents' evening; her every move was under intense scrutiny. Of course, like other stories, Jane Brown's is not only about persecution, but also about support and doing significantly better than just 'surviving'. The massive attacks on her led to the mobilizing of support, from other lesbians and gay men, from Hackney National Union of Teachers (NUT) and, most significantly, from the parents of children at her school. In March 1995 the report by the Ofsted inspection team on her school was exceptionally positive. The relief felt at this is not so much a vindication of inspection of this kind *per se,* but illustrative of the fact that, as a lesbian, she needed to be exceptional to be seen as being 'acceptable'. A year later she underwent the training to become an Ofsted inspector herself, passed the course and was offered a post, only to have the offer withdrawn as a result of further media 'outrage'.

Teaching as seduction

Jane Miller (1996) shows that the feminization of teaching since the mid-nineteenth century has involved, among other things, significant efforts to control the sexuality of women teachers. There was a long period, for example, when women teachers were not allowed to be married, but rather had to occupy the positions of desexualized spinsters. So there is a long history of wariness about teachers' sexualities, which works together with the historical specificities of the present moment to produce the kind of punitive surveillance which we have described in earlier chapters.

It is, no doubt, partly because of the level of surveillance of schooling and sexuality and moral panic around the issue that, as we have already pointed out in Chapter 5, teachers are generally desexualized, in very gendered ways, through their clothing and other aspects of their self-presentations as well as through the institutions of schooling themselves. As Renee notes in the quote heading this chapter, the stereotypical teacher of the Anglophone world is not only a woman but usually imagined as 'conservative', 'with glasses', which, as we know from Dorothy Parker, is, in and of itself, de-eroticizing.[2] The ways in which teachers work to desexualize themselves within the context of their daily professional practice form a kind of protection in a potentially dangerous area of their lives. Teachers are not supposed to engage in sexual relationships with their students (quite rightly, in our view, given the power relations involved and the potential for abuse). Neither, as we have seen in earlier chapters, are they supposed to admit to their students that sexuality might constitute a significant part of their lived experience. Insofar as sexuality is legitimately speakable by teachers in the school context, it is domesticated and oblique (for example, through mention of a partner, preferably a spouse, of the opposite sex), within the ghetto of sex education (which will be discussed in Chapter 8), in the context of rebuking a student (especially a girl student) for sexualized behaviour, or within a pastoral situation where the teacher is dealing with the results of sexual behaviour by or towards a student (a situation in which the teacher's options are limited by statute).

There are many senses in which teachers' sexualities remain closeted, regardless of how they identify or the kinds of lives they lead. If, as Eve Sedgwick (1990) has argued persuasively, the closet can be seen as an iconographic metaphor for the late twentieth century, this is even more so in relation to education. Not only are teachers' sexualities (gay or straight), so to speak, 'in the closet', but the whole of formal education (at school and university level) in Anglophone countries can be read in this way. Yet, as we suggested at the end of the previous chapter, teaching can also be seen as a process of seduction. In using the term 'seduction', of course we do not mean that teachers literally seduce their pupils in a sexual sense – though this does happen from time to time, usually between male teachers and female pupils, notwithstanding the greater publicity given to seductions of boys by women teachers (see Chapter 4). Rather, we are seeking a metaphor to describe the kind of thrill and pleasure which can be produced by the best teaching, the kind of intensity of feeling, akin to love, that can pass between teachers and taught. This has been written about (and written off) in terms of students, especially girls, having 'crushes' on their teachers, but the importance of such feelings to pupils' construction of self can be seen in stories like Peter Redman's memory of 'Mr Lefevre' (Redman 1997) which we quoted in Chapter 1.

Jane Miller (1990) in her book *Seductions* uses this word as a metaphor for the kind of attraction which women (even feminists) may feel towards even very sexist ideas. She uses 'seduction' in order to imply the ways that sexuality spills, sometimes messily, often ambiguously, into women's lives, 'into their thought, their work and into the reports they have been able in one way or another to give of themselves' (Miller 1990: 2). She makes the point that using the metaphor of seduction helps us to understand the ways in which power is experienced in contexts of inequality, defining seductions as:

> all those ways in which women learn who they are in cultures which simultaneously include and exclude them, take their presence for granted while denying it, and entice them finally into narratives which may reduce them by exalting them.

As we have already pointed out, schools are structured in inequality, primarily through age relations, always as inflected by other inequalities such as those of class, ethnicity and gender. Children and young people who attend them as pupils/students are engaged in the important work of 'learn[ing] who they are' in a cultural institution which both includes and excludes them and in which their presence is essential (just as the presence of women is essential to society) but also, paradoxically, denied in some important senses. It could, indeed, be argued that those young people (and adults) who are the most successful in negotiating the education system, those high achievers who end up as university undergraduates and maybe even doctoral students, are the ones for whom the metaphorical seduction, by ideas and by teachers, has been most successful. And teachers themselves, having previously been seduced, re-enter the arena of schooling to perform, again, the act of seducing the minds and energies of their students. As Simon commented when we interviewed him:

> [W]e all have special people in our lives, my House Master at [my grammar school] was mine. Yeah, he made me into a teacher, not made me, but made me *into* a teacher, and he developed my political ideas. Mmm, he was a very strong influence on my life, very much so, indeed, and I'm glad he's become very successful, 'cos he deserved it.

Similarly, June Levinson (1994: 14), in a strongly evocative passage, recalls how:

> When my gaze fell upon the new fourth year English teacher, . . . it was a falling in love with a future vision of myself – fiercely academic yet thoroughly approachable, teacherly but sensual. She allowed us glimpses into her life which cast her family as solid, ordinary, working-class Mancunians and herself as surprisingly exotic. In the slides she showed us of her Indian trek, her normally tightly bound hair was flowing down her back, and she looked carefree and joyful in the embrace of her dark-skinned, Indian boyfriend.
>
> (quoted in Miller 1996)

Both of these excerpts vividly capture the influence that the loved teacher can have on a pupil. Simon's stressed, 'He made me *into* a teacher' and June Levinson's 'falling in love with a future vision of myself' bespeak an intensity of feeling normally reserved for one's most significant relationships, and, indeed, demonstrate the significance of relationships between students and much-loved teachers. For students, this can express itself in a love of a particular subject which might stay with them for life, a frequent topic in the regular column in *The Guardian* about successful people's favourite teachers. For teachers, on the other hand, one of the great rewards of teaching is the buzz of pleasure obtained when students respond positively to one's teaching. The second quote shows, too, the way these dynamics are racialized and classed. June Levinson's teacher was seductive because of the combination of the familiar ('solid, ordinary, working-class Mancunian') and 'exotic'. Her 'Indian trek' and her 'dark-skinned, Indian boyfriend' added to her attractions and the 'gaze' which 'fell upon' this particular teacher was a complex combination of colonial, maybe Orientalist, gaze and the desire to be, as well as to be with. And while the aspects of her life shared with her pupils offered a seductive combination, the very act of allowing them these 'glimpses' added to the seduction – a process which we shall discuss in more detail below, when we come to the story of 'Mr Stuart'.

Successful teaching, as Gillian Spraggs (1994: 181) has argued, is 'a kind of performative art' in which '[as] with all artists, your basic material is yourself and your experience'. In other words, successful teachers have to put enough of themselves into their performances, allow enough glimpses into their own lives, to fire the imaginations of their students. For all teachers, this is a process which can be difficult since it demands a performance which is both revealing (enough to be seductive) and masking (because of the required desexualization of teachers). Furthermore, as well as the requisite fascinating glimpses of the teacher's life, the seductiveness of successful teachers is predicated on the fantasies which their students/pupils develop about them. These fantasies may be overtly sexual, but more often they involve the kind of identification described by Simon and by June Levinson where the desire is to be like, or to be, the teacher. There are also more generalized (and gendered) cultural fantasies within the public sphere, and amongst teachers themselves, about what it means to be the ideal or perfect teacher. These fantasies range from the teacher-as-mother figure, so common in infant and primary schools, to discourses about discipline on the one hand and charisma on the other. Jenny Shaw (1995) argues that these shared fantasies are productive of anxieties, many of them (particularly, she claims, in the context of debates about single-sex schooling) about sexuality. Shaw asserts that the long-running debates around single-sex and co-educational schooling:

serve as a defence mechanism which aims to suppress the subversive potential of sexuality . . . Once it is seen as a discourse that serves a defensive purpose it is easier to see that it is not really about academic performance but about fears and fantasies which have become attached to schooling, sexuality, separation and merging.

(Shaw 1995: 129–39)

Virtually everyone has been to school and has had teachers whom s/he either loved or feared, sometimes both. Our fantasies and fears relate to these earlier experiences of schooling, and – taken together with the seductiveness of ideas, with the erotic charge of successful teaching, and with all the transferences and counter-transferences involved in relationships between teachers and taught – are also deeply implicated in what seems like an almost obsessive drive to desexualize schools.

The extreme nature of the wish to erase sexuality from schools is revealed, especially, in moral panics about sexuality and schooling (discussed in Chapter 4) and also in some of the parliamentary debates about schooling, sexuality and sex education (see Chapters 3 and 8).

However, this drive is, as we show in this book, largely unsuccessful. Not only is sexuality part of the coinage of relations amongst pupils/students, it is also a major factor in many interactions between teachers and students, and is, as we argued in Chapter 5, one of the major resources for resistance to schooling on which pupils draw (see also Kehily 1993). Teachers, it seems from our evidence and those of other researchers (see, for example, Rogers 1994), frequently use sexual taunts to enforce their control, especially of boys. 'Don't be such a Nancy-boy' was a frequently cited example, used particularly when boys were unwilling to perform particular versions of masculinity during, for instance, physical education. Similarly, in the stories we were told by young people and others working on the Sexuality and Education Research Project about the ways they resisted schooling, sexuality featured strongly. Many of these stories, such as the 'Christmas kiss' story discussed in Chapter 5, featured a kind of sexualized play which challenged the authority of the teacher. For straight teachers, this is complicated enough. For those who identify as lesbian, gay or bisexual, such 'games' are fraught with danger (see also Spraggs 1994).

The limits of discretion: Neil's story

One of these dangers is that of being 'outed' against one's will. Most lesbian and gay-identified teachers find this, at the very least, an alarming prospect (although, as we shall see, coming out deliberately can be done, in certain circumstances, with considerable success). There are widespread mythologies about lesbians and, even more so, gay men as marauding and dangerous, liable to prey sexually on young people. These were pervasive during the age of consent debates discussed in Chapter 3 and, indeed, seemed to be the main reason why MPs voted for reducing the age of consent of gay men only to 18, two years older than the age of consent for women and for heterosexual men. In dominant discourses, then, it is axiomatically problematic for lesbians and gays to become teachers (or to work with children/young people in other capacities). This means that the teaching performance, using one's own life as the material for it, becomes immediately more complex. In discussing these complexities, it is important to keep in mind that they are inherent in the wider problematic of the simultaneous absence and presence of sexualities in schools. Indeed, the argument of this chapter is that the positioning of lesbian and gay teachers is illustrative of, and contributes significantly to, the discursive framing of sexualities in schools.

When teachers come out as lesbian or gay (or when they are 'outed' against their will), they take a number of risks: of loss of credibility; of incurring homophobic abuse; of being pilloried in the popular media; of losing their privacy; and even of losing their jobs. All the lesbian or gay teachers we interviewed during the course of our project, whether they were out at school or not, spoke of the risks both of coming out *and* of staying in the closet. Neil, for example, told us a long story about how:

> I live very close to the school I work at, not actually in the catchment area – that was a deliberate choice. But two gay friends do live in the catchment area, and, horror of horrors, some new neighbours moved in . . . and then it turned out that the children had been allocated a place at the school I teach in . . .
>
> Although I'm out [outside of school], I'm not sort of camp or anything like that, and, so far as I was concerned, [my friend's new neighbours] had got nothing to worry about, and certainly wouldn't have known anything about it. As far as my friend's situation is concerned, his other half is supposed to be a lodger as far as the neighbours are concerned. He lives with his lover. Anyway, after a couple of weeks, they started getting a lot of aggro from the neighbours including some house bricks thrown at them through the greenhouse, and all sorts. Then the children started shouting at them, things like 'poof' and, you know, the usual sort of homophobic things . . .
>
> And then, just before Christmas . . . the head summoned me. She said, 'I just wanted a word with you', and I went in and she said that this particular mother had been and complained. And I said, 'Why? I don't teach this child.' But she said, 'She thinks you are a danger to the children in your class', and I said, 'Well, why? Because I'm not adequate?', and she said, 'Well, let it just be said that she considers you

to be, to have dangerous friends, friends who could be a danger to children.'

Here, the risk of being 'outed' *at school* (as against in the rest of his life) is vividly captured in the phrase 'horror of horrors'; the safety of the closet is dubious at best. Neil's closet was immediately endangered by the chance that his friends lived in his school's catchment area and that their new neighbours' children attended his school. Merely *visiting* his friends was enough to cause Neil's status as a safe teacher to be threatened. The head's report that '[the mother] considers you to be, to have dangerous friends, friends who could be a danger to children', shows the ellipsis between having gay friends and being supposed to be gay yourself, and between being gay and being a danger to children. It also reveals a depth of anxiety about sexuality and schooling, here focused on the gay teacher (or the teacher who had gay friends), which can only be explained in terms of unconscious fears and fantasies, perhaps based on the seductiveness of teaching as a process. Neil's response was, perhaps inevitably, defensive:

> I said, 'Well I can assure you they are not', and I said, 'It is no business of hers' . . . '[W]ell I've had the complaint and I have to inform you', she said, 'I'm not complaining to you, and I'm not, um, asking you to alter anything you've done. You're 100 per cent professional, and I'm perfectly happy with what you're doing', she said, 'but I'm just warning you that this woman is out to cause trouble.' She said, 'If you want me to I'll back you up with unions, because really she [the mother] is making slanderous allegations, and we don't even know what she is saying, outside in the playground.' Because a lot of the communication that goes on is outside the actual school building.

Neil's story draws attention to the dangers of being outed, through unpredictable happenings, that might accrue to a gay or lesbian teacher who remains in the closet. It also demonstrates the role of gossip more generally in policing the actions, and the identities, of teachers. Furthermore, it shows that it is not actually within the power of individuals to avoid such gossip, however discreet their behaviour. Clearly, the neighbourhood hostility towards Neil's friends had reached a pitch of queer-bashing at which personal injuries became a distinct possibility, with 'some house bricks thrown at them through the greenhouse'. But what was more, someone had spotted Neil visiting his friends and this mother's complaint was the result of that. The head's judgement of the situation was that Neil might need the support of his union, and she was keen to back him up in this, but Neil was more inclined to hope that things would simmer down if they were let well alone. As he continued:

> I'd rather just let the matter rest, which was fine and things have plodded on really until June, June this year. I was just leaving the

school one afternoon and this particular woman, this mother marched into the school sort of wielding the pushchair and the children in tow, she had got another younger child, and, um, she starting screaming abuse down the corridor at me, just as all the children were going out of school, and parents were in and teachers were outside the rooms and whatever, um, shouting things like, uh, I was a danger to the children, that I was associated with pooftahs and queers, and, um, she would refuse to have her children taught by me and I just very calmly sort of went, 'I'm sorry, I'm not prepared to discuss this. I'm not going to enter into this, you can go and talk to the head if you want'. At which point the deputy head came out and he sort of said to me, 'Look, move away. Just go away. Don't get yourself involved.' And he managed to talk her into going into the head and, um, the head reported back to me after, that she had had the same reaction from this woman that I'd just, and the head basically said to the woman, 'Well if you are not happy with the situation, and if you are not happy with the education that we can offer then take your children elsewhere, you'd (be) perfectly right to.' And she said, um, 'We are actually a very popular school, we are actually overcrowded. There is a waiting list for children to come in', and the youngest child had a reception place for this September and the mother was warned that the reception place would be withdrawn, and she had to sign to say that she understood this, and she wouldn't be able to take up the reception place and the head even went as far as to look round other primary schools to find somewhere that would accept the family. And from that point on the head said, 'Well I do sympathise with you', she said. 'I'm sorry that you are in this situation', she said, 'it is just something that happens if you live close to the school'. I said, 'Well it's not. Because I could have lived 20 miles away but my friends still live near to the school, you know, it could just happen out of coincidence.'

There are several things going on at this point in the story. First, Neil is careful to establish his own cool and professional behaviour (however he might have been feeling, a matter which, significantly, he does not mention). Second, the mother involved apparently felt entirely justified in her homophobic abuse of Neil. She had completely accepted the logic of those popular common senses which position gays as a danger to children. Since her only evidence that Neil was gay was that he had visited his gay friends, it follows that she either thought that only a gay person would be friendly with another gay person, or she thought of gayness as a contagious disease (like HIV/AIDS; see Redman 1997). Third, the head reacted against the mother's homophobic abuse. She was not prepared to condone this overt bigotry. Furthermore, the disruptiveness of a parent making a scene (for whatever reason) in school at a time of day when a number of parents were about, just as the children were leaving school, is something which any head would wish to avoid both because of the possible effects on children and because it is liable to lead to potentially damaging gossip amongst parents not only about the teacher concerned but about the school as a whole. In such circumstances, these events led to the head taking a firm, even drastic, stand with the mother in question. Certainly, Neil felt more supported than when she had gone straight to the head with her complaints. Fourth, the head's judgement that such events are 'just something that happens if you live close to the school' and Neil's spelling out for her that the events were the consequence of his friends' residence close to the school, rather than his own, reveal that, although she was ready to stand against overt homophobia, she had little grasp of the everyday lives of lesbian and gay teachers or of the risks to them as a result of being outed through chance circumstances or of the more pervasive character of sexual gossip about teachers generally.

The support for Neil from both head and deputy was, of course, welcome. But it was not something he could be sure of in the absence of whole-school policies about support for lesbian and gay teachers when and if they come out or are outed in school. Such policies are thin on the ground, and it was as recently as 1996 that the NUT, which has a significantly more liberal record on this than the other teacher unions, finally passed a resolution saying that the union would support lesbian and gay teachers who came out.[3] We shall be arguing in the final chapter that developing policies supportive of lesbian and gay teachers and students (out or in the closet) are an important part of any struggle to improve schools in relation to sexuality.

Classrooms and closets/classrooms *as* closets: Mr Stuart's story

As is evident in Neil's story, schools, in general, are hotbeds of gossip and this gossip is frequently about sex. Children gossip about each other and about teachers. Indeed, such gossip forms an important part of their preparation for meeting new teachers. Teachers gossip about each other and about children and their families. Parents gossip about their children's teachers (and, it seems, their children's teachers' friends) and about the other families with children at the school. It was all the more surprising, therefore, to come across a situation in which there was a closing down of the usual gossip networks as occurred in Edendale School. The Year 5 teacher, Mr Stuart, came out as gay to the children in his class while Debbie was observing the class.[4] This was not a sudden decision. Indeed, he had been at the school for several years and had worked hard to achieve a situation in which coming out to pupils would be positive. He had been out to the head and other staff for a long time. He was active in lesbian and gay politics and had discussed this with the head, including the possibility that he would be outed by the press. The head had been supportive and had ensured that he would receive the support of the school's governors should such an eventuality take place. About a year later, and a year before Debbie had observed his class, he had met with the head to put forward the view that he was uncomfortable about hiding his gay identity from pupils, that it was not appropriate for him to lie to them should they ask him questions about his personal life, and that he did not feel that it was possible to deal with homophobic abuse between the children adequately without coming out to them. Again, the head had supported him and had suggested that he meet with the school's Governing Body. At this meeting, he put forward his views and successfully obtained their support for the idea that, should it be appropriate, he would come out to children in the school. Indeed, one of the parent governors commented that it was important for the children to learn that some people were lesbian or gay.

The question arose in a session on the class topic, 'Me, My Family and My History'. Mr Stuart had asked the children to work in groups to try to establish three 'facts' about boys and three 'facts' about girls. They quickly discovered that this was not possible without resort to 'rude' things such as 'girls have vaginas' and 'boys have penises'. One of the groups came up with the fact that 'girls can't marry girls' to which Mr Stuart responded that, while this was true because of the law, nevertheless 'women can love and live with women and men can love and live with men'. One of the boys immediately called out 'oh, that's disgusting'. In the course of challenging this heartfelt statement, Mr Stuart said that he was gay. The children's immediate reaction was to deny this because, as Elias said, 'Everyone says you're not gay, because your girlfriend is Ms Allen'. Mr Stuart responded by saying that he was gay and loved and lived with another man, that the children had seen his partner at school concerts and that, currently, he was feeling quite lonely because his partner was working abroad for a long period. At this one of the children said, in a puzzled tone, 'But we *saw* you and Ms Allen and you were in the greengrocers, laughing'. Clearly, the gossip networks had been active and the two teachers had been paired off in the children's minds (after all, shopping for fruit and vegetables is a very domestic act!).

Much to my surprise (and, indeed, to Mr Stuart's), his being gay did not spread around the school. Two weeks later, for example, a child in the other Year 5 class was in trouble for using homophobic insults, and had no inkling that Mr Stuart was gay. When I interviewed Samantha and Louise, I asked them about gossip:

> *DE:* D'you sometimes gossip about each other or about Mr Stuart?
>
> *Louise:* Yeah.
>
> *DE:* Who d'you gossip with?
>
> *Louise:* Just my friends really. We don't really like spread it because it's not very nice.

Samantha: And then the teachers would know, or our friends would know.

Louise: Yes, they might think it's true and then they'll ask him and then it's not true, like rumours.

DE: Like what kind of things would that be?

Louise: Well, like, rumours.

DE: Rumours, like what kind of rumours?

Louise: About, um, that two teachers like each other and that.

Samantha: Yeah, Mr Stuart and Ms Allen love each other.

Louise: Yeah, but then other people might find out and then if Mr Snowden finds out anything that it's true then he might sack them. But they're, um, they're best friends but not like, but they're best friends.

Samantha: Yeah, yeah.

It is clear, from the earlier classroom discussion and from the girls' talk about 'rumours' that there had been significant gossip and speculation amongst the children (and, perhaps, their parents) about Mr Stuart and Ms Allen's relationship. In fact, Ms Allen identifies as lesbian and the two teachers are good friends both in and outside school as well as working together in developing study programmes for the year group. The children's speculation about their relationship indicates processes of projection and the development of (heterosexualized) fantasy within this primary school which are typical of pupil/student gossip about teachers. At this stage, they are talking both about rumours of Mr Stuart's gayness and of rumours about Mr Stuart and Ms Allen. Indeed, we read Louise's response to Debbie's question, 'What kind of rumours?' as a way of side-stepping the issue of gayness. Samantha immediately picks up Louise's cue with an item of heterosexual gossip. Louise, however, is still thinking about Mr Stuart being gay, for her statement that 'other people might find out and then if Mr Snowden finds out anything that it's true then he might sack them' does not make sense on two counts: first, heterosexual, unmarried teachers who become involved with each other would definitely not lose their jobs and, as will be seen later, these girls were easily sophisticated enough to know this; and, second, her concern is about Mr Snowden finding out 'anything that it's true' and she knows that Mr Stuart and Ms Allen are 'best friends but not like, but they're best friends'. Debbie then reminds them of the classroom discussion in which Mr Stuart came out to them:

DE: Mm. 'Cos I remember that came up in class one day didn't it that, when someone said . . .

Samantha: I think it was Levi. Just because they were talking to each other a lot.

Louise: In the shop and they go to, um, they go to lunch break together.

Samantha: I think they go to lunch break.
Louise: That doesn't mean that they like each other, but they're just friends.
DE: Well, they like each other, but like each other as friends.
Louise: I think they just go to lunch break together to talk about what you're going to do and then you can do it after and things.
DE: Yeah.
Louise: And then they take another idea and they both do it.
DE: Yeah, because they've got the same year.
Samantha: Yeah and like, Mr West and Ms Humphrey do it as well.
DE: So it's the year group teachers.

In this part of the discussion, Samantha and Louise explore the nature of Mr Stuart and Ms Allen's friendship. They go over what seems to be the basis of the gossip about them, that they talk to each other a lot, go shopping together and take their lunch breaks together. Louise makes a distinction between them 'liking' each other, where 'like' stands for 'love', and being 'just friends', and then moves towards identifying the friendship as, at least partly, based on working together to 'take another idea and they both do it'. At this point, Debbie tries, once again, to get them to talk about Mr Stuart's revelation that he was gay:

DE: But what, what about, I mean, so you wouldn't want Mr Snowden to hear that Mr Stuart and Ms Allen were boyfriend and girlfriend because you know it's not true, but what about things that would be true? Would you gossip about them?
Samantha: No.
Louise: No, not really because Mr Stuart doesn't want them to know, he just wants the class to know.

By this point, it is very clear to everyone involved in the conversation that all three know they are talking about Mr Stuart being gay, but no one will name it. It is, in Eve Sedgwick's (1990) terms, an 'open secret'.[5] Here we see the girls aware of the secret but unwilling to share it openly with Debbie. Meanwhile Debbie tries to get them to talk about their secret, which, after all, they know she knows since she was in the classroom with them when Mr Stuart came out and has just reminded them of that. In her discussion of Henry James's *Billy Budd*, Sedgwick argues that:

Both the efficacy of policing-by-entrapment and the vulnerability of this political technique to extreme reversals depend on the structuring of the policed desire, within a particular culture and moment, as an open secret.

(Sedgwick 1990: 101)

We also begin to see, in their clear refusal of gossip and the reason Louise offers to the effect that 'Mr Stuart . . . just wants the class to know', just how aware the girls are of the policing of gay identities and desire through homophobia. Debbie tries to press them on this:

DE: How d'you know that? What makes you think that?
Samantha: Yeah. Maybe, if he told us and then he might not want the whole school to know.
Louise: We wouldn't have done it.
DE: Why would he not want the whole school to know?
Samantha: I dunno.
DE: To know what?
Samantha: To know anything really.
Louise: Anything, to like uh . . .
Samantha: He wouldn't tell us anything personal. Maybe he'd tell us that he, his auntie got his hair cut, her hair cut and . . .

Debbie's pressure is met with complete resistance. First there is a repetition that 'he might not want the whole school to know', and when Debbie tries, again, to probe, Samantha takes refuge in her 'I dunno'. When Debbie, in frustration, asks what it is that Mr Stuart wouldn't want known, there are two lines of resistance to naming the word 'gay'; first that Mr Stuart wouldn't want anything known about him and second that, in any case, he wouldn't tell the class anything personal. At this point, Debbie comes as near as she can, without actually using the word, to saying that Mr Stuart is gay and this finally prompts the girls to talk about homophobia (though still not saying that Mr Stuart is gay):

DE: Well, he *did* tell you about his boyfriend going to America, didn't he?
Louise: Yeah.
Samantha: Yeah, but, he doesn't want, really, everyone at the school to know.
Louise: Maybe he does but, I don't know, I wouldn't really spread it because . . .
Samantha: 'Cos, it, people go a bit funny in this school about . . .
Louise: Yeah and then they'd go, they'd jump around and tell . . .
Samantha: Their mum and dad . . .
Louise: . . . and then they'd say, 'Is it true?' or something. And maybe their mum and dad will think that he's a bad teacher and then they'll think that, 'Oh no, my son is going to be, like, um, don't want my daughter, he's going to be like that, so I'm going to take my kid away from the school' and tell Mr Snowden about him and he could be sacked.

DE: D'you think that would happen?

Samantha: No.

Louise: No, not really, 'cos, most grown-ups are, um, grown-up about it but some aren't really. Some are.

Samantha: Yeah, but, um, Mr Snowden knows, I think.

Louise: Yeah, probably does. I think most of the teachers do, but that could happen and then the parents might think that he's a bit strange.

Samantha: Strange.

Louise: So that if he's in class and they might take their child out.

DE: So you would be, like, really worried about Mr Stuart and what would happen to him? It sounds like you'd be really kind of, protecting him, yeah?

Louise: Yeah, we don't, 'cos we don't like supply teachers at all really.

Samantha: I know, 'cos we don't want a new teacher.

It is clear that the children are absolutely aware that homophobia is a feature of the 'particular culture and moment' that they have to negotiate and that gay desire is policed – hence, perhaps, the reversal involved in identifying Mr Stuart and Ms Allen's friendship as a romance. They know that 'most grown-ups are grown-up about [homosexuality], but some aren't really'; they know, or think they know, that the head teacher is aware of Mr Stuart's gay identity; they are aware of the potential dangers of coming out and seem to have made a conscious (or semi-conscious) decision to build a kind of closet around the classroom. They have done so in order to protect their teacher since they 'don't like supply teachers' and 'don't want a new teacher'. The children have a standard of comparison here. While Debbie was observing the class, Mr Stuart had been away for nearly three weeks on jury service. The supply teacher taking his place had fallen significantly below the standards that Mr Stuart set himself, particularly in relation to the respect he offered the children. We would certainly read their not wanting a new teacher as implying a positive comparison of Mr Stuart with other teachers and, indeed, of their feelings towards him.

In discussing this transcript with others in a variety of academic seminars and in-service sessions with teachers, it has been suggested that a contributory factor to the children's closeting of their classroom was that they were fearful that, as members of his class, they themselves might be tainted with the stigma associated with gayness. Certainly, this may be the case for some of them, but that is not how it felt to Debbie in this conversation. It seemed to her at the time, and it seems to us looking at the transcript, that the wish to protect Mr Stuart predominates heavily over other feelings. Earlier in the chapter we quoted from June Levinson to discuss how seductive it can be for children when a teacher shows them glimpses of their lives. Certainly, the children in

Mr Stuart's class seemed to love him (not only in this conversation, but throughout the period of Debbie's observation). The seductiveness of Mr Stuart's actions here was not erotic, but consisted of inviting these 9 to 10-year-olds to see his world from his point of view, treating them with a respect rarely accorded to children and, in so doing, entering into a kind of social contract with them: he would treat them respectfully and they would protect him. Indeed, one of the (many) negative effects of the punitive surveillance of teachers which we have described is that it is likely to undermine this kind of respect for children. It can be risky, the costs too great, and it requires a certain courage to proceed in this way when the system is stacked against you.

Mr Stuart is happy about having come out to his class, though it is a process which he recognizes he will have to go through again and again with no guarantees as to the results. He has written about coming out at school in the *Times Educational Supplement* (*TES*),[6] has appeared on television, has been reported on in some of the tabloid press and has frequently run workshops for other lesbian and gay teachers about coming out. He certainly regards coming/being out at school as providing him with a sounder and more reliable protection than trying (perhaps unsuccessfully) to remain closeted. Neither would he be happy to depend on his friendship with a woman teacher, even if, like Ms Allen, she is a lesbian, to provide camouflage for both with gossip making them appear straight. But he is also aware that the choices he has made may limit his possibilities in terms of future jobs. He would not, for example, be willing to work at a school where he could not be out (and, in any case, it might prove difficult to put this particular genie back in the bottle given his public stance) and, especially in an era where schools are very concerned about marketing themselves,[7] this could prove a problem.

Disciplining the Other, constructing the norm: Harry's story

Notwithstanding the apparent ease with which Mr Stuart, in a school with a strong and sympathetic head, was able to come out, for lesbian and gay identified teachers the fears and fantasies which abound within and about the profession are, perhaps, particularly acute. The 'horror', which Neil alluded to, of being outed is often avoided by dint of distancing oneself from anything to do with lesbian or gay sexuality. This was a telling part of Harry's account of himself as a teacher:

DE: You were saying that you felt like you had to definitely play a
         part?
Harry: Oh yes, yes!
DE: Can you tell me a bit about the part?
Harry: The part, I guess the part was to emulate the straight male
         teachers.

DE: What does that entail?

Harry: It entailed initially hitting pupils and being physically violent, or physically intimidating and (*taking a deep breath*) trying desperately not to appear soft.

DE: Yeah? Because that was the give-away?

Harry: That seemed to be the give-away, yeah . . . I think that perhaps I was also steering clear of talking about anything that would suggest, give the children an opportunity to point the finger at me, or ask that awful question, which children in school are perfectly capable of asking.

What is captured here is the strongly felt necessity to take any means available to avoid the inference that he was gay. Harry has to cut and stretch himself in painful ways in order to avail himself of the sources of recognition which he needed, to make himself recognizable as a teacher. What is clear, in this interview, is that there is more to the horror of being outed than the risk of losing one's job. The exposure of this part of his identity, one which he was not at ease with anyway, seems at least equally important here. Harry's evident distress during this part of the interview was compounded by his view that hitting children and being physically violent was both wrong in itself and constituted a truly terrible form of pedagogy. His chosen form of defence, then, was far from the seduction which we have argued earlier in the chapter is a key element in successful teaching.

The general presumption of heterosexuality, which we have identified elsewhere as a primary manifestation of heterosexism (see Epstein and Johnson 1994), works as a technology of the self in the production and policing of teacher identities. In Harry's case, the distance which he perceives as necessary to avoid the danger of being identified as gay by his pupils is achieved by dint of adopting an extreme version of a style of teaching in which he consciously (at least in retrospect) performs his gender as what he describes as 'straight macho'. Harry's performance draws, in horribly poignant ways, on (straight) male privilege. It is significant that he was able to associate himself with heterosexuality by resorting to violence. That this simply would not be available as a strategy for lesbian women tells us much about the structuring of the sexual politics of schools.

Some lesbian teachers try to 'heterosexualize' their performances in order to fit in to schools and escape identification as lesbians. Gillian Spraggs, for example, talks about teaching her subject (English) 'in a mode of rigid and safe academicism' (1994: 181). Sarah O'Flynn (1996: 86), in her examination of the many different ways in which lesbian teachers teach and survive in schools, argues that some:

seek to establish a sense in which we are the same. It involves minimising difference and literally working psychically to create that sense of similarity with the heterosexual majority. Nevertheless, having success at this needs maintenance. It involves investments of time and energy and achieving success at it in one location, doesn't necessarily mean one will be able to repeat the process elsewhere. There is a sense in which one is confined in one's job. Conversely, being completely out can also result in this.

This, as we noted above, is one of the costs to Mr Stuart of his success in coming out in his present school.

Technologies of the self: dressing not to impress

On a different note, Didi Khayyat writes about the way that she handled herself as a secondary school teacher:

> One of my students that summer, a young woman of about 19, took it upon herself to 'expose' my sexual preference. I knew that her intentions were not malicious but that she was acting out her attraction to me ... The more she goaded me about my sexuality, the more I ignored her and the more she made her accusations publicly. Because my other students liked and respected me, their response was to silence her, to disbelieve and discredit her intimations that I was a lesbian. To them, I was a teacher they liked; therefore I could not be a lesbian.
>
> (Khayyat 1992: 1–2)

Here we see simultaneously the presumption of heterosexuality and the erotic charge involved in a relationship between a successful and charismatic teacher and her students. Indeed, the (usually homo-erotic) 'crush' which the adolescent girl has on her favourite teacher is commonplace, famously in *The Prime of Miss Jean Brodie* (Spark 1969) and within the school story genre more generally, but also in many adult women's memories. But these crushes are meant to be a phase and their very ubiquity perhaps contributes to the notion which frequently meets lesbian and gay identified people when they come out, that they will 'grow out of it'. The frequency of homo-eroticism within the teacher–pupil/student relationship may also make the performance of heterosexuality a feature of much teaching, but perhaps particularly salient for lesbian or gay teachers.

Of course, it is not only lesbian and gay teachers whose sexuality is disciplined and for whom the performance of conventionally gendered heterosexuality is a requirement. The teacher's 'uniforms' discussed in the previous chapter are, indeed, heterosexually desexualized! And for women teachers, particularly, this is complicated by issues of age and appearance. Jane Miller (1996) points out that:

> Brains, looks and clothes become interchangeable terms in the covert regulation of women teachers and their potentially wayward sexuality.

Some of us asked in the early seventies if we might wear trousers to work. To do so was regarded as brazen, unprofessional and political.[8] So several already 'naturally' trousered persons gave much judicious thought to the issue. The decision eventually went our way, but was relayed to us with a list of caveats evincing a positively unseemly interest in anatomy and current fashion. Trousers could only be worn as part of what was known then as a 'trouser suit'. Bums must not be seen. And there was also a list of the kinds of trousers we might absolutely not wear: ones made of denim or jersey, for instance, and ones which were either tight or flared. It was not, of course, that any of the women who availed themselves of these new liberties bothered much with the detail. But we yielded to the convention which lets men wear what they like, so long as it includes trousers, while exercising what is allowed as control over female dress in the interests of professionalism.

This may seen unimportant. It stands in, however, for some central ambiguities. The possible sexual provocations of a young woman teacher may be used to cancel her professional competence and judgement. Just as the absence of sexual provocations in an older woman teacher may exile her from the human altogether. Both are assessed not as workers but as more or less desirable women and as more or less well adjusted to a small number of fundamentally sexual roles.

(Miller 1996: 16)

In some ways, Jane Miller's account of 1970s discussion of the wearing of trousers may seem quaintly anachronistic in the 1990s. However, its continuing relevance is evidenced not only by the teacher uniforms we saw in our school observation, with denim, for example, still seeming almost unwearable by women teachers. It is also striking that mid-1990s panics about violence in schools have been accompanied by comments about the deleterious effects on children's values if teachers do not dress appropriately and even the suggestion from some Conservative MPs that teachers should be compelled by law to dress 'smartly'. Our observation would indicate that such legislation would be an unnecessary addition to teachers' disciplining of themselves through their dress. For women teachers, dressing 'neutrally', in ways which de-eroticize their bodies, may be an important strategy for trying to avoid sexual harassment from male staff and students – which, as Valerie Walkerdine (1981) has shown, can take place with boys as young as three. For them to wear clothes which drew attention to 'their potentially wayward sexuality' runs the risk of attracting the male gaze on themselves as heterosexual objects.

Both male and female teachers are expected to display an acceptable face of heterosexuality. But it seems from our research that heterosexual male teachers are less likely than either gay male or women teachers to suffer severe consequences for behaviours which are deemed inappropriate. For example, Julie King, a senior teacher in one of the schools where we did our research, recalled how:

There were like, and still are like, two members of staff and without exception each year group complained that these two male members of staff continually invaded their personal space and they found it uncomfortable and unpleasant and it made them feel very uneasy. And in fact it was reported to the head about these two members of staff and I know with one of them there had been several incidents of, more than just harassment really, quite sort of reported cases, of things like going off with a girl after being at the pub for lunch and then bringing her back a couple of hours later, that kind of thing, and the head did investigate several of these cases with the union, but nothing . . . it was very difficult to prove, in fact impossible to prove, and the head couldn't take any action because of it being . . . I mean the other person's like the union rep, he's the union rep who's very clever on sort of union issues and just could never be brought to task for it. And the other one, the other person mentioned by these girls is . . . the head of [lower] school and I reported that he was, um, that the girls were complaining about him invading their personal space and to try and respect their personal space in the future, but he does still contravene it on occasions. I mean, um, but it's nothing that, it's just sort of you know, get into a class or sort of making sexual innuendoes that make them feel very uncomfortable. With the other member of staff, for the last couple of years it's all been quiet on the western front, I think the last case . . . because there was a complaint, a parent made quite a serious complaint about him kissing a girl. But again he denied it and the union were in and there was no . . . it's a very serious allegation as you know and you've got to be able to conclusively prove it.

It is virtually impossible to imagine a similar result in respect of an equivalent parental complaint about either a woman teacher kissing a boy or a teacher of either sex kissing a pupil of the same sex, both because they would be less likely to be offered adequate union support (Bartell 1994; Spraggs 1994) and because of the high possibility, even likelihood, that their case, with or without conclusive proof, would end up being spread across the tabloid press. It would seem, then, that while the sexualities of all teachers are policed, the disciplinary process is more likely to take a coercive turn in the case of those who depart from the norm of the (white) heterosexual male.

In this chapter, we have been concerned to explore 'Teaching Sexualities' by examining the experiences of lesbian and gay identified teachers. As we have seen, the particular patterns of self-discipline in their case, engendered by the panoptical gaze of, among others, students, parents, the popular media and politics, can tell us much about the ways in which sexuality is played out in the school system. The seductiveness of successful teaching may produce anxieties which produce and feed upon scandalous stories in the popular press, particularly in relation to gay and lesbian teachers who are, it seems, automatically assumed to be dangerously attractive to their pupils. The act of teaching seduction is a delicate, complex one, vulnerable to the crudity of the disciplinary processes attendant on the surveillance of teachers. Even to discuss these issues may raise the hackles of some. We fully expect this book (and in particular this chapter) to cause a scandal about 'trendy educationists' who say that teachers should seduce children![9]

Notes

1 For the implications of this case in terms of local politics, see Cooper (forthcoming).
2 Dorothy Parker's well-known couplet reads 'Men seldom make passes/At girls who wear glasses', in Oxford Dictionary of Quotations (1977: 368, section 16).
3 Prior to this, the NUT's most recent advice to lesbian and gay teachers was that 'ordinarily personal sexuality is not a matter for discussion with pupils'. It then advised that, should the question arise, teachers should try to 'draw the questioner into a more general consideration of relationships' (National Union of Teachers 1991).
4 This discussion draws on Epstein (1997b).
5 This is a theme to which Sedgwick constantly returns.
6 In order to retain the promised anonymity of the school, we are refraining from giving the reference for this article. 'Mr Stuart' is, as with other names, pseudonymous. Obviously, his public political activities make him and his school traceable (though, interestingly, the tabloid press have not mentioned his school by name, even when writing about him as a person), but that is something he has negotiated directly with the head and governors. Debbie's undertaking, as a researcher going into the school, was not to identify the school in her writing.
7 See also Epstein (1994b) and (Epstein and Kenway 1996).
8 Debbie's first experience of school inspection by one of Her Majesty's Inspectors in the early 1970s is memorable for his main comment on the quality of teaching – that he did not like to see women teachers in trousers!
9 The British Sociological Association Conference in 1994 was on the theme of 'Sexualities in Social Context'. This produced a major outburst from the press, ranging from moral outrage in the tabloids to trivialization of the issues in even the most liberal broadsheets. We know of one paper about sexuality and education which was withdrawn, after the author had been pursued by the Daily Mail in the period immediately before the conference took place.

CHAPTER 7

Learning sexualities

Bodily turmoil and raging hormones

As we have seen in Chapters 2 and 3, one of the primary ways in which we understand the sexual in contemporary society is through recourse to discourses of the biological or the natural. In a theory of development which is based on notions of ages and stages (phases), one of the questions which causes anxiety to some is the notion that some girls and, maybe more so, boys could have their development 'arrested' during a 'homosexual phase' through contact with lesbians and gays. In this context, being gay or lesbian is seen as potentially contagious. Indeed, some of the anxieties about lesbian and gay teachers derive from this notion, which is then reinforced through the idea that adolescence is a time of massive change and uncertainty.

It is considered a truism to suggest that young people find their teenage/ adolescent years a period of confusion and experimentation around sexuality, that they (especially boys/young men) have raging hormones (especially testosterone), changing bodies and developing, but intense, interest in the opposite sex. The bodily changes which take place earlier or later during this period ('phase') clearly are an important part of young people's lived experiences, but, as others have suggested (Henriques *et al.* 1984; Steinberg 1997), we make sense of the biological through discursive practices which are deeply embedded in our culture; and the cultural sense we have of our bodily experiences shapes those experiences. Connell (1995: see especially Chapter 2), in his discussion of men's bodies and masculinities, uses the highly suggestive term 'body-reflexive practices' to explore the interconnectedness of the materiality of people's bodies and social practices (in his example, in relation to sexual practices). He suggests that there is a 'circuit of production'[1] which:

> goes from bodily interaction and bodily experience, via socially struc-
> tured bodily fantasy (involving the cultural construction of hegemonic
> and oppressed sexualities), to the construction of fresh sexual relation-
> ships centring on new bodily interactions. This is not simply a matter
> of social meanings or categories being imposed . . ., though these
> meanings and categories are vital to what happens. The body-reflexive
> practice calls them into play, while the bodily experience . . . energizes
> the circuit.
>
> (Connell 1995: 62)

Connell's 'socially structured bodily fantasy' is structured around particular sets of discursively framed narratives which, as we argued in the
introduction to Part Two, allow people to tell themselves and others who
they are and what kind of people they are becoming. In saying that people
draw on discourse to produce themselves, we are not suggesting that this
happens in predetermined ways. People may insert themselves into the
dominant discourses that we discussed in Part One in a variety of oppositional ways, or they may 'fit in' in quite conformist ways. And, of course,
they may occupy contradictory positions in discourse simultaneously, or the
way they are positioned and position themselves may change contingently,
according to circumstances.

We would argue that the 'turmoil' caused by bodily changes in 'adolescence' does not exist independently of the discourses and their attendant
social practices which mark this as a significant (and easily identifiable) stage
in a person's development towards adulthood. The emergence during the
nineteenth century of the category 'adolescent' (now often elided with the
twentieth-century category 'teenager') coincides with, and is, we would suggest, related to the emergence of, a range of regulatory institutions (like
schools).[2] It is, perhaps, also significant that 'adolescence' has emerged as a
crucial period of identity-formation, especially in relation to questions of
sexuality, in the same period as that in which, according to many scholars,
sexuality has been made a (the) key discourse through which we learn to
understand who we are.[3] We no longer just 'do' sexual acts, we are the acts
we do, or, perhaps more accurately, the acts we identify with.[4]

In this chapter we will continue the discussion begun in Chapters 5 and 6,
by exploring the cultural work that young people-as-school-students do in
the production of their identities/identifications[5] with and/or against dominant definitions of gender and sexuality. As in the last chapter in relation to
teachers, we will maintain a strong focus on lesbian/gay-identified students,
since their identifications are likely to be under the greatest pressure –
although it must be said that adolescent identities, at least within high
income countries, can all be considered to be under pressure to a greater or

lesser extent. Indeed, to use Frank Mort's (1987) useful terminology, there is a 'medico-moral'[6] common sense about the dangers and confusions of adolescent sexuality which can be found almost every day in one or other of the popular media (see Chapter 4). This sense of danger with regard to adolescent sexuality is combined with a general lack of certainty about when adolescents stop being children, an uncertainty compounded by economic conditions and social security legislation which result in widespread unemployment of school-leavers and their being unable to leave home because they can neither claim benefit nor find jobs. One result of this is that, like children, they may be deprived of sexual privacy in ways which cause problems for many, but perhaps most acutely for those whose sexuality is perceived of as, in some way, 'deviant'.

This chapter will examine the ways in which lesbian and gay students' experiences are gendered and racialized in the course of an exploration of how school students are actively engaged in the production of sexualized identities within the context of what we have labelled elsewhere the 'presumption of heterosexuality' (Epstein and Johnson 1994). Finally, the chapter will revisit anti-sexist practice in the light of our research before we move on, in Chapter 8, to considering the 'impossible practice' of sex/uality education.

You really do form very, very close friendships: lesbian experiences

It would be a mistake to elide the experiences of young lesbians and young gay men for (perhaps obviously, though this is often ignored) their experiences are gendered in a number of ways. First, in the course of our research it became clear that many of the men's narratives involved memories of early same sex experimentation and many of them would say that they 'knew' they were gay from puberty or even earlier. In contrast, the majority of the women we interviewed talked of identifying as lesbian much later. Most often, they were at university or had been in heterosexual relationships for prolonged periods (often as much as 15 or 20 years) before identifying as lesbian. On the whole, they would talk about this transition from straight to lesbian as 'realizing that I was a lesbian' rather than as 'becoming a lesbian'. We would argue that this relatively late identification as lesbian is related to the dominant discourses of (hetero)sexuality current in contemporary British society which tend to render female sexuality passive, with women as the objects of the male gaze rather than active, desiring agents – or, if they are desirous sexual subjects, they become immediately dangerous.[7] Given common-sense perceptions of lesbian and gay sexualities as being only about sex, about 'what you do in bed', identification as lesbian or gay involves a discursive assertion of active sexuality. This makes the ability to identify against the heterosexual grain in this way much more readily available to men than to women. In this context, and notwithstanding the 'permissive discourse' which emerged in the late 1960s (see, for example, Hollway 1984, 1987), it is not surprising that women might tend to insert themselves in discourses of active and 'deviant' sexuality later than men and that, therefore, girls/women might begin to experience themselves as lesbians later than boys/men experience themselves as gay.

Baby dykes and young lesbians

There is, however, some evidence that this later identification as lesbian may be in the process of change. There is a relatively recent emergence, better established in the USA than in the UK, of young women labelled 'baby dykes'.[8] It is, perhaps, significant that 'baby dykes' have appeared on the scene during a period in which transgressive female sexuality more generally has achieved substantial media coverage, not least through the popularity of Madonna.[9] It may also be that 'baby dykes' are partly about consumption and image in/of popular culture. These young lesbians, many of them still at high school, have attracted a great deal of attention from both gay and straight press. Indeed, part of the early 1990s apparent explosion of 'lesbian chic' has focused on young, 'attractive', women supposedly less politicized through an engagement with feminism than their older (and 'unattractive') 'sisters', confident, visible on the scene, and apparently invested chiefly in having a good time. Many young lesbians may play with, perform, or invest themselves in, such images, without this constituting the whole of their lives; and their experiences at school may not bear much similarity to the media images or to their own leisure time pursuits. It may also be the case that, for some baby dykes, the fluidity of identity proposed in contemporary cultural theory is felt as a lived reality in which these young women move into and out of 'lesbian' identities in ways which might not have been so easily available to older women. For some of them, both 'being a lesbian' *and* 'being heterosexual' may, indeed, be 'phases'. In this respect, academic discourses may align with queer politics and popular consumerism to open up new ways of being and of understanding who one is.

The experiences of young lesbians who come out with even two or three others in the same school are likely to be significantly different to the more common experiences of those who find themselves isolated. Maxine, for example, spoke about the importance of the lesbian head girl of her convent boarding-school in the following terms:

> And, um, she was quite open, and, er, she was quite open about lesbianism as well, and she sort of like said there's nothing wrong with it . . . And she was pretty cool. I sort of hung around with her actually, which was unusual considering I was two to three years younger than

her. But, um, she was pretty cool. And, er, yeah, she looked after a lot of the younger ones, and again I think she identified a lot of us as being lesbian as well, and that's why she looked out for us, as the head girl, which was really nice. I'll *never* forget her – she's brilliant. I still remember her a lot.

This memory speaks to the support gained through contact with another lesbian in school, maybe especially if she is slightly older, and may also give us some feeling of the difference that 'out' lesbian and gay teachers might make to school students. However, as indicated above, Maxine's experience is rare in UK schools.

Second, as Rogers (1994: 35) argues:

Young lesbians are subject to a triple invisibility: as children, they are invisible in the adult world; as women, they are invisible in a male-dominated world; and as lesbians they are invisible in a gay world.

This should not lead us to believe that the three 'invisibilities' identified by Rogers are additive in any simple way. Rather, they shape and are shaped by each other and at different moments a different aspect of identity might become more important than the others. Of course, young gay men/boys share with young lesbians the invisibility of childhood, one aspect of which is the invisibility of their sexuality, but this too is shared in gendered ways. It is, for example, well documented that the girl child in school (and elsewhere) is significantly less visible than the boy child (see, for example, Mahony 1985; Lees 1986, 1987; Holly 1989; Deem 1991; Lees 1993), although there are important debates about the extent to which being noticed is always an advantage (see, for example, Daniels *et al.* 1996). And, of course, the three invisible gendered identities (child, woman and lesbian) listed here are far from exhaustive in the catalogue of identifications which are an inherent part of schooling and of the world more generally. As we have argued in Chapter 5, racialized/ethnic and classed identities, as well as school-based identities like 'academic' or not, are imbricated in constructions of sexuality in (and outside) schools.

Homophobia and anti-lesbianism: the limits of friendship

As pointed out above, the majority of women we interviewed talked about identifying as lesbian after leaving school. Teresa was a university student, who described herself as having come from a white, working-class background and having attended a working-class co-educational comprehensive school. Her recollection of school days is one of presuming her own heterosexuality and that of others:

Certainly when you got into your teenage years, all you talked about was boys. You just did that. You just fell into it without thinking, y'know. I s'pose it wasn't until I left school and, um, about 17, 18, when I started to think about, um, for myself, rather than what my parents wanted me to do, that I began to realise that I didn't really want to settle down and get married, because that what's my friends were beginning to do . . . So that's when I left home and moved away. But I didn't realise at the time it was because I was a lesbian. It's only, like, when I got into my twenties that I thought, 'Yeah, maybe I'm a lesbian'. But at the time, when I was at school, it was just, it was something that really never even came into our conversations.[10]

This account resonates with many others, both in the statement that 'all you talked about was boys' and in Teresa's identification as lesbian after schooling was over. Later, in the same discussion, Rachel, from a liberal, white, middle-class background explains that:

All the time I was at school, . . . everything that Teresa was saying is true. I mean we went through the stage of everyone being, when they were 14, . . . and it was all exactly the same, and, uh, the boyfriends, and all those things, which I never, y'know – well, I can't say I've never bothered. I was bothered, but I never thought I should get particularly dressed up. I didn't quite see that boys were that wonderful and I was, well I had a brother and I was sensible about boys.

In Rachel's school there was an expectation that pupils would go on to university, which was certainly not the case for Teresa and her friends. This meant that Rachel's tendency to be 'sensible', not only about boys but also about schoolwork, which provided a kind of escape for her from the constant 'boyfriend' talk of her classmates, fell within an acceptable discourse of the 'academic girl'. Sue Lees (1993: 16) suggests that:

Being academically successful involves [girls] taking on, in so far as they are permitted to, attributes that are considered to be masculine. This can only be achieved at some cost, by behaving in an 'asexual' way.

However, this depends rather on the context in which the girl finds herself. Not all girls see/experience behaving 'asexually' at school or with school friends as a cost. Sometimes girls may deliberately aim to be perceived as 'asexual' by adopting the position of 'swot' and becoming academically successful. For example, some young women who have experienced sexual abuse may choose the academic route in a deliberate attempt to avoid being seen as a sex object. Or a girl's identity as academically successful may be sufficiently rewarding in itself to more than compensate for perceived asexuality. Among these rewards may be the approval of a much-loved teacher, in a situation where the seductiveness of the teacher is more important than acceptance by other students. Equally, a young woman who identifies as lesbian but is not 'out' at school may choose academic success to avoid the compulsory nature of heterosexuality within the school, and this was certainly the case with some of our informants. Indeed, Karen Harbeck (1995: 126) suggests that lesbian, gay and bisexual teens often try to be perfect in whatever they do and therefore end up as high achievers. Neither is it clear that girls who attend single-sex schools have to behave in an 'asexual' way in order to achieve academically (see and cf. Deem 1984). Furthermore, as Valerie Hey's study of girls' friendships shows, academic success and investment/participation in the 'heterosexual economy' are far from mutually exclusive (1997: 79; see, especially, Chapter 7).

Valerie Hey found that some of her informants specifically rejected single-sex schools on the grounds that this might result in them becoming lesbian. This echoes academic and political arguments from the 1970s about the need for co-educational (state) schooling to prepare young people for their (presumed heterosexual) futures (see, for example, Dale 1971). While there is no evidence either way about links between single-sex schooling and 'coming out a lesbian' (as Gabbie, one of Hey's informants, put it: 79), our evidence would suggest that single-sex girls' schools are somewhat more friendly places for those who identify as lesbians than boys-only schools are for boys perceived as gay or than co-educational schools are for either. Chris, for example, had experienced significant harassment at her co-educational secondary school, including receiving anonymous threatening letters, when she came out as a lesbian.[11] She talked about the difference that being in a single-sex environment made:

> Once I'd started sixth form, I was completely out at school. I didn't deny that I was a lesbian, and obviously people talked about it, but most of my friends were fine. It was single-sex, it was a girls' sixth form centre, separate from the main school, and I found no problem at all, 'cos I played hockey, and most of the hockey players were lesbian. Well, a lot of them were . . . so that was okay. There was no problem.

Similarly, as Maxine explained:

> I went to an all-girls convent school . . . Retrospectively talking, I reckon half the teachers were dykes and the other half were nuns. Well, the nuns were dykes too, really, and they weren't, I don't think they were particularly religious in an institutional sense, y'know. They lived in a woman-identified environment, and that was one of the few places they could do that.

Maxine's point, here, about the single-sex environment being potentially woman-identified is well made. On the other hand, she too talks about the need for some kind of dissimulation. Intense friendships were permissible; sexual feelings for other girls/women were not. Maxine had a developed analysis of the limits beyond which one could/should not go in relation to other girls:

> *Maxine:* There's a lot of feelings between young women in schoolgirl books and schoolgirl stories about how much they cared for each other and stuff. And in that situation you *do* care for people because you live with them at school . . . You really do form very, very close friendships . . . And, so you know, we got up to a lot of things and certainly, from about the age of 10 onwards we'd all piss around and sort of, like, me and a few of my friends would sort of, like, kiss each other and *pretend* that we were practising for when we met a man. D'you know what I mean?
>
> *DE:* [*Laughs*]
>
> *Maxine:* Um, but that was the justification for a lot of the girls, where it never was for me. But I kept my gob shut about it, 'cos I, I understood that what I felt was good and I really liked it, um, and I definitely fell in love with, um, a, a, another girl at the age of 10 who was the same age as me. Um, but I also knew that I shouldn't tell her and that I shouldn't tell *anybody* about how I was feeling.

Nayak and Kehily (1996) found that girls are less likely to express extreme forms of anti-lesbian or anti-gay feeling than boys in mixed-sex schools, and, as Faderman (1981) has pointed out, there is a long Anglo-American history of intense women's friendships being permissible and even encouraged. It is, therefore, not surprising that single-sex girls' schools often provide a less overtly hostile setting for young lesbians than co-educational schools do for them or for young gay men (and 'sissies').[12] It is, nevertheless, important to note that girls may be abused and/or isolated socially for being (seen as) sexually deviant by other young women, both in co-educational and in single-sex settings. As we pointed out in Chapter 5, such deviance may take many forms: being too (hetero)sexualized and, therefore, a 'slag'; not sexualized enough and, therefore, 'tight' or a 'drag'; or, worst of all, being a 'lezzie' (Lees 1993). Girls police themselves and each other, perhaps especially their friends, with regard to sexuality:

> The microcultural politics of girls' homosociality were . . . steeped in co-appraisals. Girls insisted on making each other into acceptable selves in 'suitable' appearances and dispositions (variously caring, nice, kind, attractive, confiding but not too close), positions and predispositions which went right to the heart of how girls were supposed to perform their roles as each other's friends in conditions controlled by forms of hegemonic masculinity.
>
> (Hey 1997: 130)

'I thought I was the only Asian lesbian in the world': the racialization of sexualities

It is, as Hey points out, not only hegemonic masculinities which come into play in the construction of girls' homosocial and/or lesbian identities or relationships. These are also classed and racialized. In our study, the racialization of young lesbians' experiences in schools was raised mainly by those of our respondents whose family origins were African–Caribbean or South Asian. This is not surprising, since whiteness is as much an assumed norm as heterosexuality so that the salience of racialized identity was not so clear to our white informants as it was to those of colour (and often also to those identifying as Jewish). Lara, for example, interviewed for us by Shruti Tanna, describes how:

> I thought I was the only Asian lesbian in the world. I thought I was *the* Asian lesbian and I was put on this earth to sort of start this revolution amongst Asian lesbians, for, about being gay. And that was my purpose in life. And because of this, I mean I was convinced I was the only Asian lesbian in the world, and like, you know, my image of lesbianism was like this short-haired, really butch white dyke, bovver boots style, and here was me, this little Punjabi woman, this Punjabi girl you know at that point, who, you know, loved long earrings and long hair and liked, I mean I didn't wear make-up because I absolutely hated make-up at that point, but I used to love Asian clothes.

Lara's feeling of being alone in the world is a standard part of dominant lesbian and gay narratives (as described in the introduction to Part Two). It is also indicative of the fact that there was no one who recognized her, or in whom she could recognize herself. In effect, she had to invent herself as '*the* Asian lesbian', the only one in the world! She could not be, and did not want to be, the stereotypical lesbian of her imagination. Her description of this image of lesbianism (short-haired, butch, white, bovver boots) and the incongruity of being a 'little Punjabi woman' who was also a lesbian are particularly interesting. This incongruity is not one of Lara's own invention. Notwithstanding 'lesbian chic', the iconic figure of the lesbian in popular culture is as she describes. Asian girls and women, on the other hand, are often seen through an Orientalist lens as even more passive sexually (and in other ways) than women in general, while simultaneously and contradictorily positioned as highly (hetero)sexualized exotic Others.[13] Nevertheless, Lara was able to do a project on lesbianism in the Sixth Form, supported by her sociology teacher to whom she was, she says, completely out. Later, she also came out to some of her friends but:

> [I]t was, 'No, you're not' or, 'You fancy me', all that sort of stuff, so you get all that sort of shit, somehow you fancy *any* woman. Anyway, I think they found it hard to believe because . . . I challenged all their

stereotypes about being, you have to be white, you have to be butch, you have to be all sorts of things, you have to want to be a man for some reason, all those sorts of things.

Sunita, Lara's partner, like many other women we spoke to, did not identify as lesbian until after she had left school. She describes herself as 'naive' and 'asexual', explaining this by reference to her family's religious background:

If I tell you about my family background, that might explain a few things about me. I come from a family where there are six of us – four girls and two boys. And my family were very religious, a very religious family and were heavily involved in our local temple . . . And we had a very protected childhood. Basically at school I really wasn't aware of any type of sexuality. As far as I was concerned, I would say really that I was asexual. I had no inclinations, no conscious inclinations of any sexual preference or any awareness of my sexuality even . . . The other thing was the school I went to. It was a traditional grammar school, you know, and I hadn't heard about homosexuality, I wasn't even aware of it. Er, I wasn't aware of it at school, even at grammar school, I wasn't aware of it. I mean there were guys that fancied . . . *[2 second pause].*

Yeah, I just wasn't aware of it, I wasn't aware of anything. I was just very, very naive. Too much really. And at school there had been guys that had fancied me, but I really didn't want anything to do with them . . . because I knew that, that I'd expected to have an arranged marriage, that my parents would not like me to be with guys. It was really sunk in, you know. It was, like, brainwashed into me. And although it had never been stated, 'No, you mustn't go out with a boy' or this, I knew very well what it all meant – that I wasn't supposed to mix with guys.

Sunita's experience, as related here, bears a much closer resemblance to the stereotypical image of the protected, religious, South Asian girl than does Lara's. Like Lara's, it calls into play her affiliations to her ethnic background, though Lara's reference is to place and gender ('a little Punjabi woman') while Sunita's is to religion. For both of them, their ethnic and/or religious affiliations shape their stories of their sexuality. Sunita's assertion, repeated six times, that she was not aware of sexuality serves to emphasize the place that her family's particular version of Hinduism plays in formations of her identity. Neither Lara nor Sunita refer directly to experiences of racism, though it is there in the subtext of their interview, an assumed background to this conversation between three Asian women. As with the conversation held by KOLA, discussed in the Part One Introduction, their Asianness can be assumed, as can their experience of racism.

In the second discussion recorded for us by KOLA and published as an edited transcript (KOLA 1994), the group decided to keep the focus primarily on racism in their experiences of schooling, partly because, when they read the transcript from their first discussion, they felt that the relative absence of issues of race was problematic. Part of this discussion explored the contradictory experience of coming out but still not fitting in. Ranee, for example, remembers that at university:

> going into the groups and realising that you don't fit in was an experience for me too. But going into the group actually made me say, 'I am a lesbian', which was good after years of knowing I was a lesbian but denying it to everybody. If someone came into a room and mentioned the word lesbian, I'd hit the ceiling. I'd be so uptight, so nervous, I could feel my heart in my throat. Going into the groups, the clubs and the pubs helped me say, 'Yes, I'm a lesbian'. But I also became very aware that they were predominantly white, and they didn't take anything into account about being accessible for black people because they weren't dealing with racism within the groups. So it was like getting into a group and having your identity, but also knowing that within that group they could oppress you.
>
> (KOLA 1994: 59–60)

Here Ranee is struggling to shift the narrative framework of the coming out story as an heroic conclusion to a period of struggle, a framework which assumes whiteness by assuming that once one has come out, one will have found one's 'community'. For her, the process is more complicated: going to university and finding a group to whom she could voice her lesbian identification was a simultaneous process of inclusion (in an out group) and exclusion (from an in group). Rather than a happy ending, coming out is both a partial solution and part of the struggle. We have argued elsewhere (along with many other writers) that coming out is never a once-and-for-all event, but rather a continuing process (see, for example, Epstein and Johnson 1994; Spraggs 1994; Appleby 1996). This is made particularly clear in Ranee's shifting of the narrative framework to include the racialization of her sexuality.

Maintaining a macho image: experiences of young gay men

As is the case with women, the sexual identities of men are also gendered, classed and racialized, constructed, like (and with) masculinities, in relation to each other and to femininities (see also Mac an Ghaill 1994a, 1994b, 1996; Haywood 1996; Haywood and Mac an Ghaill 1996). However, as with our lesbian respondents, the white men we spoke to did not (usually) refer to 'race' or ethnicity, though several spoke about their class position.[14] We have already pointed out that discussion in a specifically black space produced an equivalent normalization of 'blackness' to the standard naturalization of whiteness. Nevertheless, when they were specifically discussing racism, members of KOLA pointed to a situation which Robert described as 'invidious':

> It's this invidious situation, as a black gay man, of having to deal with racism every bit as much as a heterosexual black person, but not having the confidence that you can turn to the black community for support because of all those issues around shame and fighting for our dignity anyway, and not wanting the extra burden of homosexuality or the stigma of that attached to us.
>
> (KOLA 1994: 60)

Several of our informants drew attention to the ways that heterosexuality, conventional gender relations and the naturalization of whiteness are often (re)produced through both the taught and hidden curricula.

Doing a thing on weddings: racialized heterosexuality

Ayo,[15] for instance, told us a story about how, while in the infant school, his teacher organized some 'mock weddings'. He did not remember the particular occasions of this event, but it seems likely, from his age, that it took place at the time of the marriage of Prince Charles and Princess Diana – a time when infant and junior teachers up and down the country were undertaking projects about 'weddings' and 'marriage':[16]

Ayo: We were doing a thing on weddings.

DE: So, what, you were about 6 or 7?

Ayo: Yeah, and they decided that we should all play at getting married.

DE: *They* decided? The teachers?

Ayo: Yeah. As a fun thing to do, I suppose . . . And we, some, I think two other 'couples' or, you know, speech marks *[demonstrating quotation marks with his hands]*, they progressed up an imaginary aisle and had confetti and things thrown at them and this girl who I was supposed to get married to didn't want to, and she started screaming the place down, and I was really rattled.

DE: Yeah? Do you know why she didn't want to?

Ayo: No, it was just she didn't want to. And she started blubbering all over the place, and I remember this was just a lesson.

DE: Did she just not want to get married? Did she not want to do the getting married bit, or did she not want to do the getting married bit to you?

Ayo: I definitely think it was to me. And I was told it was to me. Some of the other kids were saying, 'Look, she didn't want to do that', and it made a really deep impression. I thought, oh, she doesn't like me . . . After the break period, the teacher got, I think had done things, or whatever, made things happen, and it was all done very quickly and rushed. You know, let's get this over with so everyone's satisfied, so we rushed through this pretend ceremony and stuff, and that was it.

DE: Did the kids sort of enjoy that? Did they think it was sort of . . .

Ayo: Yeah, they thought it was a giggle . . . And you know there were actual dresses and stuff, brides' dresses and little doll things that they got dressed up in and we were dressed in our ordinary clothes I think. We didn't do any black history.

Here we see the mutual reinforcement of compulsory heterosexuality and of conventional gender relations inescapably intertwined. The playing out of the heterosexual marriage ceremony in its traditional (white, British) form with 'an imaginary aisle and . . . confetti and things thrown at them' assumes the desirability of marriage and institutionally heterosexist forms of relating and reinforces the fantasies of imaginary futures which children (and particularly girls) often express.[17] Furthermore, the dressing of the girls in 'brides' dresses' while the boys remained in their ordinary clothes represents a further reinforcement of particular ways of being girls and boys; girls wear pretty, frilly clothes while boys are more careless about their appearance. Ayo's apparent leap from the weddings to the statement that 'we didn't do any black history' is not random. The particular form of wedding played out was, as we have already pointed out, traditionally white British, while the objection of the little girl to marrying him seems not to have been an objection to getting married as such, but a rejection of Ayo himself. Whether this hostility was, as seems likely, founded on racism is neither here nor there in terms of the way Ayo understood it. His immediate shift to black history is a clear indication that he experienced and continues to experience this episode as an example of racism. In retelling the story here, he is redefining it retrospectively, for himself and for Debbie, in ways we discussed in the introduction to Part Two. The significance of this story from childhood for Ayo seems to be the particular discursive intertwining of racism, sexism and heterosexism in a particularly powerful (and to Ayo painfully memorable) form. From his adult stance as strongly identified both as black and gay, both naturalizing assumptions of whiteness and heterosexuality carried in this role-play signify the distance which he feels and felt as a child from what was considered to be norm.

Ostensibly white

Michael was another informant who had a highly-developed political analysis. He was a 'nun', a member of the queer activists' group, 'Sisters of

Perpetual Indulgence', and delighted in the transgressiveness of dressing in nuns' costume, and roller-skating through the centre of London (and elsewhere). He took part in a student focus group discussion facilitated by Alistair Chisholm and in the course of the conversation talked about being called 'homo' while still very young when he held hands with another boy.[18] He talked extensively about the changes which impinged on him because his father's job took him to several different countries as a small child. He characterized one primary school, run by Dominican nuns, as promoting sexual naivety:

> You're completely naive when you're in a convent school. You have absolutely no idea. People sort of whispered about sex in the playground but I mean the sort of idea there was basically variations on the theme of the stork and they had no idea where babies came from. They had no idea what anything did really, I mean, I think we pretty much thought you'd go to a supermarket and bought babies.

As can be seen, the lack of information which the children had did not prevent them from 'whisper[ing] about sex in the playground' but evidently the whispers were based on little and inaccurate information. It seems that what the children *were* aware of was that sexuality was, somehow, taboo. Michael found returning to what sounds like a fairly rough British state school something of a culture shock because, as he recollects:

> [Y]ou've got all these really wise know-it-all kids, or they think they know it all anyway. They've all, you know they've all seen porno movies, and they've seen the magazines, and they know all the words for everything and it was really quite, it was culture shock for me, I just wasn't used to that. I mean it would probably be the same thing if I'd been to a convent school in this country, but it was just coming from that really really sort of sheltered, pure background and then suddenly you're in the playground with people who are saying things like shit and fuck and, I mean I didn't even know these words existed . . .
>
> [Y]ou're suddenly thrown into this medium 'cos it's totally alien, and also I was getting a lot, I was getting a lot of racist abuse as well because people would find out that my mother was Indian. Because I look ostensibly white, I mean I could be Italian or something, people would automatically assume that I'm white and then it was almost worse in a way because if I looked Indian or I looked black or whatever then they'd know from the start, but somehow they'd sort of make friends with you and then know you were, you weren't even white, you weren't English, and you weren't born there. And, um, you'd just get all this stuff about, I used to, I was called mongrel and half caste and, um, got into fights with people. I spat in people's faces; I nearly pushed somebody's head through a window once.

In this part of the group discussion, Michael moved swiftly from his story of being called 'homo' and not understanding the term at the time, though he recognized it as a term of abuse, through his general naivety about sexual matters and on to being the butt of racist abuse. It is interesting to note that, in his account of the racist abuse, a key moment was when others found that he was not, as he appeared, 'white'. This is particularly interesting when related to the issue of homophobia, since the fact that it is not necessarily possible to tell whether someone is gay or not seems to be deeply threatening within popular imagination. Indeed, this threat may come from deep psychic fears related to early repressions of the homo-erotic within ourselves and to unconscious fear of the 'return of the repressed' (cf. Dollimore 1991). In line with most other contemporary theorists, we have argued throughout this book that identities have to be worked at and the boundaries policed in order to be held in place (see and cf. Rose 1983; Hall 1990, 1996b; Redman 1997). What this means, in effect, is that older, disruptive and repressed desires constantly threaten to erupt, disorganizing our sense of ourselves, of our identity, in the present. If this is the case, then the revelation that others are 'perverse' – for example by desiring people of their own sex – is likely to be deeply disturbing. It is too close for comfort, too much like our own repressed desires, and the fact that this 'perversion' may be, to all intents and purposes, invisible, makes it all the more threatening and likely to destabilize our own boundaries. This dynamic is particularly visible in some of the contributions to parliamentary debates discussed in Chapter 3 and in the scandals of the popular media discussed in Chapter 4.

One thing that really screwed me up

It is interesting, given the stress on team sports and the proposed expansion of the (quasi-military) cadet corps in British schools in the late 1990s, that many of the young gay men we spoke with detailed an intense dislike of team sports. Here, for example, are Stephen, Michael and Jamal discussing school sports:

Jamal: And one thing that really screwed me up about school was PE [physical education] and Games because it was really shit I remember. Um, just the thought, because I used to think about guys all the time and getting changed in a room full of men . . .

Michael: Oh I know!

Stephen: And showers!

Jamal: Yeah, and I used to start sweating, you know thinking, Oh my god, everybody's looking [all laugh].

Michael: I used to wear my underwear in the shower.

Jamal: I never used to have a shower, I just used to pretend . . . But

> the one thing I really hated about school was the PE and
> Games and how undermining that was you know.
>
> *Michael:* It is isn't it?
>
> *Jamal:* Bloody hell, yeah. And just cause you can't kick a football or
> you can't play rugby you're incapable, that's how I was
> really made to feel, I was inadequate as a human being 'cos
> I can't kick a football, you know . . .
>
> *Stephen:* I think a lot of it though is not being good at sport is that you
> internalise a lot of things that tell you, you know, you're not
> really masculine therefore you can't do anything that is mas-
> culine, and you just internalise it. And also there's a sort of
> thing there of, um, that men, you're in a completely differ-
> ent situation to heterosexuals where, um, what you fancy is
> the same as you but they're also your sexual rivals and so
> you're in a very sort of awkward situation with other men
> especially when you're trying to get some concept of self as
> you grow up and, and so I tended to react very very badly to
> team situations.

Stephen's analysis about the internalization by gay boys (and sissies) of
not being masculine is interesting, but it is important to note that boys who
identify as heterosexual as adolescents and throughout their lives can also
find school sports, and especially the showers, excruciating. One of the
reasons for this may be the way that masculinities are produced and policed
through, for example, comparison of penis size and other body parts.
Another is the combination of the need that boys (and men) seem to have to
boast of their sexual prowess with the need to disguise any homo-erotic
desire they might feel. Later in the same conversation, Michael remarks that:

> It's just really embarrassing and you think, Oh my god, oh my god I
> might get a hard on and everyone would know, and you have to be
> really really careful and get quite shy, well I did anyway. What I really
> objected to was the sort of mentality surrounding sports, not actually
> the sports themselves but just the sort of matiness, the sort of hetero-
> sexual laddishness that went with it.

They didn't bother me

The 'heterosexual laddishness' to which Michael refers is an important part
of the policing of heterosexuality that takes place in male homosocial settings and it is interesting to note that, in those cases where lesbian and gay
respondents spoke about having no problem with being out at school (and
as school students), this was in the context of being able to carry off particular gendered styles which are usually coded heterosexual. For example,
Simon told Debbie that:

I . . . came out at a very early age. I was rugby captain, very macho, very masculine, didn't have any problems with anybody picking on me. When you're six foot two, six foot one, six foot at a very early age, you don't tend to have many problems . . .

Simon is very clear, here, that his ability to come out while still a school student without being, as he put it, 'picked on' rested on his size and perceived macho version of masculinity in what was, as he described it later, 'a very traditional school . . . very boys-only, very rugby-oriented, very win, win, win, very academic'. Rugby clubs and rugby teams (sometimes, interestingly, referred to as 'rugger buggers') are, like the United States 'jock', notoriously misogynistic and, at the same time, notoriously hyper-heterosexual. In Chapter 8 we will be examining the necessity felt by so many boys to appear to be 'macho studs' in relation to sex education. There is a connection, here, between the costs of compulsory heterosexuality to women and to subordinated groups of boys. Simon and his first lover could come out because they were big, tough and could therefore not be perceived as gay.

This theme of his macho appearance and, at times, behaviour as a protection against being victimized for his gay sexuality reappeared frequently throughout the interview:

People just left us alone. You just didn't mess with Simon and Peter, 'cos they would beat you up. But we never, ever had to beat anybody up whatsoever. When you were as tall and as powerful as we were, people just didn't mess, you know.

On occasions, he had recourse to homophobic abuse against boys who were not sufficiently macho:

Simon: But thinking back to when I was 13/14/15, if people weren't strong enough to play rugby for the school, then my biggest upset is that, 'Oh, you're a pooftah, you Nancy boy', you know.

DE: And you would actually use those words?

Simon: And I know that I used those words, yeah. If people, if people weren't strong enough to support the school, then I would certainly have a go at them. People who wanted to be in the school play, rather than play football, would get a lashing. And, you know, that's adolescence for you, you know, you, you would attack, perhaps rather than being attacked yourself . . .

DE: So, I'm interested in this business of the use of the abuse, and the use of the rugby team macho image as a protection . . . but also using the abuse itself as a protection for yourself. Is that fair?

Simon: We, whether we were doing it knowingly or not, we felt that if we maintain this image, if we maintain this macho image, and we attacked others, we would be left alone, and nobody would attack us, you know. 'Look at Simon and Peter. They're not queer. Why don't we all strive to be like Simon and Peter?', you know.

It is illustrative of the heterosexual presumption, as it operates in school contexts, that Simon and Peter's friendship was, apparently, not taken to be a gay relationship. In his very sports-oriented grammar school, the pair were taken as a model to aspire to. One can well imagine teachers drawing attention to them in this way, which is extremely unlikely to have happened had their gayness been acknowledged within the school. Unlike Harry, in the previous chapter, they were able to find a way of being recognized which did not require them to cut and stretch themselves out of recognition to themselves. From the perspective of a gay man now involved in all kinds of gay activism (for example the organization of Gay Pride), Simon remembered moments of homophobia with some embarrassment (hence, perhaps, the use of the word 'upset'). What is interesting, however, is that what was being required here both of him and by him was a version of masculinity which was not only apparently heterosexual *because* it was macho, but one which is particularly unfriendly to women. Furthermore, other, less macho ways of inhabiting masculinity were derided – 'People who wanted to be in the school play, rather than play football, would get a [homophobic] lashing.'

Sexuality and anti-sexist practice

Máirtín Mac an Ghaill citing Sue Lees (1987: 180), draws attention to the fact that:

> For the students, the assimilation of non-macho behaviour to feminine behaviour was illustrated in relation to the ubiquity of the term 'poof' which, in 'denoting lack of guts, suggests femininity – weakness, softness and inferiority'.
>
> (Mac an Ghaill 1994a: 165)

This was illustrated time and again both in our interviews and in our observations of classroom behaviours. Frequently, the homophobia expressed towards non-macho boys was in terms of the assertion of their similarity to girls. This took place at all levels of schooling, from the Early Years to the Sixth Form.[19] Indeed, it is interesting to note that the behaviour of 'tomboys' within the primary context is much more acceptable than the behaviour of 'sissies'. This, we would suggest, is because for a girl to be more like a boy can be interpreted positively, while for a boy to be more like a girl is, almost invariably, seen as problematic because being a girl is, in some sense, disreputable. Insults like 'poof' and 'Nancy-boy' are used, then, to control not only the sexuality of boys but also the forms of masculinity they are likely to adopt, at least within the school context. Interestingly, Mac an Ghaill (1994b: 93) gives an example of a boy who was enabled to occupy a non-macho version of masculinity (including the achievement of academic success) by virtue of his previous association with a 'hard' gang and his consequent reputation as a 'hard man'.

Boys frequently seem to survive by dint of appearing 'hard' and macho, especially in boys-only schools. At the conference (held in April 1995) of the London Association for the Teaching of English, Debbie attended a workshop on anti-sexist work with boys. Here the facilitator, Rav Bansal, pointed out that as soon as he started overtly anti-sexist work in his single-sex boys' school, he was labelled as gay and that, in order to retain any kind of credibility, he took care to drop remarks about having a girlfriend. Furthermore, in the tape of a lesson which he played for the workshop, we heard him clearing the air for discussion of feelings and sexism with the remark that 'we know that none of us here are gay'. As he explained, he was distinctly uncomfortable about this but felt that it was the only way in which the boys in the class would even begin to entertain the ideas with which he was confronting them.

The extreme homophobia and misogyny of single-sex boys' schools and classes have significant implications for practice, to which we shall return, in relation to sex education, in the next chapter. There is clearly a moral and pragmatic dilemma here. If, as seems to be the case, sexism, homophobia and heterosexism are inseparable, it may well be that anti-sexist practice is impossible in the absence of policies and practices which reduce the anxiety which boys seem to feel about the possibility of being labelled as gay. Furthermore, in recent moral panics about the supposed 'underachievement' of boys, one area which has been almost entirely missed is the association of studiousness with being gay and/or sissy in school(boy) cultures. The cultural work which is done in schools to promote heterosexuality and heterosexism is, it seems, disadvantageous not only to girls and sissy and/or gay boys, but to conventionally heterosexual boys intent on asserting their 'normal' masculinities.

Conclusion

The experiences of the lesbian and gay students whose stories constitute the substance of this chapter tell us something, too, about how heterosexualities are constituted. From the reductive, biological discourses which frame adolescence, through the racialized and gendered positionings of our informants, to the brief excursion into the realm of anti-sexist school practices, one theme runs through the chapter: the policing of sexual desire(s) and the constraints under which young people make themselves. In making themselves in conditions not of their own choosing, students become invested in certain ways of being in relation to the dominant discourses which are always already in place. For most students, social recognition, a key element in identity formation, is generally obtainable only within the terms of dominant discourses. Identify formation is, then, neither a kind of voluntaristic supermarket where different sexual (and other) identities can be taken off the shelf and bought or rejected at will, nor is it completely determined by 'socialization' or any other means. The processes of 'Learning Sexualities' take place through the telling, to self and others, of 'sexual stories' about oneself. Some of these stories are dominant, others oppositional, both reacting against dominant discursive frameworks and drawing on emergent ones. Here, we have focused on the oppositional, the lesbian and gay-identified student, but always in relation to the dominant of normative heterosexuality. In the next chapter, we shall be returning to the problematic of heterosexuality, exploring the ways that sex education reproduces dominant sexual discourses to the disadvantage of girls, women and subordinated boys.

Notes

1 See Johnson (1986) for discussion of the 'circuit of cultural production'. See also du Gay *et al.* (1997) for a later adaptation of the idea of this circuit.

2 See Stainton Rogers and Stainton Rogers (1992: Chapter 9) for an interesting discussion of the construction of the category adolescence from the mid- to late nineteenth century onwards.

3 See, for example, Foucault (1978) and Weeks (1985, 1991) for discussions of the historical emergence of sexual categories, and Sedgwick (1990) for a sustained exploration of the significance of the homo/hetero divide and of the metaphor of the closet. Plummer (1995) explores the ways in which certain sexual stories gain currency in historically specific circumstances while others are untellable (and unhearable).

4 It is not, for example, necessary to be involved in sexual relationships or to be active sexually to identify as lesbian, gay, bisexual or, indeed, heterosexual.

5 See Hall (1996b) for a discussion of the advantages of using the term 'identification' in preference to the term 'identity'.

6 'Medico' because of assumptions about flowing hormones and their effects in creating rampant teenage lust; 'moral' because of the fears of teenage sexuality becoming uncontrollable and, therefore, the considerable energy spent on trying to control it through a range of strategies ranging from public disapproval to legislation.

7 There is an enormous feminist literature dealing with women and (mainly hetero)sexuality. See, for example, Cartledge (1983); Vance (1984); Hollway (1987); Holly (1989); Collins (1990); Holland *et al.* (1990); Walkerdine (1990);

Holland *et al.* (1991); Jackson and Scott (1996); Leonard and Adkins (1996); Richardson (1996).

8 We would like to thank Diana Paton for pointing this out to us.

9 See Schwichtenberg (1992) for discussion of the polysemic meanings of Madonna texts and the significance of Madonna.

10 See Alistair *et al.* (1994) for an edited version of this discussion.

11 See Epstein (1997a) for further discussion of this in the context of a consideration of masculinities in schools.

12 There may also be a classed aspect to this. Valerie Hey's (1997: 128) ethnography indicates that middle-class girls 'had more material and sexual freedom' than working-class girls, notwithstanding the significant degree of regulation they all lived out.

13 See Parmar (1987: 99) for a discussion of:

> [t]his contradictory imagery of Asian women – represented on the one hand as sexually erotic creatures, full of Eastern promise and on the other as completely dominated by their men, mute and oppressed wives and mothers.

These contradictory representations can be seen as Orientalist. While Said's (1978) generative text deals hardly at all with women, several feminist authors have engaged with his ideas to explore the many ways in which Orientalism is gendered (Miller 1990; Chatterjee 1996; Lewis 1996).

14 This may also have had something to do with the politics of many of our university student informants, several of whom were involved in socialist groups of one description or another.

15 While Ayo's parents were from Nigeria, he himself was born in London and identified as Black, British and gay.

16 My memory of being a classroom teacher in an infant school at this time was that I was the only member of staff to resist undertaking a whole-school project on 'Weddings' (but not divorces!)

17 It is extremely common for little girls, asked to draw themselves as grown-up, to illustrate themselves as brides. Little boys, on the other hand, will frequently illustrate themselves in the pursuit of some kind of 'masculine' job, for example as astronauts or train drivers.

18 See Epstein (1997a: 111–12) for a discussion of this story.

19 See Epstein (1995) for further discussion of this point in relation to primary schooling.

CHAPTER **8**

An impossible practice?
Sex/uality education in schools

On 24 February 1997, the *Today* programme on BBC Radio 4 broadcast a feature about new research, just published, about young people's 'sexual conduct' (Ingham 1997). This was the first of several programmes on radio and television over the following two weeks to feature this particular research. The focus of the coverage was the finding that sex education is more successful in the Netherlands than in the UK in reducing the number of unwanted teenage pregnancies. Not for the first time, a researcher in the area of (hetero)sexuality and sex education had found that:

> ... the major complaint by young people regarding content [of sex education] related to the over-emphasis on biological aspects and a relative neglect of emotional and relationship issues, and much greater coverage of more 'sensitive' issues, such as homosexuality, abortion and abuse, was consistently called for.
>
> (Ingham 1997: 11)

In contrast, Ingham said, young people in the Netherlands described earlier and more liberal sex education, with many more of them reporting that it had begun in the primary school and covered many of the issues which British young people identified as missing. The study confirmed yet again (Fisher, Byrne and White 1983; Fine 1988; Ray 1994) that, contrary to the common-sense beliefs expressed in the popular press, and in debates on sexuality and sex education in Parliament which we discussed in earlier chapters, liberal and open approaches to sexuality and to sex education are more likely to contribute to reducing the rate of unwanted teenage pregnancies than those emphasizing morality or abstinence. According to

Ingham, the very much lower rate of teenage pregnancies in the Netherlands does not reflect a striking difference in the ages at which various events take place (first sexual feelings, 'deep kissing', fondling and so on), but rather a much greater comfort with sexuality, more confidence in negotiating sexual encounters and, importantly, less expectation that particular gender roles must be performed in particular ways in heterosexual relations (1997: 13). Of course, a reduction in 'unwanted teenage pregnancies' (unwanted by whom?) is an excessively narrow definition of what sex education is for. However, Ingham also points out that young women in the Netherlands were less likely than those in the UK to report regrets about their first sexual experiences; that young Dutch men were more likely than British young men to say that relationships were important to them; and that early sexual relationships in the Netherlands generally lasted longer both before and after sexual intercourse took place than in the UK. Overall, he suggests that 'the immediate context in which first intercourse occurs is related to (and may be the result of) the greater comfort with, and "respect" for, members of the opposite sex experienced by young people in the Netherlands' (1997: 13).

Approaches to sexuality and to sex education in the Netherlands are characteristically considerably more liberal than they are in the UK (or the USA). There is, for example, no discriminatory legislation against lesbian or gay sexuality, but rather a high level of state and public support for lesbian and gay equality, demonstrated by state funding for lesbian and gay centres and the 'homo-monument' in central Amsterdam, dedicated to lesbians and gay men killed in the Nazi concentration camps during the war. The age of heterosexual and same sex consent is set at 16. However, there is statutory provision that sex involving partners between 12 and 16 will not be prosecuted unless complaint is made by the young person or her/his representative. Sex education in the Netherlands begins at primary school and is much more open than it is in the UK. Relationships, pleasure and desire are up for discussion as well as different methods of contraception – and, indeed, it is regarded as part of good practice that young people should experience buying condoms, bringing them back to school and then discussing how they felt, whether they were embarrassed, and why. The results of these liberal approaches in school and more widely seem to be that Dutch young people tend to handle sexuality with more confidence and in more safety than comparable young people in the UK. Within the British context, Ingham reports similarly that early, unprotected intercourse within brief relationships was more likely among young people from what he terms 'moralistic' and 'laissez-faire' families than from 'realist/humanist' families. He defines 'moralistic' families as those where abstinence outside marriage is regarded as the only proper course of sexual action and 'laissez-faire' families as those in which adults show no interest at all in young people's activities. Evidence from the US also suggests that young women attending schools which promote sexual abstinence as the only acceptable course are more likely than those in schools with more liberal sex education programmes to become pregnant in their teens (Trudell 1993). In other words, situations where young people were unlikely to be able to discuss with significant adults questions of sexuality (either because they would be disapproved of, or because they felt there was a lack of interest), were more likely to enter into 'unsafe' (both physically and emotionally) sexual encounters than those who were able to have such discussions.

In this chapter, we bring together the concerns of the rest of the book, showing how the public and political discourses about sexuality and schooling which we explored in the early chapters and the more specific constructions of sexuality in schools examined in the last three chapters coalesce and are negotiated in the sex education classroom. For many sex education teachers, the findings of Ingham and others described above will come as no surprise. But these teachers are working in situations where, in every lesson, they have to walk a tightrope. If they are too open, even where they restrict themselves to answering pupils' questions, they risk public recrimination conducted in the media (as demonstrated in Chapter 4) and Parliament (Chapter 3). Their attempts to educate students about sexuality take place in a context complicated by the homophobia of many students, the macho performances of many boys, the wish of many girls (and boys) to be desired, the official taboos on talking about sexuality in school, and the need to make the sex education classroom a (relatively) safe space in which all their students can talk about sexuality. For sex education teachers, even more than for teachers in general, they are 'damned if you do and damned if you don't'. It is for this reason that we have entitled the chapter, 'An Impossible Practice?' The chapter will draw on published and unpublished material from other researchers,[1] on observation in a single-sex girls' school and a co-educational school and on interviews, to explore the ways in which teachers walk this particular tightrope.

The biggest casualty of the National Curriculum

I think the biggest casualty of the National Curriculum, especially in science, has been the opportunity to explore the social implications of sex and sexuality. At the moment although . . . there are still aspects of it on the syllabus they're very much the mechanical biological aspects of it, and opportunities to discuss things like contraception and families and values have largely gone. Because of the time constraints, I feel very, um, I feel [2 second pause] bad about this actually, because I think there is, um, it's something we have an obligation . . . to make sure that pupils have access to this kind of information.

(Jennifer Kidd, Head of Biology, Heathlands School)

There are many paradoxes in the legal status of sex education. As pointed out in Chapter 3, it is compulsory for all secondary schools to provide sex education, but it has been excluded from the National Curriculum apart from those places where it features in the science curriculum. Parents may withdraw their children from sex education, but not from National Curriculum science. In the latter context, curriculum content, as laid down in the Education Act 1993, and within the science curriculum itself, is restricted to, as Jennifer Kidd puts it, 'very much the mechanical biological aspects of it'. At the same time, Circular 5/94 (DfE 1994) advises schools that sex education should be taught within a framework which stresses relationships:

> The purpose of sex education should be to provide knowledge about loving relationships, the nature of sexuality and the processes of human reproduction.
>
> (DfE 1994: para. 8)

However, within the terms of the law, the desired stress on relationships can be avoided by parents on behalf of their children as can information about HIV and other sexually transmitted diseases (which are not included in the science curriculum), but mechanical biology cannot. Young people in schools, even if they are over the age of consent, do not have a right of appeal against parental decisions to withdraw them from sex education. If they remain at school after the age of 16, they can, in theory, take their parents to court (and it is likely that the European court would rule in their favour!), but this is clearly not a practical proposition! Any 'unresolved disputes' between parents must also be referred to the courts (DfE 1994: para. 36), but the child must be withdrawn from sex education pending a court decision. If young people attend further education colleges, however, their parents lose the right to make decisions about their sex education. It is no wonder that conscientious teachers, like Jennifer, 'feel bad' and find themselves caught on the horns of what she described as 'a real dilemma'.

Jennifer's school had experienced what it means to be taken up by the popular press when:

> [W]e had, uh, a very thorough programme looking at . . . 'cos I remember wanting to talk about incest on the curriculum and the head being a bit reticent about it, and there was a girl in my year group whose father had just been convicted for incest with her and two of her sisters and it was in the local newspaper . . . and the school actually, although it wasn't named, but it was criticized by the judge for saying that there'd been nothing on the curriculum about incest.
>
> (Jennifer Kidd)

It is unclear what the judge thought the school should have had on the curriculum about incest. Did he, for example, imagine that telling the students about incest would help to prevent it, or that schools are in a position to impact significantly on the family lives of their pupils? Or was he saying, simply, that having incest dealt with in the curriculum would lead to earlier disclosure by its victims? And did he think that this would be an easy path for a school to take? In any event, the school's response was to:

> [contact] the Rape Crisis Centre who gave talks to the whole year group about personal space and invasion of personal space, and then leading into incest. We had, I remember, I was amazed by how many students actually had personal experiences, not . . . there were three or four cases of incest that presented, but, you know, of over-amorous uncles and other situations that they'd been in. So we formed a group with the school and the Rape Crisis Centre to try and equip these students to assertively deal with these, with this unwanted overtures from male relatives and family members. And it was great, it was very successful. The . . . and for many years we linked in with the Rape Crisis Centre.
>
> (Jennifer Kidd)

Hearing of this, one of the national tabloids sent reporters to wait outside the school gate, called the head and asked, 'Why is there so much incest at your school?', and, according to several of the teachers, including the head, made the lives of teachers and students a misery:

> The angle that they were taking was that, 'Well if this is necessary what's happening at this school that girls are so vulnerable?' and so, 'that there's such a high incidence of, you know, incest and rape taking place'. They were like frothing, getting quite frothy at the mouth about the whole thing.
>
> (Jennifer Kidd)

As Head of Biology and as Head of Year, Jennifer had particular responsibilities with regard to sex education and, as a result of the incest case, had developed, with her colleagues, a wide-ranging programme for sex education, influenced by feminism, which raised issues around girls' rights not to be subjected to sexual harassment and violence as well as questions about sexuality in relationships and negotiating sex. With the introduction of the National Curriculum, the Education Act 1993 and falling expenditure on schools and on sex education, much of this had fallen by the wayside, much to Jennifer's regret:

> I think the more work you do on sex and sexuality the more students feel [you are] accessible, feel they can talk to you about it, and much more things manifested then than ever do now. Things like pregnancies and incest, they manifested much more frequently at that time.

And I'm sure it's not because it's happening less, just that there are no sort of inroads, or few perceived inroads for the students.

While it may be easy to criticize the approach developed by the school as being overly concerned with the victimization of girls at the expense of exploring the pleasures of sexuality (see, for example, Fine 1988) or the dialectic between pleasure and danger (see Vance 1989), it is important to recognize the radicalness of the kind of work undertaken at Heathlands School. Contacting the Rape Crisis Centre, an avowedly feminist organization, was a brave step and, as can be seen, did not go unpunished. There were ongoing effects from the school's experience at the hands of the media in that context. For example, several years later, the head was initially extremely wary about allowing us to do research in the school, and was particularly worried about the possibility that we might be focusing on lesbian and gay students[2] and the possible interest that this might spark in the media. Of all the teachers concerned with sex education with whom we spoke during our research, only one did not mention the school's experience over the incest case, and she had only been in the school for a term before we arrived.

(Preventing) reproduction and (creating) dis-ease

Jennifer's concerns in our interview with her were largely about the legislative framework which made it difficult for her and her staff to offer the kind of sex education which they would have preferred, one which included social contexts and social costs – although, as we have noted above, the primary discourse of sexuality in use is one about dangers (of pregnancy and male violence). It is important to remember that these dangers are very real. Nevertheless, this stress on sexuality as danger contributes substantially to those constraints on sex education which are produced *within* the school and the classroom. We have discussed, in Chapter 5, some of the more general effects of the combination of attempts to desexualize schools at the official level with the prevalence of sexuality at the informal level. There we pointed to the burden of representation of sexuality in the school which certain pupils, like Tracy, were made to bear. In that chapter we referred to an incident in a sex education lesson, when Tracy produced a condom. Here we wish to consider further how sex education, specifically, is constrained and produced in contradictory ways by the attempted desexualization of schools.

As we have argued earlier, the sex education classroom forms a kind of ghetto within which sex is supposed to be discussed, in contrast to other spaces within the school where such discussion is taboo, conducted (figuratively if not literally) 'behind the bike-sheds' (also the mythical venue for heterosexual encounters). As we have shown in Chapter 5, one effect of the attempted desexualization of schools is that talk about sex and about sexuality becomes a key resource for student resistance to the authority of schools. Thus, although there is plenty of 'sex talk' which takes place in schools, the way sexuality figures in most interactions between students and teachers involves strategies of control and resistance, and often antagonism. The ghetto of the sex education class cannot be made immune from the general dynamic of these interactions, simply by giving permission for discussion about sex/uality in that particular school context and only that context. It is, therefore, unsurprising that within sex education lessons, talk about sex is often difficult and strained. Michelle Fine (1988) discusses in some detail what she has labelled as 'the missing discourse of desire' in relation to adolescent girls in school sex education. We have suggested, throughout this book, that this is a discourse (for girls and boys) which is more or less forcibly excluded from official school contexts, assuming, therefore, a kind of subterranean quality which erupts from time to time in a variety of forms. Furthermore, as Fine notes, even in sex education classes (where sex is to be spoken about), female desire and pleasure do not play a significant part in the official discourses of the classroom and male desire is often seen as something dangerous to girls and to be controlled by them:

> The authorized sexual discourses define what is safe, what is taboo, and what will be silenced. This discourse of sexuality mis-educates adolescent women. What results is a discourse of sexuality based on the male in search of desire and the female in search of protection. The open, co-ed sexuality discussions so many fought for in the 1970s have been appropriated as a forum for the primacy of male heterosexuality and the preservation of female victimization.
>
> (Fine 1988: 40)

Our own research would suggest that Fine's findings in the American context bear strong similarities to sex education in the context of English schools. For the most part, the sex education teachers we have observed and spoken with would fall into the category which, in Chapter 3 in relation to political positions, we labelled 'social liberal'. This perspective is well illustrated in the approaches they adopt in the classroom with which, at one and the same time, they try to open up discussion in a liberal, tolerant and relatively safe fashion and remain uneasy about sex as pleasure or desire. In this context, sex is heterosexual, male desire is dangerous and girls are victimized, as in Jennifer Kidd's account quoted above. In Heathlands School, sex education about sex as danger was often done in imaginative ways which caught the interest of the girls. For example, early on in our observation there, four of the girls spoke to Debbie at some length about the impact of a viewing of the Australian film, *Shame*, which explores issues of rape from an explicitly feminist perspective. The girls introduced the film as an example of what they considered to be the best sex education they had ever received as soon as Debbie explained to them that she was interested in sex education:

> The girls spoke enthusiastically about having seen *Shame* during their sex education class last year. They talked about how shocking and upsetting they had found it, but also how convincing. 'Women are never believed', was one comment and one of the other girls commented that this was particularly true in closed (and close) communities, like the Muslim one within which they all lived. 'It happens all the time' they agreed.
>
> (Debbie's research diary)

There are a number of interesting things going on here. First, the girls clearly valued the opportunity which use of the film had opened up for them to talk, amongst themselves (and with a researcher), about male violence. This was an opportunity which seemed not to exist in their outside-school community and which they valued partly for that reason. Their comments about the 'close/d' community within which they lived should in no way be taken as a rejection of that community. Rather, the embrace of the community (the 'closeness' of which they spoke) was, at one and the same time, stifling (closed) and a welcome source of protection within a racist world (close). The girls strongly identified as Muslim and as 'Asian', but that did not mean that they were uncritical members of the community. Second, their engagement with the film could be read as a feminist one, which located rape and sexual violence as aspects of male power. Third, this engagement was both intense and long-lived. Their conversation with Debbie took place slightly more than a year after they had viewed the film and discussed it in sex education lessons and they had leapt into the discussion with only the smallest of prompting ('I'm interested in what you think about sex education lessons' was Debbie's opening gambit). It seemed, in this conversation, that the film resonated, for the girls, with knowledges they had obtained from their own and/or other girls'/women's stories of rape and sexual violence outside the school situation and this lent its use as a teaching tool particular power. Sexuality as (male) danger was clearly an important issue for them.

Of course, male desire *is* often dangerous to women and children, and girls, young boys and women *are* often victimized through the exercise of male power in the realm of the sexual, but this is not all there is to be said on the subject. As Fine (1988: 42) comments:

> The fact that schools implicitly organize sex education around a concern for female victimization is suspect . . . for two reasons. First, if female victims of male violence were truly a social concern, wouldn't

the victims of rape, incest, and sexual harassment encounter social compassion, and not suspicion and blame? And second, if sex education were designed primarily to prevent victimization but not to prevent exploration of desire, wouldn't there be more discussions of both the pleasures and relatively fewer risks of disease or pregnancy associated with lesbian relationships and protected sexual intercourse, or of the risk-free pleasures of masturbation and fantasy?

In nearly 30 years of teaching and research, we have never observed a sex education lesson in which the pleasures and relative safety of lesbian sex were discussed, and neither have any of our colleagues with whom we have discussed this. It would be very surprising, given the political and media discourses surrounding sexuality and education, if we ever did! Nor have we ever observed a lesson in which masturbation was mentioned in terms of pleasure or as a form of safe sex.[3] Fine's analysis of the 'missing discourse[s] of desire' and pleasure is a helpful starting point, but we wish to push her argument a bit further. As our analysis of dominant discourses of sexuality in earlier chapters shows, pleasure in sexuality is seen as 'naughty but nice' for men, and evidence of degeneracy in women.[4] However, when children are brought into the picture, as they inevitably are in schools, discourses of childhood innocence combine with versions of sexual pleasure as 'naughty but nice' in ways which strengthen views of sexuality and, in particular, sexual pleasure, as corrupting. In this context, a discourse of desire and pleasure is not merely 'missing', but is actively excluded if not forcibly expelled. Thinking of it in this way helps us to understand the vehemence of moral panics around sexuality and education discussed in Chapter 4 and also the dilemma of sex education teachers.

Sex education, then, is focused on the twin poles of the mechanics of reproductive biology and the dangers of pregnancy and sexually transmitted diseases. With these foci, sex education can hardly fail to reproduce (hetero)sexism. The positioning of girls within conventional narratives of heterosexuality is achieved through a strong focus on the dangers of penetrative heterosex and their responsibility to resist, saying 'no' to the marauding depredations of heterosexual young men. Michelle Fine's argument, quoted above, that such sex education 'seriously miseducates young women' could equally be applied to young men/boys who are positioned by these discourses of the dangers of male desire squarely within what Wendy Hollway (1987) has called the 'male sex drive' discourse. Being so positioned is actively productive of those heterosexual masculinities which sexually endanger young women: there are ways in which boys may seek to 'live up to' (or down to) their generic reputations as 'studs', who all 'want the same thing' from the girls of their acquaintance. It is also problematic for those boys who, for a variety of reasons, are uncomfortable with such positioning.

Macho studs: sex education and boys

A strong concern in relation to education in the mid- to late 1990s has been about boys, who, it is said, are 'underachieving', prone to 'mess about', and are generally disruptive. As with so many other aspects of schooling, some of this may come to a head within the context of the sex education class-room. Just as this is the one school space where discussion about sex is required rather than forbidden, so too is it almost the only space within which feelings constitute part of the subject material. But feelings are, for the most part, forbidden to boys in schools and to (appear to) be a macho stud is, for the most part, required. Of course, this does not mean that every boy is, or appears to be, a 'macho stud'. There may be other strategies available to boys in certain circumstances as, for instance, in the example quoted from Redman and Mac an Ghaill in Chapter 1, where moving into the sixth form opens up possibilities for boys to position themselves as masculine in intel-lectual ways ('intellectual muscularity'). Being good at sport may also be a resource open to some and we wrote earlier about young gay men who were able to be open about their sexuality because they were over six feet tall and in the school rugby team – they were, it seems, 'macho' but not 'studs' in the heterosexual economy of their school (Chapter 7, see also Epstein 1997a).

Nevertheless, to be identified as a sissy is to invite homophobic abuse, whether or not one defines oneself as gay, often in the form of more or less ritualized humour. Kehily and Nayak (1997) argue that the use of humour and insult constitutes a regulatory practice by young men in schools through which they establish and exhibit heterosexual masculinities. The forms of humour and insult employed are, they suggest, primarily either sexist (for example, the teasing and harassment of girls or insults to other boys via insulting their mothers or sisters) or homophobic abuse of young men who did not display 'hyper-masculinity':

> Humour is an *organising principle* in the lives of young men within school arenas. Humour was seen as a regulatory technique, structur-ing the performance of masculine identities. Young men who did not circumscribe [sic] to the hyper-heterosexual practice of masculinity were ridiculed through humorous rituals. Consequently, those who worked hard at school, or exposed sexual vulnerabilities in relation-ships with young women, were targets for banter and abuse . . . [H]umour was a style for the perpetual display of 'hard' mascu-linity and also a means of displacing fears and uncertainties.
>
> (Kehily and Nayak 1997: 84)

It does not, therefore, come as a surprise to find that boys tend to use sex education lessons as a place for the particularly strident exercise of hyper-heterosexual performance, for the sex education class is the place, *par excellence*, where uncertainties and fears about heterosexuality might (inadvertently) surface. And, of course, the positioning of young men as predatory in sex education discourses about sexual danger (for young women) precisely reinforces both the psychic and social investments of young men in these 'hard' masculinities and their fears about not 'performing' adequately as heterosexual men.

Measor *et al.* (1996) observed two single-sex sex education lessons in the same school. In each case, the lesson plan was the same, but the reaction of the boys and the girls was entirely different. While the girls' lesson was 'a picture of conformity' (277) and real interest, they describe the boys' lesson in the following terms:

> There were about the same number of boys in the group as there had been girls, but the room seemed to be filled to overflowing with people, noise, chaos and disruption, pushing and shoving. Bags were thrown and so were some half-serious punches; chairs squeaked and scraped, boys squirmed and desks rattled.
>
> In the combined teaching, teaching practice supervision and research experience of the researchers, we had rarely seen such high levels of disruption in a class and we have struggled to find language to provide an evocative picture of the situation. Sue [the family planning nurse conducting both lessons] tried constantly to create order and discipline in the class, demanding silence and asking for attentive behaviour; she was unable to secure it . . .
>
> There was, it occurred to us as observers, an atmosphere almost of panic in the room. Boys continued to react strongly to the sight, smell and feel of the [contraceptive] devices throughout the lesson. The horseplay and throwing of contraceptive devices around also persisted.
>
> (Measor *et al.* 1996: 278)

We have quoted from this article at some length, in part because, notwithstanding their struggle to find the right words, Measor and her colleagues have, indeed, drawn an evocative picture of the boys-only sex education classroom. In our own research, we have not experienced this level of disruption, but neither have we ever observed a boys-only sex education lesson. Their description would seem to bear out our suggestion that the sex education class is a place of particular discomfort for young men, in which they find it more than usually compelling to be seen to be unquestionably heterosexual and unquestionably successful at heterosexuality by virtue of displaying their 'hardness' (figuratively if not literally).

Measor *et al.* point out that the single-sex sex education lessons which they observed took place at the request of the girls because they found the boys to be disruptive and offensive in mixed-sex lessons. They end their article by suggesting that there should be at least some single-sex classes in sex education because this resulted in better experiences for the girls and because their 'observations suggested that boys seemed to react negatively whether they were in single-sex or mixed groups at this age' (Measor *et al.* 1996: 287). They suggest, further, that it might help if more sex education for boys was provided by men, pointing out that in the schools they researched, they found only one male sex education teacher. Our own opinion, supported by such research evidence as exists, is that boys are generally likely to be more disruptive not only in sex education classes but in lessons in general when they are in single-sex classes and especially if anti-sexism is part of the agenda (Bansal 1995; Kenway *et al.* 1997).

There seems to be little evidence to suggest that sex education conducted by men for boys in single-sex classes would do more than exacerbate the generally competitive macho performances of a significant proportion of the boys unless strategies were found to disrupt and subvert the hegemonic discourses of masculinity and masculine sexualities which pervade schools. Admitting anxiety, ignorance or puzzlement is simply too risky for boys in the homophobic contexts of schools and all-male classes, perhaps especially those, like sex education, where the possibilities of 'heterosexual failure' are actively present even if not overtly discussed. Furthermore, it is common for male teachers, especially in all-male classes, to adopt a kind of 'mateyness', relying on misogyny and homophobia to help them control the unruliness produced by the hyper-masculine performances of some of the boys. As Jane Kenway and Sue Willis with Jill Blackmore and Leonie Rennie (1997: 31–2) point out:

> Joking with the male teachers [in single-sex boys' classes] is seen as a particular advantage, the class is more relaxed and not so strict and students and teacher can enjoy being sexist and uncouth with impunity. Single-sex provides new opportunities for exercising old style masculinity.

As we argued in Chapter 6, in relation to Harry's story, his adoption of violence towards his students as a strategy to establish himself as apparently heterosexual is a notable demonstration both of the different resources available to men and women teachers, but also of the pervasive homophobia of the school. It is likely, then, that a male teacher of an all-male class would/could do little or nothing to change that without an attempt, at the very least, to make schools (and male teachers!) generally less misogynist and homophobic.

We are not, here, arguing against single-sex classes, since we recognize that they do provide a better experience for girls, not only in sex education but within schooling in general. Girls' experiences are at least as important as those of boys and it is certainly not fair to ask them to bear the burden of civilizing their male peers. However, we are concerned that, as a strategy, single-sex sex education does not, of itself, answer Madeleine Arnot's (1984) question, 'How shall we educate our sons?' This remains a stubbornly difficult question to address, though there are some indications of possible ways forward. However, as Kenway *et al.* (1997: 29) point out, 'those approaches which address both *different masculinities* and *gender relations* . . . are the least common, the most necessary, but the most difficult' (emphasis in original). We would argue that the development of such interventions in sex education would need to include not only 'the missing discourse of desire' in girls, but the opening up of schools and schooling beyond the sex education class to possibilities of 'alternative masculinities'.

Anne-Mette Kruse (1997) recommends strategies for teaching boys and girls in single-sex groups for part of the time, and then bringing them back together to discuss what has happened in their single-sex groups, partly for working on certain subject areas but, more importantly for our purposes, in the development of anti-sexist work for boys and girls. Rob Pattman (1997) argues for a similar strategy in sex education, with single-sex groups discussing questions about particular items of popular culture (for example, newspaper reports) and then reporting back and debating their responses in a cross-gender group. There is a potential danger in this approach, if the tasks undertaken tend always to end up in a kind of blaming directed at boys, which is not unlikely when dealing with issues like sexual harassment. Nevertheless, it may well represent a strategy for opening up new possibilities in sex education.

Sex Education Forum (1997), in their extremely useful 'Factsheet' on the sex education of boys, draw particular attention to the importance of whole-school policies on sex education. Such policies, they suggest, 'need to include specific mention of the way in which boys' needs will be met' (3). They also stress the support that teachers need in developing approaches to sex education generally but aimed at boys in particular, suggesting that specific in-service training could play a big part in helping teachers deal better with both the aggressiveness and insecurities of boys.

'Love hurts': love and sex

Although, as we have argued above, the discourse of desire is more or less missing from sex education in schools except in the context of male desire as danger, there is a discourse of 'love' which at certain moments might shade into a discourse of desire. For the most part, however, 'love' is seen as an embarrassment, especially by boys. This is in line with the strong prohibition on boys' expressions of 'soft' emotions (anger is allowed) in school contexts. In Chapter 4, we discussed the ways that the male sex drive discourse coexists with the 'have/hold' discourse (Hollway 1987) in popular culture. Clearly, discourses of love are also related to the have/hold discourse, a discourse which calls on boys/men to 'protect' and girls/women to 'love and cherish'. Hollway describes how, positioning themselves with the have/hold discourse, the couples she researched placed the emotional work of their relationships primarily on women, and how this might be disrupted in certain circumstances when men took on the caring role. Within informal contexts in the school, girls may well partake in extensive discussions and fantasies about love and romance and certainly use popular cultural resources, like girls' magazines and love stories (sometimes distributed free with the magazines) to do so (see also Kehily 1996). However, girls too may express embarrassment at the notion of 'love', within the context of sex education (but not in the context of informal discussions about boyfriends). In one (girls-only) lesson which we observed, the teacher began the lesson with the reading of two poems about 'love'. Her announcement that this was how the lesson would start produced several 'oohs' from the class in tones which seemed to assume that this could be expected to be a lesson involving the opportunity (at least) for rather risqué jokes. Several girls immediately fell into giggles which it took them some time to control.

As became clear from the discussion in the small groups in which they were required to work, most of these students equated 'love' with heterosexual relationships. One group had written on their paper, 'Love hurts'. It was this comment which the teacher picked up in the whole-class discussion following the brainstorm:

Teacher: [reading from the sheet of paper] 'Love hurts', what does it mean?
Anne: [giggling in an embarrassed way] He doesn't love you. You can't tell him.
Jill: If someone dies when you care about it, it hurts.
Teacher: What's the difference between caring and loving, being in love and love?
Whole class collapses in giggles
Teacher: [after shushing the class several times] Can anyone share an experience of love with us?
Prolonged silence
Jill: Nobody knows what love is.
Brenda: [calling out] I do!
Teacher: Explain that a bit more.
Brenda: I'll come back to that, Miss. It's vanished.

Here we see a teacher perhaps beginning to introduce, through a discourse of love, the 'missing discourse of desire', but the attempt does not work. It seems that the context even of girls-only sex education in school is not conducive to open discussion of desire. Indeed, such a discussion might be particularly difficult because of the need which girls feel to guard their reputations against the charge of being 'slags' (Lees 1993), even (maybe especially) within the context of a single-sex classroom. It might also have something to do with the one-sided revelation of personal experience which is being required of the girls here. This is a difficulty for teachers of sex education. Teachers regularly (quite casually and without thinking twice about it) do draw on their heterosexual relationships for examples of things they have seen, done or experienced to make their lessons come alive for their students. However, within the context of sex education this is made all but impossible by the firm positioning of sex within the realm of the private (notwithstanding the efforts of feminists to make the personal political). The desexualization of schooling adds to this, and, as we argued previously:

> Reflection on the conditions required for two adults, even in the context of intimate relations, to communicate openly and effectively about sexuality may help us to understand some of the dimensions of the problem for the sexuality educator. The ability to discuss and to recognize the reality of the other's experience depends upon a mutual struggle to subvert existing power relations. But sex education in schools occurs within the context of grossly unequal relations ... [L]iberal methods prescribe that the students' own experience is, at least, a starting point. Students are likely to resist such one-sided revelations.
>
> (Epstein and Johnson 1994: 219)

It is not surprising, then, that attempts to open up discussions of sex and of desire founder on the embarrassment of the students (and teachers). One strategy which teachers can employ to defuse this is by distancing the lesson from the revelation of the personal through fictionalizing devices. Mary Kehily (1997), for example, describes a co-educational sex education class in which the students were given the task of writing fictional letters as if to magazine 'agony aunts'. Most of the problem letters she discusses are written by girls and most of them turn on problems produced for girls in their relationships with boys: fear of being pregnant, fears for reputation, fears of abandonment, fears of having become infected with HIV, fears of violation form the substance of their letters. Kehily discusses only one letter written by a boy, which is about the demands made on him by his girlfriend, who wants him to spend more time with her and less with his mates. There is also one letter, written by a girl, which posits a boy with homosexual desire. Of course, the nature of the fantasies explored in these letters lies partly within the genre of the problem page letter, as does the advice which the class proffers in discussion of each problem, which seems almost always to have involved recourse to some form of counselling. But it is, none the less, striking that the predominant emotion imagined by the girls is fear, and desire, where it does appear, is implied rather than stated. For example, one letter reads, 'I have recently slept with my boyfriend and everything was perfect' (Kehily 1997: 4). However, even this letter goes on to detail a story of infidelity (on the part of the boy) and fear of pregnancy and disease. The only letter which seemed to be overtly about desire was the one about being gay. Kehily's account of the class's reaction to this letter makes it clear that this provided the occasion for an unusual loss of classroom control by the teacher as the boys shouted their defiance of any possibility of their experiencing gay desire, while the girls seemed to take pleasure in claiming the power in the classroom by teasing the boys. Here the teacher's attempt to open up the discussion for more liberal views of gayness foundered on the heterosexism and homophobia of the school culture and on the defensiveness of the boys.

Liberal discourses in the age of AIDS

If liberal possibilities seemed to be difficult to achieve with respect to homosexuality, our research showed pupils more open to the expression of liberal ideas in relation to HIV. In East City School, we observed a series of four lessons with a co-educational class about HIV. These lessons seemed to have two aims: first, to open up a discussion of 'safer sex', and second, to appeal to the sympathy of the students for people with AIDS. The first lesson consisted of watching a video of an episode of *Different Worlds*, an American show from the Cosby stable, about young people, most of them African–American, in high school. The episode, which featured a girl who had contracted HIV from having had unprotected sex with her regular boyfriend, engaged the students' serious attention and, as one of the girls commented afterwards, 'It hit me that one day you're lying on the grass and five years later you're dying.' For the most part, the class went along with the preferred reading of this episode, which was clearly that one should not be mean to people with AIDS. Several of them were quite judgemental about the unkindness of the fictional students in the show, but none admitted to being able to imagine themselves as becoming HIV-positive.

The second lesson in the series consisted of the giving of information about the transmission of HIV, followed by an exercise in which the students were asked to write their reactions on 'Post-It notes',[5] which they then stuck on to prepared sheets of paper carrying six different statements:

1 We've all got to stop having sex.
2 Drug addicts deserve what they get.
3 If it's gonna get you, it'll get you.
4 If I got AIDS I'd kill myself.
5 Real men don't get AIDS.
6 AIDS isn't my problem.

As they moved around the classroom, sticking their Post-It notes on to the bigger sheets of paper, several of the students were anxious to assert both their knowledge about HIV and their liberal credentials in relation to it. Thus, nearly all the comments were definitely on the liberal side, expressing sympathy and support of those who are HIV+ and suggesting that safer sex was the way to deal with the fear of infection. However, in relation to the second statement, when HIV was linked to the taking of drugs, students' notes suddenly became extremely moralistic. Here the majority of written reactions were in agreement with the statement that drug addicts deserved what they got, with only three students writing more sympathetic reactions:

> No they do not you might be lucky and a lot of people are under pressure and might do it to help them. Their lives might not be as good as ours.
> Not really. I sympathise with them.
> <u>Not</u> true.
> (Original emphasis and punctuation retained)

The last two lessons in this series were devoted to the preparation and performance of sketches about AIDS by small groups of students. Without exception, these sketches showed the students as extremely understanding and supportive of a person with AIDS, sometimes with someone represented as a 'stranger' voicing more illiberal opinions. This may be a measure of the success of the AIDS lobby in combating early representations of AIDS as the 'gay plague'(Redman 1997) and in enlisting sympathy for victims of the disease. However, taken in conjunction with the generally illiberal responses to drug-takers with AIDS, it can also be read as a kind of conformity to what were seen by the students as the values of the teacher, powerfully set up in the episode of 'Different Worlds' shown in the first lesson. This is not to dismiss the liberal views expressed as meaningless, for just as the performance of homophobia and misogyny help to entrench and reproduce them, so too with more liberal discourses. Bernstein's (1971) dictum that 'Education cannot compensate for society' is clearly as true in relation to gender and sexuality as it was, when he wrote it, in relation to class. Nevertheless, schools can, in certain circumstances and perhaps in small ways, contribute to producing alternative discourses through which young people and their teachers can come to understand the world.

Informal sex education: educating ourselves

Mary Kehily (1996: 7) argues that:

> [P]opular cultural forms were frequently used as a resource by young people and provided a framework for discussing issues of sexuality. Plots from the soaps such as *Brookside* and *EastEnders*, characters from soaps such as Hannah in *Neighbours*, episodes of *Byker Grove* and TV personalities such as Barrymore were cited and used as reference points in discussions of sexual relationships, physical attraction, parental constraints and homosexuality. These cultural references acted as a vehicle enabling sensitive topics to be articulated and

provided a way of looking where personal experiences could be juxta-posed with media experiences.

She goes on to discuss the ways in which girls, in particular, use teenage girls' magazines as a resource for a version of collective self-education, buying the magazines, sharing them, discussing them, using them in friendship groups for humour and for information. Like everything else, this is a gendered activity. Boys might look at such magazines, but would risk being called 'sissy' if they admitted to it (though they might admit to looking at men's magazines with their diet of sport and sex).

These magazines have caused some outrage in the popular press and Parliament. William Oddie (1997), for example, writing in the *Daily Mail* talks about one article from *Mizz* as being 'nothing more than a guide to behaving like a tart', and uses the occasion to attack the 'liberal sex edu-cation/"health"' establishment, referring back to older 'scandals', like that leading to the withdrawal of the Health Education Authority's *Pocket Guide to Sex* for young people (discussed in Chapter 4). What strikes us, examin-ing the magazines, is that, in contrast to school sex education, a discourse of female desire is strongly present, and, of course, this is partly what Oddie is objecting to in the quote above. However, it should not be assumed that this is entirely progressive. In some ways, there is a reversal here, with men (boys) being the sex objects in ways usually associated with women, with pictures of half-dressed 'gorgeous boys' or 'hot bods' occupying a significant amount of space. At the same time, girls need to make themselves attractive to boys/men, to be desirable as well as desirous in quite conventional ways. Furthermore, it seems that girls must learn about boys and their problems as well as dealing with their own. For example, one issue of *Bliss* came with a free booklet entitled *Steamy Boys' Confessions* (Tobin 1997), which includes 'confessions' about problems with sweatiness and spots, as well as about being 'bad' or 'soppy'. The magazines are, moreover, entirely hetero-sexist. There is no possibility, within their discursive frameworks, for girls to experience same-sex desire or pleasure.

Nevertheless, the girls' collective use of such resources gives them a greater sexual literacy and opens up possibilities for their use in sex education. As we have seen in this chapter, the use of a popular television programme in deal-ing with AIDS helped the teacher set up a significantly more open space for discussion than is usually to be found in sex education classes. We would agree strongly with Mary Kehily when she suggests that, for girls at least:

> Contemporary popular culture, for example soap operas, teenage magazines, problem pages and music videos can be a useful resource for teaching and learning. They offer pupils and educators the [chance] to critically explore public images of sexuality.
>
> (Kehily 1996: 8)

While boys seem to make less collective use than girls of popular cultural resources, they, too, are familiar with them. Jane Kenway and Lindsay

Fitzclarence (1997) propose the use of 'narrative therapy' to help boys develop 'alternative narratives' to those that are hegemonic around violence. This strategy involves not only 'naming the dominant plot', e.g. 'being tough', but also finding exceptions to the dominant plot and developing narratives which move towards a 'counter-plot' (131). Such exceptions are to be found in popular culture. For example in *EastEnders*, Tiffany and her baby are, at the time of writing, living with Tiffany's gay brother and his boyfriend in a 'pretended family' relationship. This is clearly a better environment for the baby than would be provided by a reconciliation with Grant, with his history of domestic and other kinds of violence. This is very much the view expressed by both boys and girls with whom we have discussed this *East-Enders* story.[6] We would argue that there is a need to use popular culture in sex education, to build on the resources which students already have, in contexts which allow them not only to explore gender difference but also intra-gender differences, not only heterosexual, but also same-sex desires and pleasures.

Sex education which locates itself within biological discourses of reproduction cannot fail to be heterosexist in nature. At best, any possibility of non-heterosexual relationships can only be tagged on at the end. Furthermore, such an approach means that sex education automatically becomes about the dangers to girls/women from boys/men. Such an approach, as we have demonstrated, results in boys feeling that sex education is for girls, encourages heterosexism, homophobia and misogyny. It is, then, clearly disastrous for sex education to begin with reproduction and its prevention, with sex and its dangers. Rather, sex education should begin with relationships, respect and difference, taking up questions of reproduction along the way rather than privileging them from the start.

Notes

1 We would particularly like to thank Mary Kehily for allowing us to use unpublished material from her work towards her PhD.
2 See Redman (1994) for further discussion of this wariness.
3 Kehily (1997) has discussed sex education lesson in which students wrote letters to fictional agony aunts and then discussed the advice they would give the writer. One of these letters was about a 'flasher' who masturbated in front of a girl. This lesson is discussed in greater detail later in this chapter.
4 There are, of course, many feminist analyses which point to the 'madonna/whore' dichotomy which positions women as either chaste, moral mothers and wives or as wicked, immoral and loose women (see, for example, Coward 1984; Vance 1989).
5 These are small, sticky sheets of paper with a level of 'stick' which allows them to be temporarily stuck on something, removed and stuck on something else.
6 By the time of publication, Tiffany and Grant are living together, having renewed their marriage vows in a church blessing.

CHAPTER 9

Conclusion: sexuality and education otherwise

In this book, we have made a detailed critique of dominant discourses around sexuality and schooling. But we have also identified some discourses and practices which seem to us to hold out some hope for developing what one might call 'sexuality and education otherwise'. We want to end the book by pulling through the theoretical and political positions which have informed our analysis throughout. These positions and practices are not merely personal. We see plenty of evidence of similar ideas and practices: in the ideas of lesbian, gay and feminist activists, in the voluntary organizations and their coordinating and campaigning bodies like the Sex Education Forum, in academic theorizing and research, in some episodes and storylines in popular culture, and certainly in some of the ways our 'families' (in narrower and larger senses), friends and allies live their daily lives.

In our boldest moments, we can identify a cluster of ideas and practices which are 'emergent' in the sense in which Raymond Williams uses this term in an often-quoted series of essays which reflect on Gramsci's concept of hegemony (Williams 1977: Chapters 6, 7, 8 and 9). Williams identifies three moments or aspects of historical formations: the dominant or hegemonic, the residual and the emergent. Dominant or hegemonic ideas and practices are those which, for most people, seem to be common sense, almost incontrovertible – for example, that conventional families are the most 'natural' way of organizing reproduction, child care and mutual support. The residual are those ideas which, in some respects, seem to have had their day, to be almost quaint, but have left traces and still influence our everyday lived experience. The idea that women who have children while single are 'miserable sinners' would fall into this moment, despite

significant attempts to resurrect it. The emergent aspects of a historical formation are those ideas which are new, almost waiting to happen. A notion
of full equality for lesbians and gay men is one example of this – although
it seems that it is being accepted by more and more people. Williams
stresses that the residual and the emergent may be incorporated into the
dominant, the first as an aspect of 'selective tradition' – those things we
choose, collectively, to remember and honour in, for example, the National
Curriculum – the second as a source of renewal. The case of the residual fits
many of the sexual phenomena we have been discussing. Williams uses the
example of religion:

> Thus organized religion is predominantly residual, but within this
> there is a significant difference between some practically alternative
> meanings and values (absolute brotherhood, service to others without
> reward) and a larger body of incorporated meanings and values
> (official morality, or the social order of which the other-worldly is a
> separated, neutralising or ratifying component).
>
> (Williams 1977: 122)

Contemporary debates within the Christian churches about gender and
the priesthood (absolute sisterhood?) or about homo-erotic sex and love or
about the social creation of poverty would be cases in point.

The emergent is, most plainly, the fact 'that new meanings and values, new
practices, new relationships are continually being created' (123). But there
are distinctions to be made here too, between the 'merely novel' within the
dominant culture and the 'emergent in the strict sense', that is, elements that
are 'alternative or oppositional'. One aspect of the emergent is rooted precisely in what the dominant social order 'neglects, excludes, represses, or
simply fails to recognize' (125). It is these elements which form the basis for
opposition, though also for incorporation and change within the dominant
order. As we have seen in Chapter 2, Jacques Derrida engages with very similar processes in his idea of 'the trace' (compare the residual) and 'the supplement' (compare the emergent). Williams is particularly close to Derrida
when he makes the intriguing suggestion that often 'what we have to observe
is, in effect a *pre-emergence* [original emphasis], active and pressing but not
yet fully articulated', present for example in the tension we may feel between
'what is actually being lived' and 'what it is thought is being lived' (126 and
131). As we suggested earlier, it may be that certain elements of sexual life
or discourse – for example the recognition of homo-erotic feelings in the life
of *everyone* – constitute such a 'pre-emergence' or 'that dangerous supplement' which has the potential to transform the whole field.

What are the elements, or some of them, in sexual life and discourse which
we see as active, pressing, underarticulated perhaps, but capable of trans-
forming the field, untangling perhaps some of the knots we have examined?
We want to highlight four such leading elements, which are as often

experienced as feelings or intuitions. At the social level they are 'not yet fully articulated'. This can mean that they are, as yet, in a practical state, things people do intuitively but without theorizing them, and not fully developed in explicit knowledges. But it can also mean – and here we add to Williams – something like the opposite of this: ideas which are elaborated all right, often unbearably so, but are restricted to particular social groups or practices, to academic theorizing and research for example. Sometimes the priority is not to elaborate them further theoretically, still less say something 'new', but actually to grasp practically, to practice them or make them practicable. So long as this practical elaboration has not been achieved (if it is achievable) it remains possible to deride and marginalize such insights, as 'only theory'.

1 The social production of sexuality/sexualities

According to much contemporary cultural theory and research, sexual categories and what counts as the sexual domain are produced in the play of culture and of power. They are not given outside discourse – in 'biology' for instance, which is, itself, a discourse. In other words, as we argued in Chapter 1, culture is decisive in the meanings we make of our bodily experiences. Sexual and other discourses refer to and work upon the body, changing its meanings, and also, over very long historical periods (but speeding up today), changing bodies materially too. Indeed, if we think about transsexual people, it seems as if it is easier to change one's body significantly, through surgical and hormonal intervention, than it is to change one's gender identity. Thus, although there always is a bodily moment in the relay of sexual relations, always some given possibilities and limits, bodily differences must be *made* to mean, can be made to mean *differently,* and can be imbued with more or less *significance*.

The relationship between procreative functions and sexual activity is an excellent example here. In everyday practice this is not a necessary link: very little sexual activity is procreative in intent; much sexual activity is not procreative in form. This is true for lesbians and gay men, but it is also true for most heterosexual sex. Even more startling disarticulations exist in (often specialized, restricted, unelaborated) scientific and medical discourses. Donor insemination, a very old and 'low tech' practice, and the new reproductive technologies mean that sexual intercourse is not necessary for conception to occur. These practices could easily be disarticulated from notions of the heterosexual nuclear family, as donor insemination sometimes is when used by lesbians, with or without the help of clinics. More 'high tech' practices, like *in-vitro* fertilization (IVF), are policed to produce heterosexual families (Steinberg 1997). In their case, sexual activity is displaced, technologically mediated, where mothers are adjudged 'fit' by doctors, usually only when they are in heterosexual relationships which, at least, approximate marriage and (always) with male consent. The recent story of Mrs Blood, whose wish to conceive using her dead husband's sperm almost foundered on his lack of written consent, is a case in point. While next-of-kin can give or withhold permission, regardless of the wishes of the deceased, for the use of any organs for transplant, Mr Blood's sperm were not at the disposal of Mrs Blood, who had to go through several court procedures before receiving permission to take the sperm out of the country. In the eventual outcome, we see another example of an association between sexuality and nation – other countries may allow the use of a dead man's sperm without his written consent, but it cannot be done in the UK. Overall, the emergence of new reproductive technologies as possibilities, like the emergence of contraception as a (not unproblematic) reality, must already change the way we think about the sexual. In any case, the sexual and the procreative are not in everyday experiences (still less in science or social theory) anything like so closely related as dominant discourses still (residually) insist.

Many practical – educational and political – implications flow from this leading contemporary thesis. It follows that biologistic accounts of the sexual are themselves constructions, which can be questioned. As we have shown in Chapter 8, their use as the basis of curricular or institutional distinctions is clearly flawed, producing problems both for young women and for young men. As we have seen throughout this book, conceptions of the sexual as biological are clearly open to interrogation. This is especially important since young men and women are so often pressured to live the sexual *as though it were* biologically given. As we have seen, the male sexual drive discourse often underpins the idea that men have a right to sexual satisfaction, an underlying premise of so much abusive sexual behaviour. Furthermore, sex education which starts with the biology of reproduction is inherently problematic because it cannot be anything other than heterosexist and therefore sexist (Butler 1990; Epstein 1996b).

It follows too that we can start to understand schools not as places that reflect natural distinctions, but as one of the places where sexual (among other) identities are produced. Of course, the sexualities and the sexual are produced in many different sites, often with competing versions and representational forms. This includes all the practices of everyday life as well as the kinds of public discourses we explored in Part One. But schooling plays an important part in this process. It is actually constitutive of sexual problems and possibilities, especially around the dynamics of adulthood and youthfulness, of teacher and taught. Much of this book has been an exploration of these processes, taking the standpoint of some of the sexual identities which are usually relatively marginalized – and commonly most insightful about schooling sexualities as a whole.

Sexual identities are formed in schools whether they have elaborated sex education programmes or not. Indeed, from our point of view, there is something quite awkward about sex education as a separated, specialized practice – although it needs to retain a place where it is consciously taught. A further practical implication is that better or worse outcomes will depend on practices that go right across the formal and hidden curriculum and policies for the school as a whole. Sexuality is present throughout the formal and informal curriculum anyway. As we have suggested in Chapter 8, there are opportunities within the formal curriculum to address the construction of versions of gender and sexual identities in public representation, including the media, popular culture and politics. School policies for everyday interactions on sexual issues are also helpful. As we saw in the story of Mr Stuart, when teachers are self-reflexive about their involvement in sexual discourses and practices, things shift. In his case, we saw a confluence of his own critical reflexivity, with that of the head and other colleagues, to produce policies for the school which, in turn, allowed his pupils the chance to do their own thinking in this area. We certainly believe that to teach thoughtfully about sexual (as many other) matters is to accept change in yourself.

2 Sexuality, sexual difference and power

Sexuality and sexual differences are not only socially produced, they are also invested with power. If the first thesis constitutes a thoroughgoing critique of the (re)naturalizations of moral traditionalism, the second thesis constitutes a critique of classic liberal inheritances. A contrary stress on power and 'empowerment' marks the impacts of feminist and lesbian and gay activism and of research which takes its agenda from these sources. Researchers and activists have examined the ways in which homosexualities and femininities are subordinated to male heterosexual agendas in the larger culture, including sex education programmes. They have also come to recognize how boys are stranded, mute or obstreperous in an activity for which girls are altogether better prepared through their informal cultures of talk and their readings of magazines and other popular cultural forms. As we have shown, an exploration of these informal cultures shows emergent as well as residual elements and this provides ambiguous resources for teaching. On the one hand, popular cultural forms reinvest in traditional, oppressive values. On the other, they sometimes pull the rug out from under these very values. In both cases, their use can make teaching a great deal easier.

The informal and differentiated cultures of boys and girls show not only differences (and similarities) between them, but also differences within each category. Male experience is not homogeneous, any more than female experience is, and our examination of the experiences of gay students shows how important it is to address the specificities of masculine experiences of the sexual. At the same time, we have shown that the often 'superior' feminine knowledges of sexuality, drawn from girls' collective making of meaning in informal cultural spaces, are still usually organized around the pleasing of men. More generally, as we have shown, it is important to see that power always runs both or all ways: that concrete situations always involve different relations of power, which recognize and disorganize differently according to the discourses in play. Girls can take power (more than symbolically) but do so according to the resources offered in other social relations. There are definite problems with the simpler power models which were dominant in social–radical thinking in the 1970s and early 1980s and still guide activism in some spheres, as we have seen in our discussion of the strategy of outing as an element in gay politics which presupposes fixed sexual identifications and reproduces, while valuing differently, quite familiar forms of homophobia.

Throughout this text we have been especially concerned with the ways in which sex/gender differences are intertwined with the relations of power that run between children and adults, especially in and around the school context. In the politics of sexuality it seems to be especially important to take the side of children – without endorsing everything that children do! Of the aspects of contemporary policy that anger us, many concern children. We are thinking especially of the coercion of children implied in dominant models of parenthood or in the representation or treatment of criminalized children, or of the overriding of children's voices and knowledges in matters of child sexual abuse, or of the bland neglect of the personal effects of heightened scholastic competition on the experience of childhood, or of the relative spatial confinement of contemporary children robbed of independent movement. These pressures bear most heavily on children who are oppressed in other aspects: as children with inclinations to same-sex desire, or as children disadvantaged in education already for reasons of class, ethnicity or race.

3 Addressing pupils' sexual cultures

Much of the research for this book was done via ethnographic approaches. One advantage of such ways of finding out about schooling and sexuality is that it involves taking children seriously, not absorbing them into 'families' and (ungendered) parents, but listening to what they say. Doing this makes it impossible to make the kind of overarching claim for childhood innocence, for example, so beloved by the popular press. Rather, we have drawn attention to the multi-layered complexities of the sexual cultures of schoolchildren and brought into question some common-sense assumptions about 'protection', arguing, rather, for a stance which accords to children rights – to knowledge, to control of their own lives and bodies, to support.

Perhaps there are three main implications for sex educators here. First, young people clearly learn – unevenly and differently – their own lessons about sexuality. This takes place in their own informal cultures, separate from, but in relation to, adult interventions. This does not mean that they do not need protection, sometimes, from the power of parents, other adults and other children, but vulnerability follows from unequal power (including physical force) and from imperfect knowledge, not from 'innocence'. The argument that a careful sexuality education is a corruption of innocents cannot be sustained. Second, teaching that fails to take account of the sexual knowledges and identities that are already in process among young people will produce unintended consequences, or fail to engage with youthful interests. It will also be readily mocked. Third, a knowledge of youth sexual cultures and forms of popular cultural representation are essential in devising effective teaching strategies. Popular cultural forms are, aside from peers, the most important raw material (already processed) of sexual knowledges and outlooks for young people. Teachers can treat them as points of departure without stopping there, helping students to deconstruct the embedded meanings and common senses of, for example, girls' magazines or music videos. Important too is a knowledge of the characteristic sexual dynamics of the school, especially the tendency of sexuality to be positioned for many pupils as a kind of 'playground' in contestation with the official (including 'progressive') knowledges of the school. It is possible to notice, honour and recognize these knowledges, which, as we have seen, may show great subtlety and care for others, without endorsing the frequently sexist or homophobic contents – to take them, in short, their good sides and bad, as a ground of further intervention. As Rachel Thomson (1994) has put it: it is important to involve young people, 'recognising and respecting the reality, diversity and cultural specificity of their experience'. This, as we have indicated above, implies a strong concern with children's rights and their moral autonomy.

4 Understanding difference differently

One of the key emergent forms in sexual politics is the move towards understanding inequalities and, especially, the self-empowerment of subordinated groups through, for example, lesbian and gay or black activism. Some of the most interesting contemporary theoretical approaches to sexual and other identities come out of a kind of activist discomfort with some of the more simplistic assumptions about the monolithic nature of power which has sometimes seemed to constitute a kind of oppositional common sense. For example, black and other anti-racist feminists, lesbians and disabled feminists have raised questions about too easy versions of feminism which see men as having all the power and women as having none. As 'academic activists' have thought through these questions, many have come to stress, as we have done in this book, the complex interdependence of opposed categories, and the ways in which more powerful groups are deeply implicated in relations of inequality.[1]

Sexual categories are not understood passively, as diversities that coexist, but dynamically, as differences that interact and produce each other within structures of power. It is possible to split off sexual identities mentally as though they can be performed outside these relations. As we saw in Chapter 3, Neil Kinnock can split off homosexuality from 'the family', and 'tolerate' it, but splitting is vulnerable to the homophobic question, 'Doesn't toleration ("promotion"?) threaten "the family"?' Lesbians and gays can be split off as a 'community' and separately funded, as happened in the days of the Greater London Council, but as the abolishing of the GLC and scares about HIV and AIDS show, this accommodation is unstable in both political and psychic ways. It is easily breached by a recognition of connections, even if these take a hysterical form: the demonization of the person with HIV or AIDS as the 'monstrous other' in a threatening horror narrative for example (Redman 1997). Similarly, the flows of fascination and anxiety are hardly containable, as we have seen, when homosexuality is discussed in a predominantly heterosexual context, in a sex education lesson for instance. Nor is splitting only a heterosexual defence. There is a long-term tension in the history of lesbian and gay cultures between 'minoritizing' or separatist versions of identity and 'universalizing' versions (Sedgwick 1990). Both strategies may see lesbian and gay sexualities as challenging heterosexual norms and institutions (see, for example, Rich 1980). But 'minoritizing' strategies construct lesbian and gay identities as very separate from straight identities and from each other in ways that may reinforce the gender divide. 'Universalizing' strategies, in contrast, deconstruct the interconnections of gendered and sexualized categories, stress the instability of these boundaries and seek to transgress boundaries on both gender and sexuality. What makes it 'universalizing', in this context, refers not to seeing one dominant experience as representing the whole, but rather that 'queer' presents a subversion of the whole sexual landscape.

Throughout this book, we have explored the interconnectedness of sexualities: in the histories of sexual movements, in questions of nation, in the discursive frameworks for politics and the media, in school-based experiences and practices. In dominant binaries like heterosexual/homosexual and man/woman, identities are necessarily defined in an ambivalent, shifting and internal relation to each other. Moreover, these two particular binaries – of gender and of sexuality – are also complexly interlocked (Rubin 1984; Butler 1990, 1993; Sedgwick 1994). Looking at these processes through the lens of hegemonic masculinities in conventional heterosexuality, boys must mark out their differences from girls, but also from boys who are made to represent some deviant form of masculinity, typically associated with homosexuality. The question of homosexuality remains fascinating, however, as the abusive predilections of male heterosexual cultures suggest.

Heterosexual identity is constituted by an imaginary expulsion of homosexual desire which is externalized as Other, as Not Me, along with, for example, racialized categories. Imagined, active but held at bay as well is some (racialized) version of the 'feminine'. But this is not the end of the story, for expulsion is, in one sense, in vain, because heterosexual male identity needs an internalized version of the feminine and must handle the confusions of the homosexual in order to preserve the ongoing sense of difference.

The obsession with homosexualities among defenders of 'the family' requires an explanation of this sort: why, if defenders of 'the family' see it as natural, are they so fearful of the threat? Why do they continue to offer up the dangerous, beguiling figure of the assertive and seductive homosexual on the surface of their polemic? In these dialectical relations, boundaries are both fixed *and* destabilized. More assertive performances of homosexual identity will, for example, produce heterosexual disturbances and new forms of containment, expulsion or identification. Under some circumstances, the binaries themselves – as 'pure' identities, straight or gay – break down, diversify. All these processes are visible in today's sexual exchanges. As we have shown, these processes are also at work in the face-to-face relationships of school, particularly in the boy homophobias and misogynies through which heterosexual masculinities are constituted. Indeed, we have argued that patterns of homophobia as expressed in parliamentary politics resonate with and replay the schooling experiences of elite men (see and cf. Mac an Ghaill 1994b).

We have been preoccupied, in this book, with conservative obsessions around sexualities, but also with liberal failures to engage with the power relations and the emotional charge that they entail – for example in Neil's story in Chapter 6. As we have pointed out, the very defensiveness of conservative selective traditions suggests that *heterosexuality* is fragile at many different levels. But there are ways in which liberal politics may recuperate heterosexuality in unexpected ways through its incorporation of versions of lesbian and gay identities which can be 'tolerated', as we demonstrated in Chapter 3 in our discussion of Nigel Hawthorne (see also Rubin 1984).

Such understandings make nonsense of attempts to exclude homosexualities from educational curricula or anywhere else. Culturally and psychically, they are ineradicably and bountifully present. The problem is how to handle interaction in ways that contain self-defeating splittings off or hysterical expulsions, that equalize and educate. Conservatives are right to see sexualities as interdependent – to see the celebration of 'queer' as affecting 'the family'. We see this threat as part of the emergent moment in contemporary sexual politics, welcoming it as a way of changing sexual boundaries and their resulting power relations. The desire to be a powerful man is not, however, fixed in nature. Like other identities, it is fluid, subject to change once the defended boundaries are made conscious and the psychic and social policing abandoned. When/if this happens, the 'threat' can become a 'promise', a way forward to more egalitarian and ductile sexual and gendered relations. In this way sexual diversity can become a resource for making up some new, and better, possibilities.

This book has involved an intensive, multi-layered engagement with the kinds of common senses about sexualities which we are schooled to take for granted. It is an example of the kind of work that can be done. As such, it is part of emergent strategies and counter-hegemonic discourses. As we have demonstrated, these are also visible in everyday life and, particularly, in popular culture. The straight/gay distinctions are among the most striking of our sexual differences. They are central to the disciplining and excluding mechanisms of dominant discourses. They are hedged around by inhibitions in the school and other contexts. They are also shifting and unstable in contemporary popular culture and ways of life. For all these reasons the borderlands between lesbian and gay and straight sexualities and identities are both peculiarly 'dangerous' and particularly generative of emergent forms and novel solidarities. While it is still rare, schools, teachers and students already work across these boundaries in respectful and liberatory ways. The very contradictions in the dominant which we have identified provide the ground for change. It is our hope that this book will contribute to that change.

Note

1 See, for example, Stallybrass and White (1986); Butler (1990); Rutherford (1990); Dollimore (1991); Bhabha (1994).

References

Alistair, Dave, Rachel and Theresa (1994) So the theory was fine, in D. Epstein (ed.) *Challenging Lesbian and Gay Inequalities in Education*. Buckingham: Open University Press.

Anderson, B. (1991) *Imagined Communities: Reflections on the Origin and Spread of Nationalism* 2nd edn. London: Verso (first published 1983).

Anthias, F., Yuval-Davis, N. and Cain, H. (eds) (1992) *Racialized Boundaries: Race, Nation, Gender, Colour and Class and the Anti-Racist Struggle*. London: Routledge.

Appleby, Y. (1995) 'Voices from the heart-land: lesbian women and education', unpublished PhD thesis. University of Sheffield.

Appleby, Y. (1996) 'Decidedly different': lesbian women and education. *International Studies in Sociology of Education*, 6(1): 67–86.

Arnot, M. (1984) How shall we educate our sons?, in R. Deem (ed.) *Co-education Reconsidered*. Milton Keynes: Open University Press.

Avis, J., Bloomer, M., Esland, G., Gleeson, D. and Hodkinson, P. (1996) *Knowledge and Nationhood: Education, Politics and Work*. London: Cassell.

Ball, S. J. (1990) *Politics and Policy Making in Education: Explorations in Policy Sociology*. London: Routledge.

Bansal, R. S. (1995) ' "Looking over your shoulder": a study of anti-sexist discussions in an all-boys classroom', unpublished MA course work. University of London Institute of Education.

Barker, M. (1981) *The New Racism: Conservatives and the Ideology of the Tribe*. London: Junction Books.

Barrett, M. and McIntosh, M. (1982) *The Anti-Social Family*. London: Verso.

Bartell, R. (1994) Victim of a victimless crime, in D. Epstein (ed.) *Challenging Lesbian and Gay Inequalities in Education*. Buckingham: Open University Press.

Benjamin, J. (1990) *The Bonds of Love: Psychoanalysis, Feminism and the Problem of Domination*. London: Virago.

Bernstein, B. (1971) Education cannot compensate for society, in School and Society Course Team at the Open University (eds) *School and Society: a sociological reader*. London: Routledge and Kegan Paul in association with The Open University Press.

Bhabha, H. K. (1994) *The Location of Culture*. London: Routledge.

Billig, M. (1995) *Banal Nationalisms*. London: Sage.

Bland, L. (1995) *Banishing the Beast: English Feminism and Sexual Morality, 1885–1915*. London: Penguin.

Boswell, J. (1990) Revolutions, universals and sexual categories, in M. Duberman, M. Vicinus and G. Chauncey (eds) *Hidden from History: Reclaiming the Gay and Lesbian Past*. New York: Meridian.

Brah, A. (1996) *Cartographies of Diaspora: Contesting Identities*. London: Routledge.

Butler, J. (1990) *Gender Trouble: Feminism and the Subversion of Identity*. New York and London: Routledge.

Butler, J. (1993) *Bodies that Matter: On the Discursive Limits of 'Sex'*. New York and London: Routledge.

Cartledge, S. and Ryan, J. (eds) (1983) *Sex and Love: New Thoughts on Old Contradictions*. London: Women's Press.

CCCS (1981) *Unpopular Education: Schooling and Social Democracy Since 1944*. London: Hutchinson.

Chatterjee, I. (1996) Slavery and the household in Bengal 1770–1880, unpublished PhD thesis. University of London.

Clare, M. and Johnson, R. (forthcoming) Method in our madness? power and identity in memory work method, in S. Radstone (ed.) *Memory and Method*. London: Dent.

Collins, P. H. (1990) *Black Feminist Thought: Knowledge, Consciousness and the Politics of Empowerment*. London: Harper Collins Academic.

Connell, R. W. (1987) *Gender and Power: Society, the Person and Sexual Politics*. Cambridge: Polity.

Connell, R. W. (1995) *Masculinities*. Cambridge: Polity.

Cooper, D. (1994) *Sexing the City: Lesbian and Gay Politics Within the Activist State*. London: Rivers Oram Press.

Cooper, D. (forthcoming) Governance troubles: school authority, gender and space. *British Journal of Sociology of Education*.

Corrigan, P. (1989) *Schooling the Smash Street Kids*. London: Macmillan.

Coward, R. (1984) *Female Desire*. London: Paladin.

Currie, E. (1994) *A Parliamentary Affair*. London: Coronet Books.

Dale, R. (1971) *Mixed or Single Sex School? Volume 2: Some Social Aspects*. London: Routledge and Kegan Paul.

Daniels, H., Hey, V., Leonard, D. and Smith, M. (1996) *Gender and Special Educational Needs: End of Project Report*, R.000235069. Swindon: Economic and Social Research Council.

Davidoff, L. and Hall, C. (1987) *Family Fortunes: Men and Women of the English Middle Class*. London: Hutchinson.

Davies, B. (1993) *Shards of Glass: Children Reading and Writing Beyond Gendered Identities*. St Leonard, NSW: Allen and Unwin.

Davin, A. (1978) Imperialism and motherhood. *History Workshop Journal*, 5(Spring): 9–65.

Dawson, G. (1994) *Soldier Heroes: British Adventure, Empire and the Imagining of Masculinities*. London: Routledge.

Deem, R. (ed.) (1984) *Co-education Reconsidered*. Milton Keynes: Open University Press.

Deem, R. (1991) Governing by gender? School governing bodies after the Educational Reform Act, in P. Abbot and C. Wallace (eds) *Gender Power and Sexuality*. London: Macmillan.

D'Emilio, J. (1992) *Making Trouble: Essays on Gay History, Politics and the University*. New York: Routledge.

Department for Education (1994) *Education Act 1993: Sex Education in Schools*, Circular No. 5/94. London: Department for Education.

Derrida, J. (1976) *Of Grammatology*. Baltimore: Johns Hopkins Press.

Dollimore, J. (1991) *Sexual Dissidence: Augustine to Wilde, Freud to Foucault*. Oxford: Clarendon Press.

Duberman, M., Vicinus, M. and Chauncey, G. J. (eds) (1990) *Hidden from History: Reclaiming the Gay and Lesbian Past*. New York: Meridian.

du Gay, P., Hall, S., Janes, L., Mackay, H. and Negus, K. (1997) *Doing Cultural Studies: The Story of the Sony Walkman*. London and Thousand Oaks, CA: Sage.

Durham, M. (1991) *Sex and Politics: The Family and Morality in the Thatcher Years*. Basingstoke: Macmillan.

Dyer, R. (1996) *White: Essays on Race and Culture*. London and New York: Routledge.

Edgar, D. (1988) *The Second Time as Farce: Reflections on the Drama of Mean Times*. London: Lawrence and Wishart.

Education Group II (Cultural Studies Birmingham) (1990) *Education Limited: Schooling and Training and the New Right since 1979*. London: Unwin Hyman.

Edwards, R. (1990) Connecting method and epistemology: a white woman interviewing black women. *Women's Studies International Forum*, 13(5): 477–90.

Epstein, D. (1993) *Changing Classroom Cultures: Anti-Racism, Politics and Schools*. Stoke-on-Trent: Trentham Books.

Epstein, D. (1994a) Introduction: lesbian and gay equality in education – problems and possibilities, in D. Epstein (ed.) *Challenging Lesbian and Gay Inequalities in Education*. Buckingham: Open University Press.

Epstein, D. (1994b) Lesbian and gay equality within a whole school policy, in D. Epstein (ed.) *Challenging Lesbian and Gay Inequalities in Education*. Buckingham: Open University Press.

Epstein, D. (1995) 'Girls don't do bricks.' Gender and sexuality in the primary classroom, in J. Siraj-Blatchford and I. Siraj-Blatchford (eds) *Educating the Whole Child: Cross-Curricular Skills, Themes and Dimensions*. Buckingham: Open University Press.

Epstein, D. (1996a) Corrective cultures: *Romeo and Juliet*, Jane Brown and the media. *Curriculum Studies: The Sexual Politics of Education*, 4(2): 251–72.

Epstein, D. (1996b) Keeping them in their place: hetero/sexist harassment, gender and the enforcement of heterosexuality, in L. Adkins and J. Holland (eds) *Sexualising the Social*. Basingstoke: Macmillan.

Epstein, D. (1997) Boyz own stories: masculinities and sexualities in schools. *Gender and Education*, 9(1): 105–15.

Epstein, D. (1997) What's in a ban? Jane Brown, Romeo and Juliet and the popular media, in D. L. Steinberg, D. Epstein and R. Johnson (eds) *Border Patrols: Policing the Boundaries of Heterosexuality*. London: Cassell.

Epstein, D. and Johnson, R. (1994) On the straight and the narrow: the heterosexual presumption, homophobias and schools, in D. Epstein (ed.) *Challenging Lesbian and Gay Inequalities in Education*. Buckingham: Open University Press.

Epstein, D. and Kenway, J. (eds) (1996) *Discourse*, 17: 3.

Esland, G. (1996) Knowledge and nationhood: the New Right, education and the global market, in J. Avis *et al.* (eds) *Knowledge and Nationhood: Education, Politics and Work*. London: Cassell.

Evans, D. (1993) *Sexual Citizenship: The Material Construction of Sexualities*. London: Routledge.

Faderman, L. (1981) *Surpassing the Love of Men: Romantic Friendship and Love between Women from the Renaissance to the Present*. London: Women's Press.

Faludi, S. (1992) *Backlash: The Undeclared War Against Women*. London: Chatto and Windus.

Fanon, F. (1986) *Black Skin, White Masks*. London: Pluto.

Feminist Review Collective (1994) *Feminist Review: The New Politics of Sex and the State*, 48(Autumn).

Feminist Review Collective (1997) *Feminist Review: Consuming Cultures*, 55(Spring).

Fine, M. (1988) Sexuality, schooling and adolescent females: the missing discourse of desire. *Harvard Educational Review*, 58(1): 29–53.

Firestone, S. (1970) *The Dialectic of Sex: The Case for Feminist Revolution*. New York: Bantam Books.

Fisher, W. A., Byrne, D. E. and White, L. (1983) Emotional barriers to contraception, in D. E. Byrne and W. A. Fisher (eds) *Adolescents, Sex and Contraception*. Hillsdale, NJ: Lawrence Erlbaum.

Foucault, M. (1977) *Discipline and Punish: The Birth of the Prison* (trans. Alan Sheridan). Harmondsworth: Penguin.

Foucault, M. (1978) *The History of Sexuality* (trans. R. Hurley), *Volume 1: an Introduction*. Harmondsworth: Penguin.

Foucault, M. (1980) *Power/Knowledge: Selected Interviews and Other Writings 1972–1977*. Hemel Hempstead: Harvester.

Frankenberg, R. (1993) *White Women, Race Matters: The Social Construction of Whiteness*. London: Routledge.

Franklin, S., Lury, C. and Stacey, J. (1991) Feminism, Marxism and Thatcherism, in S. Franklin, C. Lury and J. Stacey (eds) *Off-Centre: Feminism and Cultural Studies*. London: Harper Collins.

Fuss, D. (1989) *Essentially Speaking: Feminism, Nature and Difference*. New York and London: Routledge.

Gallop, J. (ed.) (1995) *Pedagogy: The Question of Impersonation*. Bloomington, IN: Indiana University Press.

Gellner, E. (1983) *Nations and Nationalism*. Oxford: Blackwell.

Gilroy, P. (1987) *There Ain't No Black in the Union Jack: The Cultural Politics of Race and Nation*. London: Hutchinson.

Gittins, D. (1982) *Fair Sex: Family Size and Structure 1900–39*. London: Hutchinson.

Griffin, C. (1985) *Typical Girls? Young Women from School to the Job Market*. London: Routledge and Kegan Paul.

Griffin, C. (1993) *Representations of Youth: The Study of Youth and Adolescence in Britain and America*. Cambridge: Polity Press.

Hall, S. (1988) The toad in the garden: Thatcherism among the theorists, in C. Nelson and L. Grossberg (eds) *Marxism and the Interpretation of Culture*. Basingstoke: Macmillan.

Hall, S. (1990) Cultural identity and diaspora, in J. Rutherford (ed.) *Identity: Community, Culture, Difference*. London: Lawrence and Wishart.

Hall, S. (1991) The local and the global: globalization and ethnicity; Old and new identities, old and new ethnicities, two chapters in A. King (ed.) *Culture, Globalization and the World System*. Basingstoke: Macmillan.

Hall, S. (1996a) For Allon White: metaphors of transformation, in D. Morley and K.-S. Cheng (eds) *Stuart Hall: Critical Dialogues in Cultural Studies*. London: Routledge.

Hall, S. (1996b) Introduction: who needs 'identity'?, in S. Hall and P. du Gay (eds) *Questions of Cultural Identity*. London: Sage.

Hall, S., Critcher, C., Jefferson, T., Clarke, J. and Roberts, B. (1978) *Policing the Crisis: Mugging, the State and Law and Order*. Basingstoke: Macmillan.

Hall, S. and Jacques, M. (1983) *The Politics of Thatcherism*. London: Lawrence and Wishart.

Halperin, D. M. (1990) Sex before sexuality: pederasty, politics and power in classical Athens, in M. Duberman, M. Vicinus and G. Chauncey (eds) *Hidden from History: Reclaiming the Gay and Lesbian Past*. New York: Meridian.

Harbeck, K. M. (1995) Invisible no more: addressing the needs of lesbian, gay, and bisexual youth and their advocates, in G. Unks (ed.) *The Gay Teen: Educational Practice and Theory for Lesbian, Gay and Bisexual Adolescents*. New York and London: Routledge.

Hartsock, N. (1987) Rethinking modernism: minority vs majority theories. *Cultural Critique*, 7: 187–206.

Haywood, C. (1996) 'Out of the curriculum': sex talking, talking sex. *Curriculum Studies: The Sexual Politics of Education*, 4(2): 229–49.

Haywood, C. and Mac an Ghaill, M. (1996) Schooling masculinities, in M. Mac an Ghaill (ed.) *Understanding Masculinities*. Buckingham: Open University Press.

Heath, S. (1982) *The Sexual Fix*. Basingstoke: Macmillan.

Henriques, J., Hollway, W., Urwin, C., Venn, C. and Walkerdine, V. (1984) *Changing the Subject: Psychology, Social Regulation and Subjectivity*. London: Methuen.

Hey, V. (1997) *The Company She Keeps: An Ethnography of Girls' Friendships*. Buckingham: Open University Press.

History Workshop (1990) *History Workshop Journal*, 30(Autumn).

Hobsbawm, E. and Ranger, T. (eds) (1983) *The Invention of Tradition*. Cambridge: Cambridge University Press.

Hoggart, R. (1957) *The Uses of Literacy*. London: Chatto and Windus.

Holland, J., Ramazanoglu, C. and Scott, S. (1990a) *Sex, Risk and Danger: AIDS Education Policy and Young Women's Sexuality*. London: Tufnell Press.

Holland, J., Ramazanoglu, C., Scott, S., Sharpe, S. and Thomson, R. (1990b) *'Don't Die of Ignorance' – I Nearly Died of Embarrassment*. London: Tufnell Press.

Holland, J., Ramazanoglu, C., Scott, S., Sharpe, S. and Thomson, R. (1991) *Pressure, Resistance, Empowerment: Young Women and the Negotiation of Safer Sex*. London: Tufnell Press.

Hollands, R. G. (1990) *The Long Transition: Class, Culture and Youth Training*. London: Macmillan.

Hollway, W. (1984) Gender difference and the production of subjectivity, in

J. Henriques *et al. Changing the Subject: Psychology, Social Regulation and Subjectivity*. London: Methuen.

Hollway, W. (1987) *Subjectivity and Method in Psychology*. London: Sage.

Holly, L. (ed.) (1989) *Girls and Sexuality: Teaching and Learning*. Milton Keynes: Open University Press.

hooks, b. (1984) *Feminist Theory From Margin to Center*. Boston, MA: South End Press.

hooks, b. (1994) *Teaching to Transgress: Education and the Practice of Freedom*. New York and London: Routledge.

Ingham, R. (1997) *The Development of an Integrated Model of Sexual Conduct Amongst Young People*, End of Award Report No. H52427501495. Economic and Social Research Council.

Jackson, S. and Scott, S. (eds) (1996) *Feminism and Sexuality: A Reader*. Edinburgh: Edinburgh University Press.

Johnson, R. (1986) The story so far: and further transformations?, in D. Punter (ed.) *Introduction to Contemporary Cultural Studies*. London: Longman.

Johnson, R. (1991) A new road to serfdom? A critical history of the 1988 Act, in Education Group II (Cultural Studies Birmingham) *Education Limited: Schooling and Training and the New Right since 1979*. London: Unwin Hyman.

Johnson, R. (1993a) Everyday life – national and other identities, in U. Bechdolf (ed.) *Watching Europe: A Media and Cultural Studies Reader*. Amsterdam and Tübingen: Amsterdam Cultural Studies Foundation and Tübingen Vereinigung Fur Volkskunde E.V.

Johnson, R. (1993b) Towards a cultural theory of the nation: a Dutch–British dialogue, in B. Henkes, A.-M. Galema and H. t-Velde (eds) *Images of the Nation*. Amsterdam: Rodopi.

Jones, K. (1989) *Right Turn: The Conservative Revolution in Education*. London: Radius.

Kehily, M. (1993) 'Tales we heard in school: sexuality and symbolic boundaries', unpublished MSocSci thesis: University of Birmingham.

Kehily, M. (1995) Self-narration, auto/biography and identity construction. *Gender and Education*, 7(1): 23–31.

Kehily, M. (1996) More sugar? Young people, teenage magazines and sexuality. *Sex Education Matters*, 9(Summer): 7–8.

Kehily, M. J. (1997) *Agony Aunts and Uncles*, Paper given at British Sociological Association Conference, York.

Kehily, M. J. and Nayak, A. (1996) 'The Christmas kiss': sexuality, storytelling and schooling. *Curriculum Studies: The Sexual Politics of Education*, 4(2): 211–28.

Kehily, M. J. and Nayak, A. (1997) 'Lads and laughter': humour and the production of heterosexual hierarchies. *Gender and Education*, 9(1): 69–88.

Kelly, L. (1992) Not in front of the children: responding to right-wing agendas on sexuality and education, in Arnot, M. and Barton, L. (eds) *Voicing Concerns: Perspectives on Contemporary Educational Reforms*. London: Triangle Books.

Kenway, J. (1987) Left right out: Australian education and the politics of signification. *Journal of Education Policy*, 2(3): 189–203.

Kenway, J. and Fitzclarence, L. (1997) Masculinity, violence and schooling: challenging 'poisonous pedagogies'. *Gender and Education*, 9(1): 117–33.

Kenway, J., Willis, S., Blackmore, J. and Rennie, L. (1997) Are boys victims of feminism in schools? Some answers from Australia. *International Journal of Inclusive Education*, 1(1): 19–36.

Khayyat, M. D. (1992) *Lesbian Teachers: An Invisible Presence*. Albany, NY: State University of New York Press.

Kitzinger, J. (1988) Defending innocence: ideologies of childhood. *Feminist Review*, 28: 77–87.

Kitzinger, J. (1990) 'Who are you kidding?' Children, power and sexual assault, in A. James and A. Prout (eds) *Constructing and Reconstructing Childhood*. London: Falmer Press.

KOLA (1994) A burden of aloneness, in D. Epstein (ed.) *Challenging Lesbian and Gay Inequalities in Education*. Buckingham: Open University Press.

Koonz, C. (1988) *Mothers in the Fatherland: Women and Family and Nazi Politics*. London: Jonathan Cape.

Kruse, A.-M. (1997) Single-sex settings: pedagogies for girls and boys in Danish schools, in P. F. Murphy and C. V. Gipps (eds) *Equity in the Classroom: Towards an Effective Pedagogy for Girls and Boys*. London: Falmer Press and UNESCO.

Laclau, E. and Mouffe, C. (1985) *Hegemony and Socialist Strategy: Towards a Radical Democratic Politics*. London: Verso.

Langan, M. and Schwarz, B. (eds) (1985) *The Crisis of the British State*. London: Hutchinson.

Lawrence, E. (1982) In an abundance of water the fool is thirsty: sociology and black pathology, in CCCS Race and Politics Group (ed.) *The Empire Strikes Back: Race and Racism in Contemporary Britain*. London: Hutchinson.

Lee, R. (1993) *Doing Research on Sensitive Topics*. London: Sage.

Lees, S. (1986) *Losing Out: Sexuality and Adolescent Girls*. London: Hutchinson.

Lees, S. (1987) The structure of sexual relations in school, in M. Arnot and G. Weiner (eds) *Gender and the Politics of Schooling*. London: Hutchinson/The Open University.

Lees, S. (1993) *Sugar and Spice: Sexuality and Adolescent Girls*. London: Penguin.

Leonard, D. and Adkins, L. (eds) (1996) *Sex in Question*. Basingstoke: Macmillan.

Levinson, J. (1994) 'Autobiographical writing: gender, culture and classrooms', unpublished MA thesis. University of London Institute of Education.

Lewis, R. (1996) *Gendering Orientalism: Race, Femininity and Representation*. London and New York: Routledge.

Mac an Ghaill, M. (1988) *Young, Gifted and Black*. Milton Keynes: Open University Press.

Mac an Ghaill, M. (1989) Beyond the white norm: the use of qualitative research in the study of black youths' schooling in England. *Qualitative Studies in Education*, 10(3): 273–85.

Mac an Ghaill, M. (1994a) (In)visibility: sexuality, race and masculinity in the school context, in D. Epstein (ed.) *Challenging Lesbian and Gay Inequalities in Education*. Buckingham: Open University Press.

Mac an Ghaill, M. (1994b) *The Making of Men: Masculinities, Sexualities and Schooling*. Buckingham: Open University Press.

Mac an Ghaill, M. (1996) Deconstructing heterosexualities with school arenas. *Curriculum Studies: The Sexual Politics of Education*, 4(2): 191–210.

McKinnon, C. (1982) Feminism, Marxism, method and the state: an agenda for theory. *Signs*, 7(3): 515–44.

McKinnon, C. (1987) *Feminism Unmodified: Discourses of Life and Law*. Cambridge, MA: Harvard University Press.

McNeil, M. (1991) Making and not making the difference: the gender politics of Thatcherism, in S. Franklin, C. Lury and J. Stacey (eds) *Off-Centre: Feminism and Cultural Studies*. London: Harper Collins.

McRobbie, A. (1978) Working class girls and the culture of femininity, in CCCS Women's Studies Group *Women Take Issue*. London: Hutchinson.

McRobbie, A. (ed.) (1989) *Zoot Suits and Second-Hand Dresses: An Anthology of Fashion and Music*. London: Macmillan.

McRobbie, A. (1991) *Feminism and Youth Culture: From 'Jackie' to 'Just Seventeen'*. London: Macmillan.

Mahony, P. (1985) *Schools for the Boys? Co-education Reassessed*. London: Hutchinson.

Measor, L., Tiffin, C. and Fry, K. (1996) Gender and sex education: a study of adolescent responses. *Gender and Education*, 8(3): 275–88.

Melia, J. (1995) An honest human body: sexuality and the continuum of resistance. *Women's Studies International Forum*, 18: 547–59.

Miller, J. (1990) *Seductions: Studies in Reading and Culture*. London: Virago.

Miller, J. (1996) *School for Women*. London: Virago.

Millett, K. (1970) *Sexual Politics*. New York: Avon Books.

Milliband, R. (1964) *Parliamentary Socialism: A Study in the Politics of Labour*. London: Merlin Press.

Mitchell, J. (1966) Women: the longest revolution, in J. Mitchell (ed.) *The Longest Revolution: Essays in Feminism, Literature and Psychoanalysis*. London: Virago (collected 1984).

Mitchell, J. (ed.) (1986) *The Selected Melanie Klein*. Harmondsworth: Penguin.

Mort, F. (1987) *Dangerous Sexualities: Medico-Moral Politics in England Since 1830*. London: Routledge and Kegan Paul.

Mort, F. (1996) *Cultures of Consumption: Masculinities and Social Space in Late Twentieth Century Britain*. London: Routledge.

Mosse, G. (1985) *Nationalism and Sexuality: Respectability and Normal Sexuality in Modern Europe*. New York: Howard Fertig.

National Lesbian and Gay Survey (n.d.) *Directive A: Perceptions of Homosexuality* (unpublished archive material).

National Union of Teachers (1991) *Lesbians and Gays in Schools: An Issue for Every Teacher. NUT Guidance on Lesbian and Gay Issues in Education*. London: NUT.

Nayak, A. and Kehily, M. (1996) Masculinities and schooling: why are young men so homophobic?, in D. L. Steinberg, D. Epstein and R. Johnson (eds) *Border Patrols: Policing the Boundaries of Heterosexuality*. London: Cassell.

Oddie, W. (1997) A year ago these magazines – aimed at young girls – pledged to clean up their act. Today, they are sleazier and more irresponsible than ever. *Daily Mail*, 14 February.

O'Flynn, S. (1996) 'Teaching it like a lesbian: the multiple ontologies of the "lesbian teacher" and her survival in school', unpublished MA thesis. University of London Institute of Education.

The Oxford Dictionary of Quotations – 3rd edn (1979) Oxford: Oxford University Press.

Parker, A., Russo, M., Sommer, D. and Yaeger, P. (eds) (1992) *Nationalisms and Sexualities*. London: Routledge.

Parker, D. (1979) News item, in *Oxford Dictionary of Quotations*. Oxford: Oxford University Press.

Parmar, P. (1987) Hateful contraries: media images of Asian women, in R. Betterton (ed.) *Looking On: Images of Femininity in the Visual Arts and Media*. London: Pandora.

Pateman, C. (1988) *The Sexual Contract*. Cambridge: Polity Press.

Pattman, R. W. (1997) 'Sexual discourses and sex education in post colonial Zimbabwe', unpublished PhD thesis. University of Birmingham.

Plummer, K. (1995) *Telling Sexual Stories: Power, Change and Social Worlds*. London: Routledge.

Radford, J. (1995–6) Twin leaks and Hackney outings: the Kingsmead School affair. *Trouble and Strife*, 32(Winter): 3–8.

Radhakrishnan, R. (1992) Nationalism, gender and the narrative of identity, in A. Parker (ed.) *Nationalisms and Sexualities*. London: Routledge.

Ramazanoglu, C. (ed.) (1993) *Up against Foucault: Explorations of some Tensions between Foucault and Feminism*. London: Routledge.

Ray, C. (1994) *Highlight: Sex Education*. London: National Children's Bureau/Barnardo's.

Redman, P. (1994) Shifting ground: rethinking sexuality education, in D. Epstein (ed.) *Challenging Lesbian and Gay Inequalities in Education*. Buckingham: Open University Press.

Redman, P. (1997) Invasion of the monstrous others: heterosexual masculinities, the 'AIDS carrier' and the horror genre, in D. L. Steinberg, D. Epstein and R. Johnson (eds) *Border Patrols: Policing the Boundaries of Heterosexuality*. London: Cassell.

Redman, P. and Mac an Ghaill, M. (1997) Educating Peter: the making of a history man, in D. L. Steinberg, D. Epstein and R. Johnson (eds) *Border Patrols: Policing the Boundaries of Heterosexuality*. London: Cassell.

Reinhold, S. (1994) Through the parliamentary looking glass: 'real' and 'pretend' families in contemporary British politics. *Feminist Review*, 48: 61–79.

Rich, A. (1980) Compulsory heterosexuality and lesbian existence. *Signs*, 54: 631–60.

Richardson, D. (ed.) (1996) *Theorising Heterosexuality*. Buckingham: Open University Press.

Roediger, D. (1994) *Towards the Abolition of Whiteness*. London: Verso.

Rogers, M. (1994) Growing up lesbian: the role of the school, in D. Epstein (ed.) *Challenging Lesbian and Gay Inequalities in Education*. Buckingham: Open University Press.

Rose, J. (1983) Femininity and its discontents. *Feminist Review*, 14: 5–21.

Rubin, G. (1984) Thinking sex notes for a radical theory of the politics of sexuality, in C. Vance (ed.) *Pleasure and Danger: Exploring Female Sexuality*. London: Pandora.

Rutherford, J. (ed.) (1990) *Identity: Community, Culture, Difference*. London: Lawrence and Wishart.

Said, E. (1978) *Orientalism*. New York: Vintage.

Schlesinger, P. (1991) *Media, State and Nation: Political Violence and Collective Identities*. London: Sage.

Schwichtenberg, C. (ed.) (1992) *The Madonna Connection*. Boulder, CO: Westview.

Science and Technology Subgroup (1991) In the wake of the Alton Bill: science, technology and reproductive politics, in S. Franklin, C. Lury and J. Stacey (eds) *Off-Centre: Feminism and Cultural Studies*. London: Harper Collins.

Sedgwick, E. K. (1985) *Between Men: English Literature and Male Homosocial Desire*. New York: Columbia University Press.

Sedgwick, E. K. (1990) *Epistemology of the Closet*. Berkeley: University of California Press.

Sedgwick, E. K. (1994) *Tendencies*. London: Routledge.

Segal, L. (1990) *Slow Motion: Changing Masculinities, Changing Men*. London: Virago.

Sex Education Forum (1997) *Supporting the Needs of Boys and Young Men in Sex and Relationships Education,* Forum Factsheet no. 11. Sex Education Forum.

Shaw, J. (1995) *Education, Gender and Anxiety*. London: Taylor and Francis.

Smith, A. M. (1994) *New Right Discourse on Race and Sexuality: Britain 1968–1990*. Oxford: Blackwell.

Spark, M. (1969) *The Prime of Miss Jean Brodie*. Harmondsworth: Penguin (first edition 1961).

Spraggs, G. (1994) Coming out in the NUT, in D. Epstein (ed.) *Challenging Lesbian and Gay Inequalities in Education*. Buckingham: Open University Press.

Stacey, J. (1991) Promoting normality: Section 28 and the regulation of sexuality, in S. Franklin, C. Lury and J. Stacey (eds) *Off-Centre: Feminism and Cultural Studies*. London: Harper Collins Academic.

Stainton Rogers, R. and Stainton Rogers, W. (1992) *Stories of Childhood: Shifting Agendas of Child Concern*. Hemel Hempstead: Harvester Wheatsheaf.

Stallybrass, P. and White, A. (1986) *The Politics and Poetics of Transgression*. London: Methuen.

Steinberg, D. L. (1997) *Bodies in Glass: Eugenics, Genetics, Embryo Ethics*. Manchester: Manchester University Press.

Steinberg, D. L., Epstein, D. and Johnson, R. (eds) (1997) *Border Patrols: Policing the Boundaries of Heterosexuality*. London: Cassell.

Thatcher, M. (1989) *The Revival of Britain: Speeches on Home and European Affairs 1975–1988*. London: Aurum Press.

Theweleit, K. (1987) *Male Fantasies Vol. 1: Women, Floods, Bodies, History*. Cambridge: Polity.

Thomson, R. (1993) Unholy alliance: the recent politics of sex education, in J. Bristow and A. Wilson (eds) *Activating Theory*. London: Lawrence and Wishart.

Thomson, R. (1994) Moral rhetoric and public health pragmatism: the recent politics of sex education. *Feminist Review*, 48: 40–60.

Tobin, L. (ed.) (1997) *Steamy Boys' Confessions*. London: Emap Elan.

Trenchard, L. and Warren, H. (1984) *Something to Tell You*. London: London Gay Teenagers' Group.

Trudell, B. (1993) *Doing Sex Education: Gender Politics and Schooling*. London: Routledge.

Unterhalter, E. (1996) States, Households and the Market in World Bank Discourses 1985–1995: a Feminist Critique, *Discourse: Feminist Perspectives on the Marketisation of Education*, 17(3): 389–401.

Vance, C. S. (ed.) (1984) *Pleasure and Danger: Exploring Female Sexuality*. London: Pandora.

Walkerdine, V. (1981) Sex, power and pedagogy. *Screen Education*, 38: 14–24.

Walkerdine, V. (1990) *Schoolgirl Fictions*. London: Verso.

Walkerdine, V. (1996) Popular culture and the eroticization of little girls, in J. Curran, D. Morley and V. Walkerdine (eds) *Cultural Studies and Communications*. London: Arnold.

Walkerdine, V. (1997) *Daddy's Girl*. Basingstoke: Macmillan.

Ware, V. (1992) *Beyond the Pale: White Women, Racism and History*. London: Verso.

Weber, S. and Mitchell, C. (1995) *'That's Funny, You Don't Look Like a Teacher': Interrogating Images and Identity in Popular Culture*. London and Washington DC: Falmer Press.

Weeks, J. (1977) *Coming Out: Homosexual Politics in Britain from the Nineteenth Century to the Present*. London: Quartet.

Weeks, J. (1981) *Sex, Politics and Society: The Regulation of Sexuality since 1880*. Harlow: Longman.

Weeks, J. (1985) *Sexuality and its Discontents*. London: Routledge.

Weeks, J. (1986) *Sexuality*. London: Tavistock.

Weeks, J. (1991) *Against Nature: Essays on History, Sexuality and Identity*. London: Rivers Oram.

Williams, R. (1977) *Marxism and Literature*. Oxford: Oxford University Press.

Willis, P. (1977) *Learning to Labour: How Working Class Kids Get Working Class Jobs*. Aldershot: Saxon House.

Willis, P., Jones, S., Canaan, J. E. and Hurd, G. (1990) *Common Culture*. Milton Keynes: Open University Press.

Winship, J. (1985) 'A girl needs to get streetwise': magazines for the 1980s. *Feminist Review*, 21(Winter): 25–46.

Winship, J. (1987) *Inside Women's Magazines*. New York: Pandora.

Wolpe, A. (1988) *Within School Walls: The Role of Discipline, Sexuality and the Curriculum*. London: Routledge.

Women's Co-operative Guild (1978) *Maternity: Letters from Working Women*. London: Virago.

Wood, J. (1984) Groping towards sexism: boys' sex talk, in A. McRobbie and M. Nara (ed.) *Gender and Generation*. London: Macmillan.

Yuval-Davis, N. and Anthias, F. (eds) (1989) *Woman–Nation–State*. London: Macmillan.

Zarkov, D. (1995) Gender, orientalism and the history of ethnic hatred in the former Yugoslavia, in H. Lutz, A. Phoenix and N. Yuval-Davis (eds) *Crossfire: Nationalism, Racism and Gender in Europe*.

Zizek, S. (1989) *The Sublime Object of Ideology*. London: Verso.

Acts of Parliament

Education [No. 2] Act 1986

Education Act 1993

Local Government [Amendment] Act 1988

Index